WITHDRAWN
HARVARD LIBRARY
WITHDRAWN

Shaun J. Sullivan, O.F.M.

KILLING IN DEFENSE OF PRIVATE PROPERTY

Dissertation Series 15

SCHOLARS PRESS FOR THE AMERICAN ACADEMY OF RELIGION

Killing in Defense of
Private Property

AMERICAN ACADEMY OF RELIGION

DISSERTATION SERIES

Edited by

H. Ganse Little, Jr.

Number 15

KILLING IN DEFENSE OF
PRIVATE PROPERTY

by

Shaun J. Sullivan, O.F.M

SCHOLARS PRESS
Missoula, Montana

KILLING IN DEFENSE OF PRIVATE PROPERTY: THE DEVELOPMENT OF A ROMAN CATHOLIC MORAL TEACHING, THIRTEENTH TO EIGHTEENTH CENTURIES

by

Shaun J. Sullivan, O.F.M.

Published by

SCHOLARS PRESS

for

The American Academy of Religion

Distributed by

SCHOLARS PRESS
University of Montana
Missoula, Montana 59801

ANDOVER-HARVARD THEOLOGICAL LIBRARY
HARVARD DIVINITY SCHOOL

KILLING IN DEFENSE OF PRIVATE PROPERTY:
THE DEVELOPMENT OF A ROMAN CATHOLIC
MORAL TEACHING, THIRTEENTH
TO EIGHTEENTH CENTURIES

by

Shaun J. Sullivan, O.F.M.
Franciscan School of Theology
Berkeley, California 94709

Ph.D., 1973
Graduate Theological Union,
Berkeley, California

Advisor:
John T. Noonan, Jr.
University of California
Berkeley

Copyright © 1976

by

The American Academy of Religion

Library of Congress Cataloging in Publication Data

Sullivan, Shaun J
  Killing in defense of private property.

  (Dissertation series - American Academy of Religion ; no. 15)
  Originally presented as the author's thesis,
Graduate Theological Union, 1973.
  Bibliography: p.
  1. Justifiable homicide. 2. Right of property
— Moral and religious aspects. 3. Christian ethics
— Catholic authors — History. I. Title. II. Series: American Academy of Religion. Dissertation series - American Academy of Religion ; no. 15.
Law   241'.6'97   75-38843
ISBN 0-89130-067-8

PRINTED IN THE UNITED STATES OF AMERICA

Printing Department
University of Montana
Missoula, Montana 59801

TABLE OF CONTENTS

	Page
INTRODUCTION	ix

Chapter

I. THE GENERAL JUSTIFICATION FOR TAKING HUMAN LIFE . 1
    Conflicting Biblical Evidence 2
    Resolution of the Conflict 8
        Public Authority 9
        Private Individual 17
        Due Moderation 34
    Conclusion 37

II. LAW: ADULTERERS, CLERICS, SERMON ON THE MOUNT . . 39
    Adultery 39
        Thirteenth Century 40
        Fifteenth Century 44
        Sixteenth Century 45
        Seventeenth and Eighteenth Centuries 47
    Clerics 49
        Thirteenth Century 50
        Fourteenth Century 57
        Fifteenth Century 60
        Sixteenth to Eighteenth Centuries 62
    Old and New Testament Morality: Decalogue and
      Sermon on the Mount 67
    Conclusion 75

III. THE THIEF'S RIGHT TO LIFE 79
    Theft and Robbery 79
    The Text of Exodus 22:1-2 82
    Roman Law 84
    The Acceptance and Transformation of "Day-
      Night" 88
        Thirteenth Century 88

	Fourteenth Century	96
	Fifteenth Century	102
	Sixteenth Century	109
	Seventeenth and Eighteenth Centuries	113
	Interfecisti, *De homicidio*, and *Suscepimus*, *De homicidio*	115
	Interfecisti, *De homicidio*	115
	Suscepimus, *De homicidio*	119
	Some Arguments from Reason	121
	The "Higher Good" Argument	121
	The "Practice of Princes" Argument	124
	The "Deterrent to Crime" Argument	125
	Conclusion	125
IV.	THE VALUE OF PROPERTY	127
	Value	128
	Specific Norm	129
	Relative Norm	131
	Recovery	143
	Doubt	144
	Fleeing Thief	146
	Fled Thief	151
	The Evaluation of Property	156
FOOTNOTES		169
	Chapter I	171
	Chapter II	179
	Chapter III	191
	Chapter IV	209
BIBLIOGRAPHY		219

ACKNOWLEDGMENTS

Occasionally, at least, doctoral dissertation topics are chosen freely, without academic pressure. Such is the case at hand. My interest in issues of justice no doubt goes back to my family, but the particular focus of this work owes its beginning to any number of civil officials who in the panic of urban revolts declared by word and/or action that property rights were above human rights. These people stirred not only my conscience but my intellect.

The responsibility for the ideas contained here rests with me, but without the initial and critical probing, the continued guidance, inspiration, confidence, and knowledge of Dr. John T. Noonan, Jr. of the University of California, Berkeley, there would be no ideas before you at all.

Gratitude is also due to Mr. Al Henon of the University of California Press, who allowed me to use the material of Lauro Martines' <u>Violence and Civil Disorder in Italian Cities, 1200-1500</u> prior to its publication. Similar thanks go to Dr. Bernard S. Jackson of the University of Edinburgh, whose ideas on theft in the Old Testament were generously made available. Dr. David Dabue of the University of California, Berkeley, and Rev. Robert Dailey, S.J. of the Jesuit School of Theology, Berkeley, deserve credit for their enlightenment in moments of darkness. To Rev. Kevin Wall, O.P. and Rev. Richard Hill, S.J., who served on my dissertation committee and responded to my study so helpfully: thank you.

The entire endeavor would not have been possible without the provision of means and opportunity provided by Rev. Alan McCoy, O.F.M., Provincial, and my brother Franciscans of the St. Barbara Province. To them and to my many "brothers and sisters": I thank you for your confidence and support.

Special thanks are due to Rev. Kenan Osborne, O.F.M.,

President of the Franciscan School of Theology, Berkeley, whose sometimes not-so-gentle prodding was a necessity, and to Rev. Armand Quiros, O.F.M., who more than once helped me break a Latin knot.

Finally, I want to thank Mrs. Suzanne Bidou for her many hours of typing drafts of this study. Her encouragement and generosity were surpassed only by her uncanny ability to read my handwriting.

The final typing of this work is to the credit of Ms. Ruth Halley.

INTRODUCTION

Certain moral questions have a long history. There are periods within that history when particular aspects of the issue are more prominent than at other times, but the question remains one which attracts the energies of scholars and ordinary people alike. One such issue is the subject of this study: the taking of a person's life in order to protect property.

To kill in defense of property may embrace a wide range of activities: warfare, capital punishment, the exercise of policing powers, the individual's effort to prevent the loss of what is his. It is the last activity which is the particular case to be examined here. May an individual, an ordinary private citizen, kill to protect his private property?

It is certain that many would answer this question with a "yes," perhaps fewer with a "no." What is to be explored here is the history of both "yes" and "no" as it occurred in the ethical tradition of the Roman Catholic Church between the thirteenth and eighteenth centuries. It was during this period, from the Scholastics to the emergence of the moral system of St. Alphonsus Ligouri, that the ethical teaching of the Roman Catholic Church achieved the form and content which continues to guide and to oblige that Church's adherents up to the present.

The six-hundred year period under examination will be dealt with through representative canon lawyers, theologians, and moralists: the men of great influence and stature in the tradition. The teaching they offered as basis for sound ethical behavior will be viewed in light of the sources from which it emerged, the processes of reasoning employed, and the social context in which the teaching came to birth and was followed.

May a private person kill to protect his private property? Whether the answer is affirmative or negative, we need to know the reasons for the answer so that its validity may be judged. If the answer is "yes," we also need to discover if there are any qualifications on that "yes." The initial question involves what are accepted as two basic rights of man: the right to property on the part of the owner and the right to life on the part of the thief. The question is thus ultimately one of comparative values. Which right is to be preferred? The answers to the question and an evaluation of those answers given by six hundred years of Roman Catholic moral tradition are the subject matter of this book.

CHAPTER I

THE GENERAL JUSTIFICATION FOR TAKING HUMAN LIFE

The purpose of this work is to examine the criteria for legitimate killing on the basis of private authority in defense of property. However, underlying this question is the more general issue of the right to licitly deprive another of life. There is need to establish the right to kill another before any specific circumstances of application may be examined.

Within the Roman Catholic moral tradition deprivation of life must be dealt with in the face of conflicting Biblical evidence. For example, the command of the Decalogue is "You shall not kill" (Ex. 20:13), but this command is countered by "Do not allow evildoers to live" (Ex. 22:18). Such conflict must be resolved if there is to be any determination of licit moral behavior. This resolution also involves, historically, the requirement of a certain consistency between the Old and New Testaments. Both are accepted as coming from a God who cannot contradict himself. Thus we will find ourselves involved in the establishment of a general moral principle that legitimates killing by determining that the commandment of the Decalogue is not an absolute prohibition; there are exceptions. Only after such determination does consideration of defense in the case of property as an exception become possible.

The analysis of the general justification for taking human life will proceed by focusing on representative Biblical texts from both Old and New Testaments which are used by central figures in the moral tradition. Then the principles employed to both justify and limit killing on the basis of the distinction between public and private authority will be expounded.

It is to be noted that in dealing with Biblical texts the sources are primarily theologians of the thirteenth and early fourteenth centuries: Alexander of Hales (d.1245), Thomas Aquinas (d.1274), Bonaventure (d.1274), John Duns Scotus (d.1308). After these men, who are considered outstanding authorities, the references to Scriptural texts become increasingly infrequent. It is almost in passing that such later men as John of Lignano (d. 1383), Jean Gerson (d.1429), and Cajetan (d.1534) make reference to any Biblical text. Most make no reference at all. While lack of such references might be attributed in certain cases to an acceptance of the prior understanding of the "masters," it would seem that what is more important is the trend toward establishing ethical norms on the basis of natural law and the capacity of man to reason, with the consequent reliance upon especially Roman civil law as an outstanding example of the exercise of human reason in the realm of law.

Conflicting Biblical Evidence

The precept "you shall not kill" is explicitly dealt with by Alexander of Hales, Bonaventure, Thomas Aquinas, and John Duns Scotus. Others do so implicitly and will be incorporated as we proceed to broaden the question of justification for killing.

The first task of Alexander, Thomas, and Bonaventure is to limit the prohibition against killing to man, excluding the killing of plants and animals.[1] Alexander proceeds to use the text of Genesis 1:26 to further establish the limitation. He understands this text to give man dominion over animals, but it does not make man lord over man. Thomas argues that lower forms of life are to serve the higher, principally as food. Bonaventure does not argue the point; he simply restricts the precept to man and says that this is contrary to the teaching of the Manicheans.

The necessity of insisting upon the restriction of "you shall not kill" to man is most probably due to the need to repudiate the teaching of the Cathars (Albigensians), as Augustine had opposed the Manicheans. The Cathars were an heretical sect whose influence perdured in Western Europe from the mid-twelfth until the first quarter of the fourteenth century.[2] The Cathars believed that natural law prohibited the killing of all animals, all irrational creatures. This belief was formally condemned in 1277 by Bishop Tempier of Paris, but Alexander, Thomas, and Bonaventure show an earlier recognition of the need to dismiss what Augustine had termed "nonsense."

As a result of treating this question, Alexander concludes that the commandment in question forbids all <u>inordinate</u> killing. The use of "inordinate" implies that some killing can be legitimate (in the context that would be of plants and animals). The elaboration of this position will be seen in Alexander's understanding of other Biblical texts.

A somewhat more extensive interpretation of this commandment is offered by Bonaventure, a student of Alexander of Hales. Bonaventure considers this precept as one of those of the Decalogue which prohibit man from inflicting injury upon an innocent person.[3] Just as adultery injures an innocent spouse and theft injures an innocent possessor of goods, so does killing injure an innocent person. Thus it is the killing of the innocent which is prohibited, not all deprivation of life. Bonaventure sanctions the killing of evildoers, provided certain criteria are met. These criteria will be discussed below.

The third Franciscan to deal with the precept is John Duns Scotus.[4] He approaches this command from a more absolutistic view: "you shall not kill" is an absolute divine prohibition. Hence no inferior may dispense with this law, and any law will be unjust that legitimates the killing of a man in a case not excepted from the prohibition by God. These "exceptions" by God may be explicit, as in certain instances in Old Testament law (blasphemy, murder, adultery, etc.),[5] or implicit. Implicit exceptions are those in which "just law generally" commands death. In this, Scotus follows Augustine,[6] who also states the criteria for "just law":[7] "those which descend from divine law as practical conclusions from practical principles, or which agree with divine law, or at least do not disagree with it." Contained here is the role of man's reason in the determination of law and that law's relationship to divine law. This role will be considered in the next chapter.

What we have here is an attempt by Alexander, Bonaventure, and Scotus to deal with what seems to be an absolute normative precept, "you shall not kill," in the face of other precepts, such as "you shall not allow evildoers to live," which decree the opposite. Alexander simply states that there must, therefore, be some legitimate taking of life; Bonaventure further determines that law can command the death of a deserving evildoer; and Scotus demands that "the deserving" be restricted to those who explicitly or implicitly are excepted from the divine precept by God.

There are other texts in the Old Testament which also prohibit the taking of a man's life. A particular group of texts (Wis. 12:10; Job 24:23; Ez. 33:11) indicates God's desire that man have the opportunity to change his evil ways through conversion and penitence. Alexander of Hales and Thomas Aquinas address themselves to these texts in a similar way.[8] Alexander teaches that those who sin against themselves be given the opportunity to repent, while those who sin against others are to be cut off from society. Thomas is more explicit, sparing life and giving time for repentance to those who do not grievously harm others, while legitimating the killing of those who do seriously harm others. Alexander's choice of words, "criminals who . . . are as rotten members" of society, would indicate the same sort of serious harm to others of which Thomas speaks.

The distinction which Alexander and Thomas make here would not seem to rule out the possibility of repentance on the part of anyone. It does deny to the more serious offender the opportunity to live out his life in a manner indicating true change of ways. Such a position tells us something of the attitude of these thirteenth-century theologians toward the sinner and their willingness to legitimate killing for serious offenses. We will examine more fully in chapter three this attitude toward the sinner,[9] and we will also discover as we go on the process by which theft is recognized as sufficiently serious to merit death. Of importance at this point is the understanding of these texts as applying in some cases and not in others. This is an example of the Scholastic method of avoiding contradictions by means of distinctions. Texts which teach incompatible positions do not contradict; they apply to different situations.

There are also New Testament passages to be interpreted if one is to justify morally the taking of human life. The parable of the weeds and the wheat (Mt. 13:24-30) and certain passages of Mt. 5 (with the parallels in Lk. 6) and 26 are explicitly interpreted. Again we find the preeminent Scholastics understanding these Biblical texts through concentration on the innocent party and by making a distinction. The distinction, however, will go beyond that of innocent-guilty or slight-serious harm; it will be a distinction between attitude (or state of mind) and action.

The parable of the weeds and wheat is cited by both Alexander and Aquinas as an objection to any justified killing of evildoers.[10] They answer the objection by stating that the parable is aimed at the preservation of good people (wheat), not evildoers (weeds). Consequently, when the good are not endangered and there is certainty as to the identity of the evil ones, these evil persons may be killed. Thomas speaks of this in general terms of the good and the evil. One is forbidden to kill the evil when this cannot be done without also slaying the good, or when the evil have many followers and to kill them would be a danger to the good. If, however, the slaying affords protection or saves the good, then the evil are lawfully put to death. Alexander approaches the issue from an interpretation of "weeds" as heretics. To kill such people is licit unless there is uncertainty in judgment between the orthodox and the heretic, or if a multitude of persons is involved, either directly or through the individual judged an enemy of the Church, as, for example, a leader with many followers.[11] Alexander wants the harm to Church and society resulting from such action against this type of situation to be avoided.

The particular focus of Alexander and Thomas, though they rely upon the tradition rooted in Augustine, can be seen as a response to the climate of hostility between orthodoxy and heresy which was a part of their thirteenth-century world (as it was a part of Augustine's world). Political and religious homogeneity were seen as essential to each other and to the well-being of the social order.

Alexander and Aquinas agree that while the taking of life is licit, the morality of any particular killing must be judged in the light of the particular focus of the parable: good people. It is their good or their harm which determines the licitness of the action brought against the evil.[12] One is even to refrain from acting if the harm done to the good is greater than the benefit attained. There is here the element of social consequences influencing the morality of an act, an element which will appear at other places in this study.

The most telling Gospel texts in opposition to deprivation of life are those in Mt. 5 (with parallels in Lk. 6) and 26. Especially the texts from the "Sermon on the Mount" had been (as they continue to be) the inspiration of reform movements which sought to recapture what was considered the simplicity and pacifity of the early period of the Church. The Albigensians, against whom orthodox theologians argued into the fourteenth century, were one sect who attacked the medieval Church for its "lust for power" and denounced all wars and crusades as sinful, the execution of criminals and heretics as murder.[13] Under such attack, it is to be expected that the traditional interpretation of these texts, thought absolutely necessary for the preservation of true religion and the social order, should be continued.

The verses of Matthew which raise questions regarding the legitimacy of killing are the following:

5:21. You shall not commit murder; every murderer is liable to judgment.

5:39. Offer no resistance to injury.

5:44-5. My command to you is: love your enemies, pray for your persecutors. This will prove that you are sons of your heavenly Father, for his sun rises on the bad and the good, he rains on the just and the unjust.

26:52. Those who use the sword are sooner or later destroyed by it.

While these statements indicate a need to examine the relationship between Old and New Testament morality, for the present it is sufficient that the response given them in the context of justified taking of life be examined.

Verses 5:21, 39, 44-5, are viewed by both Alexander, who refers to Augustine and to Gratian, and Bonaventure as prohibiting personal revenge, not as forbidding punishment or correction.[14] Alexander makes his own the opinion of Augustine on "do not resist evil":[15] "This precept pertains more to the preparation of the heart, which is internal, than to action, which is external." The intent of this statement is to avoid adding to the evil resisted by oneself becoming revengeful. There is also the desire to benefit the evildoer by taking away his freedom to do evil—"for nothing is more unhappy than the happiness of one sinning"— and to discourage others from similar evil activity. But indicative of an attitude which viewed the Church as a divine institution entrusted with the salvation of the world, no injury to God or to the Church was to be endured; opponents of God and the Church were to be "uprooted." Bonaventure, on the other hand, states that the precepts involved here do apply to both word and action, not just to the heart. They bind everyone as far as personal disposition is concerned, but they oblige only the <u>perfect</u> to external action. Thus one is to avoid lustful revenge, but he can prevent evil and even kill for the love of justice. Bonaventure's distinction between the "perfect" and the "imperfect" is based on his position that to love one's enemies and accept adversity is a sign of perfect charity. It is only those who possess this perfect charity, the perfect, who are bound to the precepts in concrete behavior. There would appear in this teaching a reflection of medieval Christianity's conviction that it is impossible to live "in the world" and be wholly Christian. The perfect living of Christianity was the call of the religious life, especially monasticism.[16]

With Augustine, Alexander and Bonaventure confront the literal statements of Mt. 5 with an interpretation that effectively vitiates them in the realm of everyday activity. This is done by Bonaventure through his "perfect-imperfect"

dichotomy and his focus on the intention internal to the
person (prevention of evil and love of justice) as legitimating the taking of whatever action may be necessary to
realize the intention. Alexander also is concerned with
intention and the prevention of evil by whatever means. He
likewise refers approvingly to Jerome's position that death
benefits a man when it is the occasion for expiation; it
benefits others by being a deterrent to similar crime.
Through such "necessities," as well as the warring, lawless,
precarious atmosphere of the thirteenth century, is reinforced the "impossibility" of the precepts being followed in
ordinary life.[17] They are counsels for the perfect. Thus
the benefits are seen to outweigh the value of accepting the
precepts literally.

     The above discussion of the justification for taking
human life has dealt with the argumentation done within an
explicit Biblical framework. It has been principally drawn
from the work of Alexander of Hales and Bonaventure, with
some reliance on Thomas Aquinas and Scotus, and with links
to Augustine and his acceptance by Gratian. The principle
sources are thus representative of men who are considered
the epitome of Scholasticism. The positions which these men
hold give rise to certain principles and avenues of approach
which will be followed in the canonical and moral tradition
of their own and later times. The link with Augustine is
less clear. We shall see that the reason for this is the
seeming inconsistency of Augustine himself.

Resolution of the Conflict

     The foregoing attempts to understand certain Biblical
texts have shown very clearly that the basic issue in the
moral tradition under examination here will not be <u>whether</u>
killing is allowed, but <u>when</u>, and <u>by whom</u>, and <u>of whom</u> it is
allowed. The Scholastics have pointed out that there can be
legitimate taking of life; God himself does so and through
law commands others to do the same. But no one is to be
killed out of a spirit of revenge. Such a decisive act as
deprivation of life is to be performed from a love for justice and to inflict beneficial punishment. Killing is a

defensive measure deemed necessary for the sake of good people and of society as a whole.

It is in terms of <u>necessary defense</u> that argumentation is conducted. We will proceed to examine these arguments according to the fundamental distinction between <u>public</u> and <u>private</u> authority. This distinction will lead us to consideration of defense as a form of post-factum punishment as well as an action aimed at prevention of harm. Once we have seen the means whereby legitimate killing is acknowledged on the part of public authority, we will turn to the basis upon which the private individual's right of self-defense is founded.

PUBLIC AUTHORITY

The major source of Church law with which the thirteenth-century scholars worked was the <u>Decretum</u> of Gratian, compiled from the Church Fathers, papal decrees, and the acts of Church councils about 1140 A.D. Added to this basic collection were the <u>Decretales</u> of Pope Gregory IX, compiled and composed by Raymund of Pennaforte and published in 1234. Both works were available to the major Scholastics. As the major source, it is to Gratian that we will turn first.

As a compilation, it is not surprising that the <u>Decretum</u> should contain contradictory passages. It was Gratian's intention to reconcile these. The question of public authority's power to inflict death exemplifies this process. Gratian acknowledges the right of legal authority to take up arms in order to revenge injury, and he interprets Mt. 26:52—"All who take up the sword will perish by the sword"—as condemning only those who have not the legitimate authority to bear weapons.[18] He illustrates this latter point by explaining that Jerome's opinion that the Church may not avenge is to be understood to mean no <u>unjust</u> avenging; the Church may <u>rationally</u> persecute heretics.

The telling word in these passages seems to be "revenge." Besides acknowledging that public authority may take revenge for injury (whether communal or personal), there is shown an attempt to control this activity. For in these passages where the public authority is given legitimation, private individuals are forbidden to bear arms in revenge. Gratian has more confidence in the likelihood of public authority acting justly and rationally than he does in the individual person.

Gratian continues the argument by citing Augustine with reference to "you shall not kill" and "all who take up the sword will perish by the sword."[19] These texts are said to prove that no one is allowed to kill, and Augustine is quoted as saying that evil people are not to be killed; they should be corrected by being whipped. In this letter Augustine writes to the Emperor Marcellianus asking that he not kill certain Donatists and Circumcelliones who had been convicted of murder and maiming. He pleads on the basis of the Emperor's faith and the mercy of Christ that these people be not punished "by the infliction of precisely similar injuries" in retaliation. Augustine wants their penalty to lead to repentance and a useful life, not that it be vindictive punishment.

In another letter cited by Gratian and dealing with the same situation, Augustine asks for a penalty less severe than death because of "our own conscience and for the testimony given to Catholic clemency."[20] He admits that some of the Church members would consider this weakness. "Nevertheless, when the feelings, which are wont to be immoderately excited while such events are recent, have subsided after a time, the kindness shown to the guilty will shine. . . ."

Augustine's intention here is to prevent the imposition of capital punishment. Gratian cites him at length, including passages which speak of "the moderation which is suitable to Christian forbearance," and the deliverance from error, not death, that is sought through the help of judges and laws.[21] The purpose of this deliverance is to preserve the evildoer from the penalty of eternal judgment. Consequently, he asks the Emperor "to forget that he has the power of capital punishment."[22] And Augustine even says that if death is inflicted, he will refrain from bringing the evildoers before the tribunal; he will have to choose to be killed by them rather than bring them to death by accusing them.

Gratian cites these passages from Augustine; he makes no comment upon them until he refers to a statement of Pope Gregory:[23] "The Church defends those guilty of blood lest it become a participant in the shedding of blood." On this sentence he does comment, and in a manner that contradicts the statements of Augustine. Gratian says:

> From this it appears that the evil are to be corrected through whipping, not by the amputation of members or by inflicting bodily death. 1) But it is objected that the Lord says to Moses "you shall not allow evildoers to live" (Ex. 22:18), and "a man who lies with a beast is to die" (Lev. 20:15). Adulterers and blasphemers known for their crime are to be stoned without mercy. Again, Moses, who accepted the Law, punished worshippers of idols with death. . . . None of those found in the Old Testament who killed the evil are called transgressors of the Law, but defenders. 2) Therefore, it is prohibited by this precept that anyone on his own authority be armed to murder anyone, not that the accused be put to death by command of the law. For he who acts by public authority destroys the evil by command of the law itself, neither is he a transgressor of that precept, nor is he estranged from the heavenly fatherland.

Gratian here returns to his earlier position: legal authority may kill. He bases his teaching upon the Old Testament and ignores the New Testament commands he had previously included through Augustine. He returns to Augustine's statement on whipping, but contradicts it. Augustine had spoken directly to the public authority and said "do not kill"; Gratian speaks of this authority as acting by command of the law when it does inflict death. The opinions are in clear opposition. Gratian opts for the Old Testament teaching; yet he is clear on the need for legal sanction and for the exclusion of private initiative.

The rejection of this teaching of Augustine by Gratian has a firm foundation in Augustine himself. He is quoted by Gratian as giving legitimation to the killing of evildoers (murderers, committers of sacrilege, or any criminal) by the command of law.[24] The issue is one of public authority and, although Augustine states his disapproval of killing others to defend one's own life, he does allow this to defend another's life, provided the defender be endowed with public authority. There is, he says, a duty to restrain men from sin. In this fashion Augustine indicates a recognition of God granting the power to kill through the instrument of the law. We may have here in Augustine the acknowledgment that while God has granted the power to kill through the law, it remains better, because of the call of the New Testament, though not binding, to avoid the use of this power. When speaking of a particular incident in which he himself is involved, he follows the "better" way and invites the authorities to do likewise; when he deals with a more general circumstance, he acknowledges the Divine granting of the power to inflict death through the law. But he remains opposed to any killing in self-defense on one's own initiative. His opposition could then be eliminated on the basis of law actually giving an individual the right to kill in self-defense.

Gratian further buttresses his opinion through two quotations from Jerome, both of which are given without comment.[25] Jerome says that to kill the evil for that in which they are evil is to act as a minister of God. This statement says that laws can punish serious crimes with death, and to act according to these laws is to act as God's agent.

These decrees collected by Gratian point to the presence of conflicting traditions among the sources of Church teaching which necessitates at least some process of reconciliation, if not a decision on an issue which involves acceptance or rejection of particular positions. We shall be dealing with this process. The sources upon which our authors depend are not always clear and so opposing positions will use the same source for their authority. The <u>Decretum</u> is a prime example of this, for, as we have seen in the case of Augustine, not even its sources are always consistent with themselves.

The sections in Gratian's work which we have examined give legitimacy to public authority killing evildoers. The basis for this legitimation is Divine law, as exemplified in Gratian's use of Old Testament examples which make public authority the Divine agent in punishing those who do evil. Further sanctioning of killing is found in the other major legal sourcebook, the <u>Decretales</u>.

The _Decretales_, published in 1234, contains the codification of legislation between the work of Gratian and itself.[26] Two of these decretals are of importance here: _Olim_, _De restitutione spoliatorum_, and _Significasti_, _De homicidio_.[27] The source of these passages is Pope Innocent III(1198-1216), during whose reign the medieval papacy reached its zenith in influence and authority. Innocent had been a student of Huguccio (Hugh of Pisa), the most famous of the decretists, at Bologna.[28] No doubt relying on the Roman law he had studied under Huguccio in both these decretals, Innocent makes use of the principle of "repelling force with force." He states that all laws allow this defensive action to repel injury, though one must employ due moderation and avoid revenge.[29] _Olim_ is specifically concerned with the employment of this principle on the part of a bishop, certainly considered a "public authority" in an age when ecclesiastical princes vied with their secular counterparts for authority in retaining the "right universal order" in both Church and society. This bishop was told that he had acted rightly in violently expelling the unjust possessor of Church property: all law allows force to repel force.

The importance of this principle will become increasingly apparent as we proceed. For the moment its value lies in being available to the thirteenth-century Scholastics and in being able to be joined to the other principles we have seen in Gratian. On the basis of "all law" public authority may take revenge for injury, may repel force with force when necessary, while acting as the agent of God in punishing those who do evil.

The notions contained in the disparate canonical decrees treated so far leave a number of questions open. When may public authority kill? Who may be killed? Why is public authority given this power? To these questions major theologians of the mid-thirteenth century addressed themselves. The circumstance envisioned is primarily one of post-factum punishment (as opposed to immediate defense), and the desire is to restrict such punishment to officials (e.g., judges, soldiers) who have the responsibility to

enforce the law, to carry out its sentences, and to protect
the members of society. It is only by such restriction that
any control can be maintained on the deprivation of life.
The doctors of the thirteenth century seem aware of the element of revenge, societal revenge, in capital punishment;
they strive to limit this revenge on the part of society exclusively to those whom societal law designates. Justice is
to be served, while personal revenge is to be avoided; thus
the judicial process is required, though, as we shall indicate, there is the recognition of situations in which this
process is impossible.

The understanding of "public authority" is intimately related to the legal system, and this system involves
a judicial process for imposition of the death penalty. For
the most part, the operation of this process is implied in
the medieval authorities through their references to judges
and those who carry out the sentences commanded by public
officials.[30] But more explicit insistence comes from
Alexander and Bonaventure.[31] Bonaventure follows his teacher
in insisting that just cause, just order, and just spirit be
present before death is a legitimate punishment. For these
two Franciscans <u>just cause</u> means that the accused merits
death because of the seriousness of his crime; <u>just order</u>
requires that there be conviction of crime and the conviction and consequent execution be carried out by those who
have this power in law; <u>just spirit</u> refers to the motivation
required: the official must act out of a love for justice,
not to gain revenge nor from "an appetite for punishment."

The inclusion of "just cause" in the requirements
for legitimate killing relates immediately to the determination of who may be killed by public authority. We have already noted Gratian's citation of Jerome that the evil may
be killed for the evil they do. But there is certainly need
to further delineate the "evil" considered sufficiently
grave to authorize death as punishment.

Alexander picks up the statement of Jerome,[32] but
then he goes on to make reference to Augustine that law or
"rational justice" determine who is to be put to death.[33]
It is curious that Alexander does not refer to Augustine's

statement in the same place that Divine law has made "exceptions" to the law forbidding killing. We have mentioned the focus of Scotus on these exceptions, and his extension of explicit exceptions by means of implicit ones. It would seem that Scotus' implicit exceptions based on "just law" and Alexander's "rational justice" both have roots in the principle of Augustine that when a law can be deduced from Divine law, is in accord with it, or at least not opposed to it, we then have just law.[34] Thus the question of who may be killed would be answered in part by saying that anyone may be killed who is guilty of a crime explicitly designated as capital in Divine law or is determined as such by civil law which does not contradict Divine law. Neither Alexander nor Scotus give any examples of what such just laws might be.

Still further light on who may be killed comes from a consideration of why public authorities have this power. The reason is quite simple, though it may be formulated variously. We have previously met the interpretation of the parable of the weeds and wheat; there the concern was seen to be the good and the protection of the innocent. Alexander shows a similar regard to prevent harm to the innocent in his understanding of Augustine's statement: "We do not prohibit the freedom of committing crimes to be taken from evil men." He interprets this as allowing death to be the means of prevention; his reason is that as obstinancy in crime increases, punishment must increase.[35] There is with obstinancy in crime a continued harm to the innocent as well as a refusal to reform. To end such harm can require the death of the criminal.

It is likewise the prevention of harm to the innocent which informs the classical formulation of Aquinas as to the reason public authority has the power to exercise capital punishment.[36] Thomas states that the reason for deprivation of life is the common welfare; the good of the whole requires the death of the part. It is because of this common-welfare purpose that the infliction of the death penalty is reserved to public officials who are responsible for the common welfare. Only these officials may decide that the common good has been injured in such a way that the cause of this injury must be sacrificed for the good of the whole. This decision involves acting for the common good in a manner which harms someone, and such decisions are restricted to those responsible for the common good.[37] Thus the process of determining just laws would have to include the consideration of the common good, as this is the purpose of civil authority sharing in the Divine power to take the life of a guilty party. That the injury considered harmful to the good of society must be of a serious nature is understood.[38]

It is clear that the power to deprive a criminal of life is to be used to benefit society. In terms of this benefit a cautionary note is interjected by Raymund of Pennaforte. Raymund, a contemporary of Alexander, Bonaventure, and Thomas, was a renowned canonist who, besides compiling the Decretales, wrote a Summa de casibus poenitentiae, in which he incorporated not simply lists of sins and corresponding penances, but pertinent doctrinal and legal matters of interest to confessors. In this work, Raymund teaches that it is sometimes more beneficial to show mercy than to punish.[39] He draws this teaching from the New Testament event in Lk. 9:51-56. In this passage the disciples are rebuked by Jesus for wanting to bring fire down on those who would not receive them. The reason for Jesus' reprimand is understood to be the bitterness of the disciples for having been rejected. They were acting not from a zeal for justice but out of a desire for revenge. Jesus, however, wanted them to willingly accept personal injury with patience and joy (as is stated in Mt. 5:11-12). This event is thus understood as teaching that revenge must not always be taken on those who have sinned. It is sometimes more beneficial to show patience and clemency. The benefit referred to is not specified, but it is benefit accruing to the innocent party. Thus we have a position like that of Alexander and Thomas in their interpretation of the parable of the weeds and the wheat. If it is more beneficial to the good to avoid harming the evil, then refrain from harming them. Justice thus gives way to mercy. But it is not clear when this is to occur, what sort of "benefit" is envisioned. It is clear, however, that the power to kill is to be used or not used in accord with what most benefits the innocent people who have been somehow harmed.

In looking to the legitimation of public authority's power to punish with death we have found that this power is understood to be a sharing in Divine authority, is to be used as a punishment for serious evil in the protection of the common good, and is to be carried out without bitterness after legal conviction of the accused. The principle of necessary defense (in this case, of the community) is the fundamental rationale and it is buttressed by the employment of the natural and Roman law principle of "repelling force with force." The position just stated will perdure throughout the period under consideration in this work. The fundamental position remains the same though variation will occur in application to particular instances and in interpretation of the meaning of particular terms (e.g., necessary, due moderation). We will be mainly concerned with such variation in its application to private individuals, not to public authority. Public authority can kill; may the private individual?

Private Individual

Through reliance on the Bible understood as Divine law and on the principle of repelling force with force considered as permissible from all laws, public authority has been justified in taking human life either as punishment or as a defense when necessary for the benefit of the common good. It will also be on the basis of legal authority that the non-official individual will be given the capacity for legitimate killing. The issue, however, is not one of capital punishment; it is a matter of necessary defense. The circumstances are not those of post-factum punishment, but of immediate defense. The actor is not a public official but a private individual. Thus Gratian states that while a judge may inflict punishment for an injury received, the person who is injured is not to seek revenge on his own.[40] To support this position such New Testament passages as Mt. 2:2 (the flight to Egypt), Jn. 18:4 (Jesus does not oppose the crowd), and Jn. 18:36 (where Jesus tells Pilate that his kingdom is not of this world) are given as proof that "injury of neighbors may not be repelled by arms." The reason for this is that "they belong to the kingdom of this world who by aid of human strength and not Divine protection strive to save themselves from imminent injury." Gratian is attempting to prevent the attacked person from succumbing to the temptation to return evil for evil; so he says that since arms are not to be sought to repel injury, law should not give this capacity to individuals.

Actually, there are two statements in this passage: (1) the aid of arms is not to be sought to repel injury; (2) the good man is not to seek revenge for injury. Is the first statement referring only to the issue of revenge in the second, or is it forbidding the use of arms in self-defense? The Gospel passages and the belittling of those who "strive to save themselves from imminent injury" would seem to outlaw all armed defense. Yet Gratian emphasizes the issue of revenge and the need to avoid it. Certainly there are other passages in the <u>Decretum</u> which legitimate defense against injury and at least implicitly allow such defense to be by use of arms.[41] We have seen that Gratian's sources are frequently contradictory; so the presence here of a prohibition which does not perdure would not be surprising. Gratian's major intent, however, is to avoid revenge; that concern will perdure. Punishment is the realm of public authority.

There has been mention of the principle of repelling force with force being acknowledged by all law. From this starting point the moral tradition will attempt to determine when such repulsion will demand and thus make legal the taking of life on the part of a private person. We will now examine the use of this principle in terms of the necessity or avoidability of killing. The question of necessary-avoidable killing involves intimately the notions of <u>due moderation</u> and the <u>possibility of flight</u>. These two phases of the question will be separated as much as is possible for the sake of clarifying the developing understanding of the terms.

Thirteenth century.—Alexander of Hales (d.1245) begins the thirteenth-century period in which the elements necessary to justify private, self-defensive killing were formulated and united in a manner that would fundamentally determine the treatment of the question for the next five hundred years. The men who came immediately after him—Hostiensis (Henry of Susa; d.1271), Bonaventure (d.1274), Thomas (d.1274), Raymund of Pennaforte (d.1275), Richard of Middleton (d.1302)—take up the issue in much the same fashion as he does: in terms of necessary defense. But there will also be particular characteristics which will need examination.

In response to the question of the legitimacy of killing in self-defense, Alexander resorts to the distinction between avoidable and unavoidable necessity.[42] Having first cited approvingly Augustine and the civil sanction of repelling force with force,[43] Alexander then quotes Augustine as to the great difference between killing "to aid necessity" and, for example, killing from revenge.[44] Necessity is termed "unavoidable" when the evil cannot be otherwise escaped; "avoidable" necessity means that through flight or some other means (seemingly any action less than killing) the evil can be avoided. To kill in a case of avoidable necessity is considered homicide; to kill when such is unavoidable is not murder.

What Alexander attempts to explain by this distinction is twofold. First, he wants to exclude revenge as a justifiable defense; revenge is attack, not defense. Secondly, he wants to point out that when possible removal of oneself from the threatening situation is to be undertaken to avoid the need to kill; the mere presence of a threat does not justify killing. In this manner Alexander undertakes to explain the meaning of the law which allows force to be repelled in kind. It is to be noted that there is an appeal to a legal foundation (Roman law and natural law) to justify necessary, self-defensive killing.

It is this legal foundation that Hostiensis explicitly expands in his comments on *Significasti*, *De homicidio*.[45] He states that all laws, "natural, civil, Divine, and canonical," permit force to repel force. Then he goes on to focus on one of the points made by Alexander: defense is permitted, not revenge. The consequence of the exclusion of revenge is that a private individual may not act against an attacker if "an interval" occurs between the attack and the response. We will deal with the dispute over the meaning of "an interval" when we discuss the teaching on killing a fleeing thief in chapter four.[46]

The other point of Alexander, avoidability through flight or another means, is pursued by Bonaventure. Following his mentor, he distinguishes between avoidable and unavoidable necessity. But, unlike Alexander, he introduces an element of partial justification in the area of avoidable necessity.[47]

Bonaventure states that if a person can flee and does not because of "shame or some other cause," his guilt is lessened, though not totally removed. (Bonaventure terms this being excused a *tanto* but not a *toto*.) This is a teaching contrary to that of Alexander, who declares killing in a situation of avoidable necessity simply homicide. Bonaventure comments that excuse is not complete because it would be better to flee if one can. Yet he has introduced here a somewhat justified taking of life when such is not absolutely necessary. His statement of cause in this circumstance is vague: "shame or some other cause." As the stated reason, "shame" appears an extremely undefined concept. Bonaventure seems to be saying that to kill in a situation when killing could be avoided has its guilt diminished simply because the one killing does not prefer to flee. This position is consistent with his opinion that the ordinary person (the "imperfect") is not bound to a morality that demands what is considered "better" activity. Not only is unavoidable necessity a legitimate reason for killing, but something of the sting of avoidable necessity is removed. One is somehow not exactly a murderer if he kills when he need not kill but decides to do so. There seems to be in this teaching a granting of some justification to killing when that is more convenient than refraining from killing. An individual is told that he may with only "some guilt" prefer to kill an evildoer to prevent his evil when the killing is not necessary. Why the person is not absolutely held to avoid the greater evil of deprivation of life can only be because of the practical exclusion of any consideration of the evildoer's right to life; his life is somewhat forfeit by the mere evil activity he performs. Yet it might also be said that Bonaventure here deals with the concrete situation of a person who kills when he did not have to kill. Whatever the reason, it is understandable that a person might so act: he is immediately concerned with defense, with his own right to life. Consequently, the guilt is reduced because of the pressure of the situation. But it seems that Bonaventure is saying more than simply that guilt is reduced. He says it is "better to flee." Does this imply that there is "good" in a homicide that could have been avoided? Is the "good" the consequence of the evil prevented? And if it is, are we perhaps dangerously close to a statement that the end achieved is of primary consideration and not the means used to achieve the end? Bonaventure does not, certainly, remove all guilt in this case of avoidable necessity; but he does seem to diminish the prohibition to the extent that the evildoer's life is overtly depreciated in value. Such a teaching continues the interpretation of the parable of the weeds and the wheat in that its attention is directed (perhaps solely) to the "good" person.

In contrast to this teaching of Bonaventure is the position of Raymund of Pennaforte.[48] After making the avoidable-unavoidable distinction and agreeing with Alexander that to kill when it is avoidable is homicide, Raymund turns to the case of unavoidable necessity. He acknowledges the licitness of killing when the need cannot be escaped, though one needs to act without hatred and with sorrow. Then Raymund declares that in such a case the person must always have "interior penitence," for it is because of a person's own sinfulness that he is faced with so serious a necessity. By this statement Raymund seems to pierce the tendency to create an absolute good-evil dichotomy which we have seen in the understanding of the weeds and wheat. He indicates that there is evil involved even in necessary killing; so it is

not a light matter and must not be lightly dismissed even
when legitimate. What is being emphasized through this insistence is that the pivotal word in legitimate killing is
"necessary"—necessary to preserve the life of the person
attacked. This thought is certainly present in the other
authors to whom we have referred, but Raymund emphasizes it
in a way the others have not; and he removes any possibility
of seeing good in the killing itself.

Preservation of the life of the innocent person is
likewise the avenue pursued by Thomas Aquinas.[49] He teaches
the theory of double effect: an action may have more than
one effect, though only one is intended by the actor. In the
case of killing in self-defense, the two immediate effects
are saving one's own life and the slaying of the aggressor.
On the basis of this principle, Thomas holds that in self-
defense one must intend only self-preservation and not the
death of the attacker. It is this intention which renders
the killing licit.

With this teaching of Aquinas, the legitimacy of killing in self-defense has moved from a simple avoidable-
unavoidable criterion, which relies upon external circumstances, to the inclusion of an internal disposition. The
internal attitude was referred to both by the exclusion of
revenge and by Raymund's demand that there be no hatred and
a presence of sorrow; yet the disposition of Raymund is itself oriented to the attacker, while the revenge criterion
is primarily negative. Thomas demands more, not just sorrow
or the absence of hatred and revenge but the positive intent
to preserve one's own life.

The arguments which Thomas uses to support his double-
effect principle are both familiar and new to our study.
Recalling the juristic maxim of licitly repelling force with
force (<u>Significasti</u>, <u>De homicidio</u>), Thomas adds that "it is
natural to everything to keep itself in being" and that a
person "is bound to take more care of /his/ own life than
another's." Again we have the situation of ideas which were
implicit in others now becoming explicit. Self-preservation
is here considered "natural," i.e., according to natural law.
Hostiensis had mentioned natural law as permitting the use of

force to repel force; Thomas says why natural law does this: self-preservation.

One further legitimation of homicide in self-defense is provided by Aquinas. He cites Ex. 22:1—"If a thief be found breaking into a house or undermining it, and be wounded so as to die, he that slew him shall not be guilty of blood"—and says that it is much more lawful to defend one's life than one's house. This passage in the Book of Exodus (including the subsequent phrases on the theft being at night or during the day) will be discussed thoroughly in the third chapter. The importance of the use of this text is the process whereby Thomas moves from the legitimation of killing to preserve a lesser value to the conclusion that therefore it has to be legitimate to kill to preserve the greater value. This form of reasoning is continued by Richard of Middleton, the final thirteenth-century Scholastic whose teaching we will examine.

Richard is in complete agreement with his contemporaries in justifying the deprivation of life on the basis of inevitable necessity, without revenge, and he ascribes to all laws the permitting of force to be repelled with equivalent force.[50] He shows, however, special reliance upon Thomas Aquinas. He repeats the teaching of Thomas in citing the text of Ex. 22, and proceeds to justify the "more licit" on the basis of the "less licit" being justified. Richard also uses this form of reasoning in another instance. Relying on an Old Testament event (the self-destruction of Samson in Jgs. 16), and applying the notion of God making exceptions, Richard teaches that just as there are times when the more serious act of killing oneself is permitted, so are there occasions when it is licit to kill another. These occasions are specified by law, as in the fundamental rule that force may be repelled to the degree necessary. Finally, Richard reiterates the preference one is to give to his own life as legitimating killing to defend life. But he goes beyond Thomas in explicitly stating as the reason for this preference the "precept of charity," which is said to tell man that it is better to love himself than his neighbor. Thus Richard seems to imply that one's own right to life precedes that same right in one who attacks that life. He

also restates the "natural law" precept of repelling force
with force and uses it to answer Augustine's preference that
killing be in the hands of public officials.[51] Augustine's
position is understood by Richard to be based on the obligation man has to love the soul of his neighbor more than his
own body. To kill an attacker is to endanger his eternal
salvation, as he is in a state of serious sinfulness.[52]
Richard answers this objection by simply stating that all
laws allow force to be repelled; so a person who so repels
acts in accordance with the law. It is possible that Richard
is simply rejecting the principle upon which Augustine bases
his opinion, but it is more likely that he stands with his
contemporaries in denying not the principle but that it is
universally binding. One is led to this conclusion from
Richard's teaching that ecclesiastical law forbids clerics
to kill in self-defense.[53] Although law generally allows
self-defensive killing, particular law may legitimately forbid it. In the case of clerics, we have a continuation of
teaching seen earlier: it is "better" to follow the Augustinian principle, yet this is not binding on all (only on the
"more perfect") because all law allows self-defensive killing.

From the teaching of these thirteenth-century authorities, with its roots especially in Augustine and the Church
law codified by Gratian and Gregory, we have seen emerge the
basic principles which justify a private person taking the
life of another. For such an act to be legitimate it must
be an act of self-defense in a circumstance which renders
the killing necessary to the defense. We have seen this
position rooted in the canonical and Roman law traditions,
which have declared the repelling of force by force to be a
principle of natural law. But this repulsion must be true
defense, excluding all revenge; and its purpose is to be the
preservation of life: a private person is not to intend the
death of the attacker. The principal Biblical justification
has been drawn from the Old Testament, and there has come to
be included the "precept of charity" as demanding preference
of one's own life to that of the attacker. Remaining throughout the teaching of this period, though at times more explicit than at others, is the notion that God excepts from

the killing prohibition and shares this with man through the instrumentality of law, natural or otherwise. It is thus as a minister of the law that the private individual may kill, not on his own authority.[54] The various components of this teaching will be present in succeeding centuries, determining the framework in which analysis and legitimation are pursued. But the components will be selectively emphasized.

Fourteenth century.—The two sources to be used for the fourteenth century, Joannes Andreae (d.1348) and Joannes de Lignano (d.1383), were both professors of law at Bologna; and each was foremost in his field during one-half of the century. It is to be expected that these men will direct their attention to the legal foundation upon which the private person's right to kill is based.

Joannes Andreae clarifies the issue of the person being a minister of law through his quoting of Roman law and the remarks of the commentator Baldus.[55] The law and commentary Andreae uses give everyone the "free faculty" to kill a highwayman or a "nocturnal despoiler of one's fields." Permission is given to subject these criminals to immediate worthy punishment so that they incur what they intended to do to others. In these cases judicial punishment is viewed as coming too late, and it is considered better to attack immediately than to take revenge later.

The importance of this law lies in its granting a person the legal capacity to _decide_ to kill someone; yet the circumstances within which the decision can be made are defined by the law. There is a freeing of the attacked from the necessity of pursuing the judicial process of conviction and punishment, as well as a desire to forestall the possibility of later revengeful action. What the law gives is the legal capacity to decide that one's circumstances fit the law and the capacity to apply the power of civil authority. The action of the private individual is not extra-legal. In this case the source of authority is civil law; we have already seen the source as Divine, natural, and ecclesiastical law. There is both clarified and extended here the notion of sharing in the power to kill (whether of Divine or public authority) through the instrument of the law.

The legal instrument emphasized by Joannes de Lignano is not civil but natural law.[56] He states that self-defense is a natural instinct to conservation; thus the legitimacy of defending oneself proceeds from natural law, not from civil nor canonical law. While this is the general principle, Lignano says that it is within the power of positive law to determine the mode of defense.

Lignano also acknowledges what seems to be a rejection of this principle of natural law which allows force to repel force. He cites as opposed to this law the texts of Mt. 5, Lk. 6, Rom. 12, and Mt. 26, all of which speak of not defending oneself. He then states that these texts do not countermand the natural law principle: whatever is consistent with charity is licit by Divine law, and defense of self is consonant with charity. To love one's neighbor as oneself is the teaching of charity, and this implies the conservation of oneself and one's neighbor. Consequently, one may defend both oneself and one's neighbor.

The demands of charity, seen before in Aquinas and Middleton, are here specified by Lignano in terms of the natural law of conservation of life. Thus defense of life is legitimated by both Divine and natural law. What the New Testament texts cited might mean given such an interpretation, Joannes does not say. He simply states that the opposite teaching from that of the texts is in accord with Divine law, and so legitimate. He makes no attempt to repeat the previous century's teaching that these New Testament passages are counsels, or pertain to internal disposition, or are binding only on the "perfect" person. The texts are dismissed because conservation of life (natural law) is implied in love of neighbor and of self (Divine law). Is it possible that these texts dismissed here might themselves be Divine law? Is the natural law principle of conservation of life "implied" in the precept of charity, and does the implied principle necessarily result in the choice of one's own life over that of a neighbor? Lignano does not pursue these questions. What he does is point out a reliance upon natural law which for him determines the meaning of Divine law and excludes the possibility of Divine law demanding something beyond the natural law. Is this consistent with his teaching that any positive law can determine the mode in which natural law is to be understood and exercised?

The rather summary treatment of the private individual's right to kill by Joannes Andreae and Joannes de Lignano shows the legal background of both men. Bologna's prominence as a center for the study of Roman law is specifically reflected in Andreae, and the increasing influence of the idea of natural law, intensified through the previous century's rediscovery of Aristotle, is evident in Lignano.

<u>Fifteenth century</u>.—The elements required for killing licitly in self-defense which we have been examining are repeated in the fifteenth century. Jean Gerson (d.1429) at Paris, Panormitanus (Nicolas de' Tudeschis; d. 1450), Archbishop of Palermo, and Antoninus (d. 1459) at Florence write in terms of natural law, inevitable necessity (though Antoninus uses the word "restoration"), and the exclusion of hatred. Gerson also speaks of charity demanding preference of self over another, while Antoninus shows his reliance upon the teaching of Aquinas on intentionality in a case of double effect.[57] But these men also interject new elements into the discussion.

The fourteenth and fifteenth centuries were times of great civil and regional strife in Western Europe. Private vendetta, casual violence over almost any disagreement, the warfare of petty and powerful princes contributed to an atmosphere of constantly threatening violence.[58] Within this situation a particularly widespread circumstance was the discrimination between "gentlemen" and the rest of the people in the bearing of arms; gentlemen could carry them, the others could not.[59]

In such a social environment and arising out of the rather rigid stratification of society, there would occur the question of the right of "less noble" persons to defend themselves against their betters. This is the question which Gerson and Antoninus answer.[60] Gerson simply states that one may repel force regardless of the quality of the person who attacks. Antoninus approaches the question by means of a "doubtful" situation: may a "weak" man defend himself against one who is "strong"? The Summa of Antoninus is considered to give a complete picture of the moral life of the fifteenth century;[61] consequently, we may infer that there was a body of opinion which would answer the question negatively. Antoninus, however, responds as did Gerson: defense is legitimate for everyone, even to the extent of killing if that is necessary.

While Gerson and Antoninus deal with social stratification and respond in an equalitarian fashion, Panormitanus appears to conclude differently. He takes up the issue not in terms of simple defense, but rather in connection with the issue of the availability of flight rendering deprivation of life unnecessary.[62] He remarks that there is a difference of opinion (those who hold the opinions are not identified) over whether a layman (the cleric is a separate case) must flee when he can to avoid the necessity of killing. Some hold that the quality of the person must be considered: there is no shame if an equal flee an equal or a subordinate a superior. Others teach that shame is always involved in flight; so there is never an obligation to flee: one may resist even when flight is possible. Panormitanus responds to the difference of opinion by saying that while a blanket legitimation of resistence may be "truer from the rigor of the law," the other is safer "in the forum of souls." He thus seems to opt for the consideration of the quality of persons, even though the law allows the other. If this conclusion is correct, the implication would then be that superior persons are not bound to flee from inferiors. Panormitanus is thus saying that the obligation to flee when possible in order to avoid killing depends on the relative social status of the persons involved and the social consequences (shame, being thought timorous, etc.) which result. Thus, while agreeing with Gerson and Antoninus that all may defend themselves, Panormitanus would seem to require only the "inferior" person to flee to avoid killing; the "superior" person need not flee because of his status and the shame involved.

Among these fifteenth-century scholars, there is one more important contribution of interest to us. Antoninus addresses himself to a case in which the evil to be avoided is of less magnitude than the evil of taking another's life.[63] He uses the example of a woman who is raped. If she does not consent, there is no sin; if she should consent, either fornication or adultery is a lesser sin than "to kill of oneself." Thus in neither case is the killing of the attacker permitted. One reason Antoninus gives for this teaching is the removal of any time for penitence on the part of the aggressor; but his chief consideration is that in this situation a lesser evil is avoided by means of a greater one if the attacker is killed. We have already met this notion in the teaching arising from the weeds-wheat parable, to the effect that the "weeds" are not to be eradicated if a great evil would result. However, it may be that the use of "to kill of oneself" is an indication that the killing is forbidden only when law does not allow it. When law does permit it, this killing would then have legal approval. Further on, Antoninus opposes the civil laws which permit a husband or father to kill his wife or daughter, or their partner, caught in adultery. We will see in the next chapter that the basis of this opposition for Antoninus is the civil law <u>Authenticum</u>, <u>Ut nulli judicum</u>, which lifts the sentence of death for adultery and allows a person to enter a monastery to do penance. Consequently, it may be that Antoninus is teaching that law will determine what is to be considered the "greater evil." Whether that position would be consistent, by itself, with the teaching as a general principle is perhaps debatable. Antoninus states that neither simple avoidance of nor fear of consent to sin which is of lesser gravity than killing can justify killing. But what is more directly the issue of this study: if consent to a lesser sin cannot be avoided by a greater evil, can the avoidance of an evil which does not involve the question of sin on the part of the innocent person have a different moral principle? The statement of Antoninus stands forth as a moral principle, and as such it can be pursued beyond the particular example employed. The question of theft provides an opportunity to do that.

   <u>Sixteenth to eighteenth centuries</u>.—During the three hundred years from 1500 to 1800, the moral teaching which permits self-defensive killing when necessary, without revenge, and on the basis of natural and all other law is consistently repeated.[64] However, in two areas pertinent to the question there is variation. One of the continuing debates up to the end of the eighteenth century concerns the obligation to flee, if possible, when attacked; and the arguments will turn on the social status of the persons involved. The other variation questions Aquinas' requirement that the private individual intend only self-defense and not the death of his attacker. It is to these issues that we will now turn.

   What was seen as an <u>implication</u> in the teaching of Panormitanus—that a "superior" person could kill to escape dishonor even when avoidance of killing was possible in another way—is accepted <u>as</u> his teaching by Sylvester Prieras (d.1523) at the beginning of the sixteenth century.[65] But he extends to everyone what Panormitanus restricted to those for whom flight would bring great shame. Thus, no person is bound to flee from injury to avoid killing an attacker. Sylvester's teaching on this point is the most liberal found in the three hundred years under consideration. It seems clear that if it were accepted, the entire notion of necessity would be undermined. Such a consequence was no doubt influential in subsequent teaching refusing to perpetuate a blanket legitimation.

   In the second half of the same century, Diego de Covarrubias y Leyva (d.1577) gives expression to the state of the question at his time. He admits the existence of a doubt whether a layman (as distinct from a cleric) needs to flee to avoid ignominy. Some teach that "he can omit flight which is injurious to him and kill the aggressor."[66] Covarrubias himself believes it wrong to kill to defend one's honor, as honor is not equal to the life of another. Yet he admits the existence of the doubt and insists that if one were to follow the other opinion there would still remain some guilt, though it would not be grave. In this fashion Covarrubias attempts to prevent the debatable position from totally exonerating the person who kills for honor, while at the same time not holding the guilt to be grave so as to remove the person who would follow the opinion from a lapse into serious sin. But he himself is clearly against killing for the sake of honor when one can avoid it by flight. The inequality of honor and life solves the dilemma for Covarrubias, but he does not impose his understanding upon others.

In the seventeenth century Lessius (d.1623), Diana (d.1663), and Busembaum (d.1668) teach that if there would be disgrace in flight, one need not flee and may kill.[67] The type of "disgrace" conceived is expressed in Busembaum's example of persons who would be disgraced—a nobleman or a military officer—and in Diana's contention that there is no disgrace for "men of inferior note" to flee. Lessius appears to agree with this teaching and to extend it to everyone, as Sylvester had. But further on[68] he says that killing for honor, while "speculatively probable," is not to be easily permitted in practice. The danger for fighting, hatred, and vengeance is too great.

Busembaum's position is repeated verbatim by Alphonsus Ligouri (d.1787) in the next century, but with a note of caution like that of Lessius.[69] While citing the previous teaching, he adds that in practice he would judge that either "never or most rarely" would it be justified to kill only to protect honor. And he specifically directs this point to the case of noblemen. He considers proposition n. 30 condemned by Innocent XI in 1679, to forbid such killing.[70] That proposition allowed killing if ignominy could not be avoided. But Alphonsus gives his opinion in this form: "I cannot understand why the contrary opinion must not be said to be proscribed by proposition 30, condemned by Innocent XI." Obviously, some did not consider it in this way. Alphonsus seems to be determined to prevent killing that is avoidable simply because of the disgrace involved in fleeing the necessity. He must have recognized the dangerous latitude of the position which obviously favored the noble and powerful in the society. Consequently, though he does not teach that it is absolutely forbidden, his use of "never or most rarely" and his understanding of proposition 30 clearly indicate which side of the issue he has chosen as his own. The status-differentiation reflected in Panormitanus and carried on by Diana and Busembaum and the liberality of Sylvester have been practically rejected by Lessius and Alphonsus, who tend to the position of Covarrubias, yet stop short of his desire to totally condemn killing to escape disgrace when avoidance of the killing is possible.

The second issue to be discussed in this period between 1500 and 1800 is that of "intention." The dominant person in this question remains Aquinas; his teaching that the private individual may not intend the death of an attacker but only self-preservation remains the norm.[71] But opposition to his teaching arises in the sixteenth century. Dominic Soto (d.1560), of Salamanca, seems to be the first to question Thomas' position, and he is followed by Navarrus (d.1586) and Molina (d.1600); the latter is then quoted by Diana in the next century.[72] Informing the opposition to Thomas are two motivating factors. The first (Soto and Molina) is primarily an attempt to justify the intending of what is a necessary means (killing) to a good end (self-preservation). The second (Navarrus and Molina) is the desire to forestall excessive and unwarranted sentiments of guilt by the person who kills in self-defense. Obviously, the second issue will be resolved if the first effort is successful.

The attempt to correct Thomas' teaching is based upon the premise that Thomas denies that the __means__ (killing the attacker) to the end (self-preservation) is licit. Soto thus argues that since the killing is a necessary means to a good end, it may be intended.[73] Molina seeks to expand this argument by saying that since defensive killing is not wrong, not against the fifth commandment, it is good. Furthermore, since the death involved is a necessary means to defense of one's own life and one may intend the end of defense and conservation of life, it is legitimate to intend as a "remote" end the death judged necessary to achieve the "proximate" end of conservation of life.

While our concern with this controversy is primarily its ultimate relationship to killing in defense of property, there is need to point out that Thomas is misunderstood by these men. When Thomas speaks of <u>intentio</u>, he has in mind not <u>means</u> but the <u>end</u>.[74] Intentio is the act of desiring to achieve an end; it is not concerned with <u>how</u> one accomplishes the task. When Thomas wants to discuss means, he uses the term <u>electio</u>: the choice of means. Soto and the others misunderstand the term <u>intentio</u>, and thus deal with a different problem than Thomas does. Aquinas wants to emphasize what a person is about—the saving of his life. Because of this focus, one is more inclined, in Thomas' view, to use moderation in defense and to avoid revenge. Soto and Molina, while not rejecting the notion of moderation (nor justifying revenge), do not emphasize it. They are concerned with means. The means is necessary and not evil (the aggression makes it not evil); thus it is good.

Although Thomas speaks of something different from what Soto and the others speak, the very difference is what interests us here. By concentrating on the end, Thomas strives to keep the notion of moderation in the foreground. The others, while not abandoning due moderation, do not emphasize it; their interest is in the means. Does this emphasis approximate (if not establish) a teaching whereby the end justifies the means? Is <u>due</u> moderation practically by-passed through a lack of consideration of the mutual injuries potentially present?[75] By restricting the private individual to desiring to preserve his own life, Aquinas demands that the end of the action be the preservation of a good, a positive objective. The others would legitimate a negative objective, the deprivation of life. Thomas thus requires the preservation of a right, while the others legitimate the direct deprivation of one. Perhaps this dispute is indicative of something we have seen before. Soto and the others would make killing a "good," which may then be desired; Thomas wants to retain emphasis upon the evil in killing. To kill in self-defense may be necessary, but for Thomas it remains a necessary <u>evil</u>, legitimated only as the consequence of a desire to achieve some good. The difference here is already apparent in its relation to the notion of "due moderation," to which we now turn.

Due Moderation

It was said earlier that the criterion of due moderation included in the principle of repelling force with force would be kept as separate as possible in our discussion. Despite this attempt, it should be clear that the meaning of this requirement has been intimately involved in the teaching on killing on the basis of both public and private authority. "Due moderation" refers to the use of only that force necessary to repel injury. Yet the issue is not resolved quite that easily. The formulation just used—"necessary to repel injury"—expresses a later concept than "the violence expressed be equal to and not exceed the violence brought." The first focuses on the injury and, as we shall see, with more concern for injury in itself than the type or gravity of the injury. The second formulation concentrates on the violence used to inflict the injury. The significance of the difference can be pointed out by recalling some of the positions we have already discussed, such as the persistent attempt to exclude hatred and revenge in acting, as well as from certain direct statements.

The first sign of divergence which appeared came with Bonaventure's reduction of guilt when a person kills rather than flees in order to avoid shame.[76] For Thomas, his contemporary, to kill in that circumstance is simply homicide; the action would be disproportionate to the end.[77] The same point of view is evident on the part of those who demanded that a person avoid the necessity of killing whenever possible. Those who justified killing when it was avoidable but would entail suffering an injury (such as dishonor) carried the teaching of Bonaventure from reduction of guilt to total absence of fault.[78]

The phrase above concerning the equality of "violence expressed" and "violence brought" is Antoninus'.[79] And we have already met his principle condemning the taking of a life to avoid a lesser evil. These two elements of his teaching emphasize his intention to require for due moderation not only the absence of excessive violence, but also a judgment on the relative evil between killing and the threatened injury. It is the latter interest that tends to disappear, as we have seen in the case of flight and dishonor. The importance of the presence or absence of this component, or the effort to equate the "evil" of killing with another "evil," will be apparent in the subsequent chapters on killing a thief.

A contemporary of Antoninus, Panormitanus, also emphasizes the importance of avoiding excessive reaction to force.[80] But he does so in terms of prior self-understanding and knowledge of the situation. Panormitanus raises the possibility of a person being certain that he cannot act with due moderation or doubtful that he can act with moderation. In both cases, Panormitanus writes, the person then cannot repel force with force. If one knows that he cannot keep his violent response within reasonable limits, he cannot employ violence as defense to violence. It is certainly possible that a person might come to such knowledge through experiencing his own reaction in similar circumstances. Given the principle of Antoninus regarding the avoidance of lesser evil by greater evil, would it not follow that a situation could itself give rise to such knowledge? Given the type or form of threatened injury and the means available to prevent it, could any attempt to prevent be excessive precisely because prevention would involve greater evil than the suffered injury? We will see that Panormitanus' approach to moderation is significant in his teaching on killing in defense of property.

Once we pass into the sixteenth century and meet the teaching of such authorities as Cajetan, Sylvester, and Navarrus, the focal point of due moderation changes.[81] From attention to the equality of the violence which occurs and the evils resulting from the use of violence, the interest shifts to the injury to be prevented. "Do that without which the injury could not be avoided" is the way Navarrus states it.[82] In pointing out this shift of focus, I am not saying that these authors have no consideration for the type or extent of injury to be repelled; they do. They do not wish to justify a very violent response to a minor attack. They will not legitimate, for example, killing to save oneself from a blow which would inflict little injury. What I want to underscore, however, is the focus and the tendency in their statements. When attention is directed primarily to the avoidance of injury, it is a simple step to then justify the means necessary to escape injury with little evaluation of the relative importance of the injuries being compared (or not compared). We will have the opportunity to see this tendency at work in the case of theft and its prevention.

One further important point is present in the evolution of the due moderation principle. We have already touched upon the concern shown by Navarrus and Molina for the consciences of people in the question of intention. The same kind of sensitivity appears in conjunction with due moderation in the work of Diana.[83] He judges due moderation to be present in a situation in which a person judges his only self-defense to be killing because nothing else occurs to him hy which he might free himself. Nor could anything easily occur, writes Diana, because the person is attentive to the present disturbance; so he can kill, and this is due moderation.

This teaching seems to be entirely valid if one were evaluating moral guilt; the circumstances render clear and precise judgment impossible. But the position does not stand as a moral principle. Extenuating circumstances can diminish guilt, but moral principles are not determined by such circumstances. One of the functions of such principles is to aid in the making of judgments. If a person fails to apply a principle because of fear or some other form of pressure, then his guilt is lessened; the moral principle is not abrogated nor is its meaning defined in terms of the action informed by the pressures. There will be other examples of this sort of thinking as we proceed. The temptation to forget the educative role of moral principles is ever-present.

Conclusion

In this chapter there has been an attempt to understand the moral justification of taking a human life. It has been shown that the basic premise for justification was the natural law principle of repelling force with force, observing due moderation. This principle was applied to both public and private individuals: the public officials for the sake of the common good, the private person in cases of self-defense. There is thus a <u>legal</u> foundation for all killing that is justifiable. This legal basis is most broad, as all laws—Divine, natural, human—are viewed as permitting force to be repelled by force.

As the fundamental principle was applied to the private individual, we have discovered a concerted effort to keep somehow within bounds the ease with which man can rise up in violence to kill. The distinction between avoidable and unavoidable necessity elucidates this effort. Because of the seriousness of killing, such action is to be taken only when it is necessary to prevent a sufficiently great evil. What evil may be so prevented is determined by law. The awareness of the need to exclude any vengeance is sharp, and because of this the sanction of legitimate authority is necessary. There is also some evidence that the killing must have a benefit which exceeds the evil of killing. But at the same time there has emerged a tendency, based on the evaluation of action almost solely in terms of the innocent person, to shift to injury as the focal point in defense rather than equality of violence and comparative harm. The dominance of a status differentiation serving to determine the recognition of legitimate killing expresses the conviction that killing is a Divinely sanctioned means for social control of evil. All of these elements will emerge in the application of these principles to the case of killing to prevent theft.

This chapter began with an examination of conflicting Biblical evidence. We saw how our authors reconciled the New and Old Testament morality by internalizing the New or making it an elitist morality not binding the common man. The internal conflicts of the Old Testament gave rise to an "exception" approach, which kept intact both the norm of the

Decalogue—"You shall not kill"—and the right to kill in certain cases. It is to the relationship of the two Testaments and the "exception" manner of understanding that we turn in the next chapter.

CHAPTER II

LAW: ADULTERY, CLERICS, SERMON ON THE MOUNT

The Catholic moral tradition, as examined, found the legal basis to justify the taking of human life in the natural law principle which allows force to repel force. From this starting point, all laws were seen to accept the principle, though different types of law—Divine, civil, ecclesiastical—would further specify details in the application of the principle. It is quite possible that in the process of specifying, the various types of law may come into conflict. In response to this conflict a hierarchy of law will be seen to emerge, through which the conflict may be resolved.

The reality of conflict within a particular type of law was evidenced in the first chapter in the efforts of the theologians and canonists to reconcile Old and New Testament morality. The attempt will be made here to further clarify that effort and to raise some questions in response to it.

Before entering the arena of abstract conflict, however, this chapter will first exhibit two examples which treat of particular cases in which killing is or is not justified. The cases at issue are whether one caught in adultery may be killed (either by public authority or by a private individual) and if it is legitimate for clerics to kill. These examples will demonstrate the interaction of the natural, Divine, and human laws.

Adultery

The morality of killing a person guilty of adultery receives consideration by a representative group of authorities spanning the period between the thirteenth and eighteenth centuries. From Thomas Aquinas to Alphonsus Ligouri the issue pivots upon the interplay between civil and ecclesiastical law, with some interjection of Biblical evidence. As was the case in chapter one, the <u>Decretum</u> of Gratian provides basic Church law on this question, and thus must be considered as a starting point.

Gratian cites a letter of Pope Nicholas I, which states that a man who kills his wife without (civil?) judgment and without such an added circumstance as adultery is to be considered a murderer.[1] Then Gratian adds that while this statement <u>appears</u> to legitimate killing a wife guilty of adultery, ecclesiastical discipline demands that "criminals be smitten with the spiritual, not the material sword." To substantiate his own position, Gratian again relies on Pope Nicholas,[2] who teaches that one may not kill his wife for the crime of adultery <u>even though</u> civil law allows this to be done. The reason given by Nicholas is that the Church is "not constrained by civil laws"; it "does not kill but gives life." As a final statement, Gratian cites the words of Augustine:[3] "It is not licit for a Christian man to kill his adulterous wife, though he can dismiss her."

The <u>Decretum</u> thus teaches as Church law the immorality of killing an adulterous wife. The contrary statement of Pope Nicholas is countered by his own words, as well as by the interpretation of Gratian, which declares the meaning of Nicholas' first statement to be only apparent. But that first citation from Nicholas contains a phrase the meaning of which will arise frequently in later authors: <u>sine judicio</u>, "without judgment." That phrase, when added to other considerations, could easily lead to the question of civil authority's power to declare adultery a capital crime and to permit a wronged husband to kill his adulterous wife. Despite the statements of Gratian, the issue was not yet settled.

Thirteenth Century

Alexander of Hales refers but in passing to the issue of adultery and killing.[4] He declares the New Law (Gospel) to be a law of "mercy and mitigation," and he gives the text of Jn. 8:11 as an indication. This verse is Jesus' statement to the woman caught in adultery: "Nor do I condemn you. You may go." Alexander goes on to say that the "law of mercy and mitigation" is in contrast to the judicial punishment of the old precepts (Old Testament), but it is not against secular power punishing. This is the extent of Alexander's teaching. Is his use of the verse from John's Gospel a statement that according to the New Law an adulterous person is not to be killed? Is the statement about civil power punishing to be understood as a legitimation of that authority's declaring death the punishment for adultery? If so, Alexander could be saying that civil law may punish with death, but the private person cannot kill. This teaching would agree with Alexander's notion of "necessary defense," for the notion of self-defense would be lacking. But he says too little to make an exact judgment.

A century after the <u>Decretum</u>, Thomas Aquinas addressed himself to the problem in terms of the relationship between civil and ecclesiastical law.[5] He teaches that a person guilty of adultery may be legitimately killed by civil authority; the person may be accused, tried, and condemned to death. The case of a private person, a husband who kills his wife for her adultery, for example, is a different matter.[6] Thomas explains that the civil law does not punish the man who kills his adulterous wife; the law considers the provocation and recognizes that as an excusing cause. However, Thomas insists, the lack of <u>punishment</u> in this instance does not mean that the civil law either commands or justifies the killing. All the civil law does is recognize factors diminishing responsibility; thus it refrains from punishing. On the other hand, writes Thomas, the Church law condemns such killing. The private individual, for example, a husband, is guilty of serious sin if he kills his wife for her adultery. Civil law does not justify, it simply refrains from punishing. Church law does not justify, and it declares the penalty to be "the debt of eternal punishment." The Church can impose a punishment where civil law refrains from punishing, writes Thomas, because it is not bound to the human law.

The teaching of Thomas appears clear up to this point. Public authority may kill a person guilty of adultery, but a private person may not. (Is there something of

Nicholas' *sine judicio* here?) Civil law does not justify the killing even though it does not punish a private person for it, while ecclesiastical law declares such killing sinful and deserving of eternal punishment. But he goes on to say that should civil law allow a private individual to kill one caught in adultery, there would be no sin in doing so. While this teaching is consistent with Thomas' idea of civil authority being able to kill or declare killing legitimate for the sake of the common good, it is in opposition to the *Decretum*, which forbade killing one guilty of adultery even though civil law would allow it. If the Church can declare a "spiritual punishment" to be applicable when civil authority refrains from imposing a temporal punishment for violating its law, can a change in civil law totally abolish the legitimation of the Church law? Thomas initially compared punishments; is the "debt of eternal punishment" solely the consequence of civil law? If the Church is "not bound" to the human law, how can that law determine the morality of an act? If the private individual cannot "intend" a death but only his own defense, would a change in the civil law make the private individual a "public authority," an agent of the civil law? The teaching of Aquinas on this issue comes from an earlier work than his *Summa*; would he have taught differently had he treated the question in the later work? Perhaps not. In Thomas' scheme all crimes are treated in the same way. Public authority may decide for the benefit of the common good to kill as punishment for particular crimes. If that authority to kill is extended to private individuals, they may without sin act as agents of the public authority. But what "might be" is not what "is" in Thomas' teaching. The state of the question as he writes is that both civil and ecclesiastical law forbid the private individual to kill the adulterous person.

While Aquinas concentrates on civil law as the determining moral factor in this issue, Bonaventure relies upon what he terms "the law of Gospel."[7] According to Bonaventure, this law forbids the killing of an adulteress; neither the public authority nor the individual may kill her. In his short statement on this question, Bonaventure's reason is "the Gospel forbids it"; to do the opposite would be against the "law of mercy." And he explicitly states that civil law cannot legitimately command such killing.

Bonaventure does not indicate what in the Gospel forbids killing an adulteress. The most obvious source of his teaching would be Jn. 8:1-11, where Jesus refuses to condemn the woman caught in adultery; Bonaventure, however, does not cite this passage. It is also possible, but unlikely, that he drew his conclusion from the general tenor of the Gospel. Such a conclusion would not be in accord with his teaching as seen in chapter one.[8]

The precise place from which Bonaventure's teaching comes may not be able to be identified, but his source is the Gospel and his conclusion is clear: an adulteress is not to be killed. His teaching also denies to the civil authority a capacity which Thomas saw it to have. The difference in the teaching of these two men, with their diverse sources, tells us the pattern of the positions held after them. Is there a "Gospel law" for this case? Is civil law or Church law the determiner of the morality of killing an adulteress? Thomas and Bonaventure answered these questions differently; so will the later tradition.

The text of Jn. 8, the likely basis of Bonaventure's "Gospel law," is the source of Scotus' teaching. He states that the punishment established for adultery in the Old Testament was revoked in Jn. 8, when Jesus refused to condemn or punish the woman.[9] It would thus be against Divine law to kill one guilty of adultery.[10]

Scotus does not elaborate his point any further; he simply accepts and declares this Gospel passage to be a statement of Divine law. Neither does Scotus give any authoritative figure as supporting his position. But it is well known that Scotus often relied upon Augustine, at least as a starting point.[11] We have already seen the inclusion of Augustine's condemnation of killing an adulteress in the Decretum.[12] Augustine also uses Jn. 8:11, to show the obligation of a husband to forgive his adulterous wife.[13] If such obligation exists and is based upon this Gospel text, it is a simple step to consider the source of the obligation to be

Divine law. Thus to kill in this case would be contrary to that law. Scotus, conceivably, could have had Augustine's teaching in mind. If he did, we will see that among the authors examined on this point, he is the only one who did. The only other direct reference to Jn. 8, will be almost three centuries later by Cajetan, who cites the text only to oppose the teaching of Scotus.[14]

Fifteenth Century

In the fifteenth century, Panormitanus and Antoninus discuss killing an adulteress only briefly, and they confine the discussion to the relationship between ecclesiastical and civil law, with some mention by Panormitanus of the need for these laws to conform to Divine law.[15] Panormitanus acknowledges the presence of civil law which allows a father to kill his daughter caught in adultery; Antoninus relates the civil law which permits a husband to kill his wife for this crime, or a father to kill the adulterer found with his daughter. Both men respond to the civil law by stating that Church law makes such actions murder; civil law cannot excuse one from the sin of murder. In making this statement, Panormitanus says that any "concession" civil law may make must be both reasonable and in conformity to Divine law. Since Panormitanus accepts the Church law's declaration of killing an adulteress to be murder, the civil law "concession" must not meet the criteria he sets down. Killing an adulteress must be either unreasonable or contrary to Divine law, or both. What failure is present, he does not say. All he says is that Church law declares the act murder. Panormitanus does not give us any particular Church law as forbidding this killing. Neither does Antoninus refer to any Church law. He cites a civil law, <u>Authenticum</u>, <u>Ut nulli judicum</u>, which punishes an adulterous person by sending that person to a monastery.[16] Antoninus understands this civil law to supercede and correct any other civil law: adultery is no longer "a matter of death."

The teaching of Panormitanus is clearly concerned only with the case of a private individual who might kill; the law he takes exception to applies to a father who would kill his daughter. Antoninus, however, is not so clear. Does he forbid only what Panormitanus forbids, or does he also prohibit public authority from passing a sentence of death for adultery?

Antoninus makes reference to the opinion of Aquinas, which we have already discussed: outside a process of judgment it is a mortal sin to kill for adultery; and civil law's not punishing is not to be taken as acknowledging the licitness of killing. Then Antoninus states that the law from Authenticum corrects that law by demanding that the adulterous person enter a monastery. What "law" is corrected? Is it the law by which public authority kills in this case, or the "law" which did not punish, or both? The private person clearly cannot kill for adultery, because, Antoninus writes, "such punishment must not be done from anger, but with maturity and counsel." Does that mean that after "maturity and counsel" enter, death may be inflicted by public authority? Antoninus begins his discussion of the question of killing for adultery by asking if a husband may kill his adulterous wife. He answers that question negatively. Perhaps he intended to do no more than that. It is likewise possible that the Authenticum is simply understood to forbid civil authority to kill for adultery. But since this is itself a civil law, it could be changed by civil authority if death was deemed necessary. Antoninus holds that the Authenticum corrects other civil laws; his major concern appears to be the private individual: such a person cannot kill for adultery. He does not seem to rule out the possibility of civil law changing, but even if it were to change it could not make the killing by a private person morally legitimate. Could public authority inflict the death penalty? The evidence from Antoninus is not entirely clear, but it would be logical on his basis of civil law to say that it could. If that is the case, on this point of public authority Antoninus agrees with Thomas. He disagrees with him regarding the private individual.

Sixteenth Century

In the sixteenth century two avenues are followed in the discussion of killing the adulterous person: the teaching of Aquinas is carried on and the opinion of Scotus is opposed. Yet there remains diversity in the question of the private person killing. Sylvester Prieras agrees with Aquinas that a private person could kill another for adultery if the civil law gave that authority; he also holds that the lack of punishment for such killing by civil authority is not a legitimation of the killing. Thus it is wrong for the private person to kill in this case.[17] Sylvester does no more than repeat the teaching of Thomas, although he acknowledges no dependence upon him. Neither does he comment upon his statement. Cajetan and Vitoria, writing commentaries on Thomas, are explicit in their dependence upon him.[18]

Cajetan and Vitoria argue this question in direct opposition to the teaching of Scotus. Both root their opposition in Thomas' principle that the individual may be killed when the death is necessary for the common good. Vitoria considers it to be "natural law that one man die lest the whole community perish"; killing for adultery is against neither natural nor scriptural law. Cajetan finds support in the weeds-wheat parable of Mt. 13, and both men proceed to challenge the opinion of Scotus. Based upon their stance that the application of moral law (the Ten Commandments)[19] depends on man's reason, Cajetan and Vitoria deny that the text of Jn. 8 does anything other than give an example of Gospel mercy. It in no way takes away the authority of civil rulers to kill for adultery.

The issue of the individual's ability to kill for adultery is not mentioned by Cajetan. It would be consistent for him to agree with Thomas: if the civil law permits it, there would be no sin involved. Vitoria, however, disagrees with Thomas.[20] He says it is impossible for civil law to give the individual the authority to kill in this situation. The reason given for this incapacity is the need for accusation and the opportunity for the accused to defend himself against the charge. Vitoria even declares that to by-pass this process of judgment would be a violation of "natural law." The violation which Vitoria sees in this instance is due, perhaps, to his judging death for adultery to be in no way an act of defense; it is a punishment. Punishment belongs to the civil power, and it requires a judicial process.

With this one important difference, these sixteenth century theologians continue the teaching of Aquinas. The important element which has emerged is the statement of Cajetan and Vitoria, taken from Thomas, that man is to determine the morality of specific acts by using his reason. If the civil law determines that adultery is sufficiently detrimental to the common good, death may be a legitimate punishment. Although Vitoria would restrict death for adultery to the civil authority after use of the judicial process, Sylvester and Cajetan would seem to agree with Thomas that civil authority could give the private person legitimation to kill in this case. The teaching thus would be based upon what man's reason determines to be needed. Once more we see the tendency evident in chapter one: to legitimate killing, to declare killing "necessary," on the basis of desire to eliminate an evil.[21] But once again we find no attempt to compare the evils (in this case those of adultery and killing). Just because the civil law can impose death for the sake of the common good, is there to be no question, no way to evaluate the judgment of the civil law? One might ask: Does killing the adulterer benefit society?

Seventeenth and Eighteenth Centuries

Lessius denies that a private person can kill an adulterer.[22] The major reasons for his position are the manifest danger that the adulterer will lose his soul (because of the lack of opportunity for repentance) and the lack of any necessity for killing. It is required that the guilty person be captured, accused, and tried. Once the legal process has taken place, an adulterer can be killed. Lessius remarks that the civil authority could appoint the parents or spouse of the condemned adulterer to carry out the execution. By his requirement that an adulterer only be killed by public authority, Lessius continues the teaching of Vitoria, though his stated sources are principally the canon law and Augustinian teaching we have already seen.

A decision is made in the seventeenth century on the

part of ecclesiastical authority which settles for Busembaum the question of a private person being able to kill for adultery.[23] Alphonsus simply repeats this position in the eighteenth century.[24] In 1665, as part of a concerted seventeenth-century papal effort, Alexander VII condemned a number of lax moral opinions. Among them was a proposition which gave permission to a private person to kill for adultery if civil law granted this to him.[25] Both Busembaum and Alphonsus understood this condemnation to settle the question of the private individual's right to kill; both remark that it is thus not morally licit for civil law to permit a private person to kill in this case. They also seem to reject the idea that the concept of "public defense" could require such killing; for they remark that it is "otherwise" in cases necessary for public defense. Both Busembaum and Alphonsus would seem to allow public authority to impose the death penalty for adultery, but they demand a process of conviction that would exclude the private person from killing. Death for adultery is thus viewed as a legitimate punishment; since there is nothing by way of defense in the case, the judicial process would be required. Vitoria's teaching is solidified.

In looking at the teaching on this issue over a span of some five hundred years, we have seen an initial dichotomy in the thirteenth century. Thomas permitted death as punishment and the possibility of civil law making private persons agents of the punishment. Bonaventure and Scotus denied the legitimacy of anyone killing for adultery. The former opinion considered abstract principles, mainly the right to kill for the common good; the latter opinion rejected killing on the basis of "Gospel law," specified by Scotus as Jn. 8:1-11. The latter opinion does not prevail. Thomas' position holds up in the authors referred to, though there is debate on the question of the private person acting as an agent of civil law. Through the use of the law of **Authenticum** in the fifteenth century by Antoninus, and the condemnation by Alexander VII in the seventeenth, the teaching ends up by rejecting Thomas' opinion and forbidding a private person to act as an agent of civil law. The prohibition is based upon both ecclesiastical and civil law. We saw Thomas' opinion that civil law could make our case one in which a person could kill with moral impunity; by the fifteenth century Church law had challenged that claim, using civil law itself to support its position. With the exception of Bonaventure and Scotus (and possibly Panormitanus and Antoninus) public authority is conceded to have the power to determine adultery a grave threat to the common good, and so deserving of death. That position appears to remain intact in the seventeenth and eighteenth centuries. The Gospel basis of opposition does not enter the question after Scotus (though there is an oblique reference by Panormitanus), except to be declared unfounded. What Scotus saw as "law," Cajetan saw as an "example of mercy" in no way binding. The difference is rooted in the visions of New Testament morality, and these we will examine later in this chapter.

Clerics

From the compilation of Church law by Gratian until the formalization of the moral system of Alphonsus Ligouri, the question of a cleric being able to kill undergoes much examination from different perspectives. Not only is the right to defend himself looked at, but also his ability to defend property and to act as an agent of the civil law. As we follow the discussion, it will be seen that the teaching develops from a more limited to a more permissive position. Of special interest will be the interplay of particular Church laws as these are understood and applied by the various authors.

There is ample use of Church law on this issue already in the thirteenth century. Before beginning the examination of the teaching of that century, a brief look at some of the laws contained in the Decretum will help to illustrate the legal background with which the Scholastics were working.[26] Further examples will occur in the various authors.

One framework in which Gratian speaks to our issue is that of "taking up arms," i.e., war; but he also includes the idea of arming oneself for a quarrel.[27] In this context,

Jesus' statement to Peter that he should put away his sword is quoted (Mt. 26:52) and its meaning is stated to be that the bearing of arms is thus forbidden to ecclesiastics. The weapons of bishops and clerics are "tears and the Word of God"; terrestrial authority is to take up arms. Because civil authority has this capacity, it is legitimate for the Church to call upon it to defend the Church from oppression.[28]

These canons from the <u>Decretum</u> cannot be said to prohibit all killing to clerics. A situation of immediate self-defense is not envisioned, for example. But these laws do forbid clerics to bear arms in quarrels and to take up weapons in a military way; the latter case is the realm of civil authority. The canons cited also point out clearly that what ecclesiastics may not do, they may ask the civil power to do. This notion will continue through the centuries. What is considered unfitting for one station in life is quite appropriate in another. It is not difficult to see the legal fiction which this notion perpetuates. If one person gets another to do what the first wants done, the first person is no less responsible for the morality of the accomplished act. Ecclesiastics cannot remove themselves from responsibility by claiming that the actual armed defense was carried out by military, not Church people.

The elements contained in these canons of Gratian, plus more specified situations and criteria, will be present as we examine the cleric's moral responsibility in killing from the thirteenth to the eighteenth centuries.

Thirteenth Century

Alexander takes up the question of a cleric being morally justified in killing from two perspectives: killing to defend himself[29] and killing as an exercise of his spiritual authority,[30] which would be a matter of punishing evildoers or acting defensively on a broader scale. In both instances Alexander prohibits a cleric from killing.

A cleric is forbidden to kill in self-defense on the basis of three canons found in the <u>Decretum</u>. Pope Nicholas I[31] teaches that a cleric who kills in self-defense must do penance before he can return to the exercise of his ministry, but, the Pope remarks, the return to his former state after penance is not to be considered as giving any license whatsoever to kill anyone. Alexander understands this canon to forbid all killing, regardless of circumstance, to clerics. He also quotes a canon of the Council of Lérida[32] which teaches the same thing: clerics are not to kill even if they are in immediate danger. Once again penance is required before the cleric who fails in this can be restored to office. From this requirement for penance, Alexander concludes that there must have been guilt in the killing. The final canon used by Alexander is one which declares killing to be an impediment to one who wants to become a cleric and has killed in the past.[33] Alexander's use of this canon to uphold his position can only mean that he infers from an impediment to entering the clerical state a prohibition on those who are already in that state.

Having built his case on these three canons, Alexander remarks that the prohibition which forbids killing to clerics is strictly ecclesiastical law. Natural law, which permits self-defensive killing when necessary, makes no distinction between clergy and laity. Whatever distinction is made between the two is the work of Church law.

The case of those having spiritual power being able to licitly put someone to death is argued at length by Alexander. Among the arguments which seek to allow killing by spiritual authorities are references to events in the Old Testament such as Moses commanding the Levites to kill those who worshipped the golden calf,[34] and Mattathias killing two men involved in pagan sacrifice.[35] The death of Ananias and Sapphira at the word of Peter is the major New Testament occurrence incorporated in support of killing.[36] Alexander answers the proposal that Peter killed these two people by stating that Peter simply declared the fact of their death; he did not kill them himself. The Old Testament examples lead Alexander into his major solution to this problem. He admits that the authority to kill belonged to the ministers of the Old Testament; the law gave them this authority. But the ministers of the New Testament do not have such power. The reason why the authority is lacking arises from the nature of the New Law, and it is twofold. A minister of the New Law must administer gentleness and love to lead men to the good, as the Gospel teaches when it says: "Do not resist evil" (Mt. 5:39) and "Love your enemies, do good to those who hate you" (Mt. 5:44). Alexander emphasizes that these things are to be accomplished by ministers of the New Law not just in their words or will; they are to put them into practice. The second reason for the prohibition is that these ministers serve the "sacrament of union." The "Sacrament of the Altar" represents, Alexander says, the union of Christ and the Church, which the union of body and soul signify. As the soul vivifies the body, so Christ through this Sacrament vivifies the Church. Thus to break the union of body and soul would be to violate the symbolism by not showing forth the union which the Sacrament represents. As a consequence of the Gospel teaching and the symbolism, Alexander says that the ministers of the New Law are not to put anyone to death. To further establish this position, he quotes Church laws[37] which impose an irregularity for killing (which forbids the minister access to the Sacrament of the Eucharist) but state that there is no guilt in the act of killing. Although Alexander understands the verses from Matthew to require practice, not just disposition but a certain mode of behavior, and the symbolism of the Eucharist to lead to exemplifying unity in what the minister does, he concludes that the prohibition is merely one of ecclesiastical law, imposing a penalty of deprivation but not binding in any way morally. For spiritual authority to kill would be "illicit," he says, but there would be no moral guilt.

In the situation of a cleric killing in self-defense, Alexander was seen to base the prohibition strictly upon ecclesiastical law; natural law does not distinguish between clergy and laity, and it allows self-defensive killing. He also said that there is guilt if a cleric kills in this case. Alexander's teaching on spiritual authority's moral legitimacy to kill is also based upon ecclesiastical law, despite his own declaration that particular texts of Mt. 5 prohibit killing by ministers of the New Law. But in this case there

is no moral guilt, just a Church penalty to be endured. Two
problems are thus created. If the Gospel prohibits killing
by a minister, how can the prohibition be based upon ecclesiastical law? If Church law recognizes moral guilt in the one
instance, why is that guilt absent in the other? The diffi-
culties are perhaps answered through the context in which
Alexander writes. The "spiritual authority" of which he
speaks seems to be a __collective__ authority, especially as
personified in the pope. This is the authority to which is
committed the __common good__ of the Church. There would be accompanying this authority the capacity to take life for the
benefit of the common good—if the Church authority were
viewed as a parallel authority to that of civil government.
Consequently, the right to kill, if not allowed, could only
be absent by means of a self-restriction on the part of the
Church. It would not be absent by the authority. Yet is it
not precisely the nature of the authority—what is referred
to as the "New Law"—which forbids the killing? The Old Law
gave the authority to kill to its ministers; the New Law does
not. How, then, can guilt be absent when the New Law is
violated? How can what is considered to be a prescription of
the New Law not be the binding force for those under the New
Law? Alexander teaches that no one can kill on his own
authority; thus the individual cleric is guilty if he kills,
because the __Church__ law takes from him a legitimation based
on __natural__ law. It is not at all clear or logical that guilt
should not also be involved in the case of "spiritual authorities." The idea of the common good is also natural law and
is also forbidden by Church law. Nor does there seem to be
any logic in basing a prohibition upon the teaching of the
Gospel and then declaring it to be a matter of ecclesiastical
law. It is rather strange that one could be guilty of homicide in killing to defend his own life and guiltless in somehow formally imposing death or in asking another to kill to
punish someone or to defend property.

    The capacity of Church authorities to call upon the
civil power to take up arms against various evildoers is
also affirmed by Alexander. He relies upon the __Decretum__ for
this teaching.[38] There was an opinion that when the pope

makes this request of the emperor, the emperor receives his authority to kill from the pope. Alexander responds that the pope does not give the emperor the authority to kill; that authority comes from the law, and thus from God. The desire to remove ecclesiastics from any responsibility in the shedding of blood remains strong.

The canonists Hostiensis and Raymund of Pennaforte both acknowledge the legitimacy of clerics calling upon secular authority when the issue is one of violence against some form of property.[39] But Raymund requires the bishop or particular church which asks to exhort the secular arm to refrain from killing, and to oppose any killing which may occur. Thus comes exoneration from responsibility.

These canonists also permit a cleric to kill in self-defense, while denying him the right to kill to protect only property.[40] Raymund, however, demands of a priest who kills in self-defense life-long penance, though he is not deposed from office. There does not appear to be any moral guilt associated with the killing by the priest, just a demand for penance: a Church punishment. Hostiensis just says that the cleric is permitted to kill to protect his own life.[41]

The teaching of Raymund and Hostiensis that there is no guilt if a cleric kills in defense of his life is the opposite of the position of Alexander. The absence of guilt is likewise affirmed by Richard of Middleton in his commentary on <u>Interfecisti</u>, <u>De homicidio</u>.[42] He also agrees with Raymund in insisting upon life-long penance, which arises from the ecclesiastical irregularity imposed. Both men consider this lifetime of penance less a punishment than being deposed from the office of priesthood.

The most obvious difference between Alexander and the others is the source upon which the disparate teaching is based. Alexander, the theologian, relies upon the <u>Decretum</u>; the others, lawyers, rely upon the <u>Decretales</u>, which were a much more contemporary expression of law. Alexander considers the penalty of "irregularity" to be a sign of guilt; the others do not. Alexander admits through his teaching that ecclesiastical law can place a moral obligation that can result in moral guilt for its subjects; Raymund and Richard deny this connection between Church law and moral guilt (at least in this context). It is possible that the change is due to a growing understanding on the part of these thirteenth-century canonists of the natural law principle of repelling force with force. This right to self-defense recognized in natural law would apply to everyone, without exception. If the Church wanted to restrict the exercise of that right by a particular class of people, it could do that only in terms of external behavior in the realm of Church-related activity. There would be no way in which the Church could attribute moral guilt to an act legitimated by natural law.

The final theologian of this period to be considered is Thomas Aquinas. He examines the morality of clerics taking life from the same dual perspective we have seen in Alexander of Hales. The discussion of the cleric being able to kill in self-defense takes place in response to an objection based upon the teaching of Pope Nicholas I, which was also quoted in Alexander.[43] Alexander understood this passage to forbid all killing to clerics, and the penance demanded led him to view such killing as sinful. Thomas, however, teaches that this law imposes an irregularity upon a cleric; there is no moral guilt in his self-defensive killing. The irregularity occurs though the act itself is sinless. The Church law in this case is viewed as strictly penal, touching only upon the cleric's ability to perform his role and requiring penance as a means of external discipline.

Thomas' examination of the broader issue of clerics killing evildoers also exhibits components already met in Alexander's work.[44] For example, Thomas responds to the case of Ananias and Sapphira by saying that Peter simply published their death sentence which had been pronounced by God; he also considers Church prelates who hold secular offices to be not responsible for killings which others carry out on their authority. But when Thomas states his reasons why clerics cannot kill evildoers, he employs somewhat different arguments to make the same point that Alexander taught. There are two reasons according to Thomas why it is unlawful for clerics to kill. First, clerics are chosen for the ministry of the altar, "whereon is represented the Passion of Christ slain." According to I Peter 2:23, Christ did not strike back when he was struck; so clerics should imitate their master. It would thus be "unbecoming" for clerics to strike to kill. The second reason Thomas gives is the entrusting of the ministry of the New Law to clerics. This law appoints no punishments of death or bodily maiming; thus to be fitting ministers clerics should abstain from these acts of punishment.

Thomas teaches that it is "unlawful" for clerics to punish evildoers with death or maiming. Does "unlawful" mean "sinful"? The phrase translated as "unlawful" is non licet, and in other places in the Summa that phrase clearly means that sin is involved in a violation.[45] Thomas is teaching, therefore, that it would be sinful for clerics to punish by killing or maiming an evildoer. The difference between this case, considered a matter of sin, and that of self-defensive killing, which carries only an ecclesiastical penalty, would seem to lie once again in what is considered "natural." According to Thomas, self-defense is an act allowed by natural law.[46] Church law could not make an act in accord with that law a sin. It is, however, the role of civil authority to punish crimes by death or maiming; the common good, which justifies these punishments, is the responsibility of these officials.[47] Since clerics are to act in a manner befitting the New Law and in imitation of Christ, they are not to exercise the power of civil office even though they may possess the authority of that office. Although Thomas finds nothing incompatible between the clerical state and princely office, he does consider the full exercise of that office sufficiently incompatible to constitute the infliction of death a matter of sin. We have already mentioned the difficulty in removing responsibility when the involvement of the cleric is remote or indirect. Thomas adheres to this position, however, in removing responsibility for a death which is imposed by a cleric holding public office as long as he does not inflict the death himself. As long as a non-cleric judges, sentences, and executes, the cleric whose public office is the authority for these actions is not considered responsible.

Thomas and Alexander are thus seen to hold exactly opposite opinions about clerics and moral guilt. Alexander finds guilt in killing in self-defense, irregularity in imposing a punishment of death. Thomas teaches the opposite. Irregularity for self-defensive killing is likewise the teaching of Hostiensis, Raymund, and Richard. These three canonists also legitimate the reliance upon secular authority in situations which are not a matter of immediate self-defense, as those involving property. While these thirteenth-century theologians and canonists do not exhibit a consensus, it is possible to see a dominance of the opinion which finds no guilt if a cleric kills in self-defense. We will see that this issue is fairly well resolved for the authorities of later centuries, while other aspects of the question continue to evolve.

Fourteenth Century

The emerging importance of the Decretales at the expense of the Decretum is further exemplified by the canonists Joannes Andreae and Joannes de Lignano. Andreae makes a brief statement in his commentary on Significasti, De homicidio, that clerics may not kill in defense of property.[48] It is permissible, however, for a bishop to call in the secular authority to regain Church property. To kill in self-defense is accepted as licit. Lignano's examination of the clerical question is somewhat more lengthy, and it shows more clearly the disputed state of the issue.

Lignano[49] offers for consideration Church laws which both permit and forbid clerics to kill to defend themselves. He cites as forbidding this defense Seditionarios[50] and Suscepimus, De homicidio.[51] The first of these declares that people guilty of sedition or usury are not to be admitted to the clerical state; the second is a decretal of Alexander III condemning two monks who killed a robber. In support of legitimate self-defensive killing Lignano makes reference to Olim, De restitutione spoliatorum,[52] in which Innocent III legitimates the violent expulsion of unjust possessors of Church property by a bishop; Si furiosus, De homicidio of Clement V,[53] which says that there is no

irregularity incurred if one kills to protect his life; and
Si vero aliquis, *De sententia excommunitatis*, which declares
that a person who strikes a cleric in self-defense is not excommunicated.[54] Underlying all these references is Lignano's
reliance upon the principle of repelling force with force.

The laws which Lignano proposes as forbidding killing
in self-defense make a very weak case for the position they
are to support. *Seditionarios* forbids admission to the clerical state of anyone guilty of sedition or the evil of usury.
To forbid self-defensive killing on the basis of this law
would require a good deal of presumption and inference.
"Sedition" certainly has nothing of defense about it; need it
involve killing at all? The exclusion from the clerical
state would have to be understood as implying that those already in the state are also forbidden. Such an implication
appears reasonable; but that which is actually forbidden in
the text has no connection with self-defense. *Suscepimus* is
also difficult to understand as applicable to this question.
It condemns two monks who killed a robber whom they had captured. The text of this decretal clearly shows that there
was no defense of life on the part of the monks. The robber
was already subdued and in their custody before he was killed.
How this law could be understood to condemn the monks for
acting in self-defense is impossible to grasp.

Lignano's response to these laws does not involve any
argumentation; he just refers to the texts mentioned above
and declares that *Si furiosus* solves the problem. That law
removes the irregularity imposed by Church law and thus
makes wholly legitimate an act of self-defense which deprives
another life. This law, promulgated in 1317, thus becomes
for Lignano (and for the authors of the next four centuries)
the primary source of legitimate killing in self-defense by
clerics. An irregularity imposed by Church law is removed by
Church law; there is no question of any moral guilt.

The decretal *Si furiosus* of Clement V, taken from the
acts of the Council of Vienne (1311-1312), firmly establishes as Church law not only the absence of moral guilt, an
opinion already strongly present in the thirteenth century,
but it also abolishes any ecclesiastical censure for a cleric

who kills in self-defense. There seem to be two possible
reasons for this removal. The first would be a consequence of
the understanding of self-defense, even by killing, to be a
matter of natural law. This was also present earlier, but it
had not been fully extended to clerics. What may have caused
it to be applied to clerics through the removal of all ap-
pearances of any wrongdoing was the last battle in the long
war with the Albigensians, a battle which took place in the
first quarter of the fourteenth century. The Albigensians
considered themselves "the perfect," and along with opposing
all capital punishment of criminals and heretics they also
promulgated the ideal of suicide. The Church's response to
this sect was in terms of social order: criminals and heretics were executed, wars were fought in order to maintain the
good order of society. It would seem that even an ecclesiastical irregularity imposed on clerics for self-defensive killing would smack of a certain sympathy with what were considered heretical notions. The cleric would appear to be
punished for doing wrong, for not allowing himself to be
killed—as one of the "perfect" would do. It was perhaps
the desire to totally separate itself from any appearance of
closeness to the heretical opinions of the Albigensians that
led to the teaching of <u>Si furiosus</u>, the extension of the
natural law of self-defense fully to clerics.[55]

That a cleric may kill to defend property is also
affirmed by Lignano.[56] Besides the bare reference to <u>Olim</u>,
<u>De restitutione spoliatorum</u> he teaches that it is licit to
repel force with force in defense of goods against all those
whom one can repel for defense of persons. It would thus
follow that since a cleric can repel force to defend his
person, he can also repel force to defend his property. (The
importance and the implications of this teaching for defense
of property will become apparent in the following chapters.)
This legitimation by Lignano is new; it goes contrary to the
teaching of Joannes Andreae, as well as that of Raymund,
Hostiensis, and Alexander. The debate is not over yet, but
the outcome is found in the teaching of Lignano.

Fifteenth Century

Panormitanus and Antoninus exhibit well the direction of thought on the question of clerical killing. Antoninus follows Lignano, to whom he makes frequent reference; Panormitanus, however, refuses to legitimate killing in defense of property by a cleric, although he moves quite close to such legitimation.

Panormitanus[57] establishes his teaching in his commentary upon Sicut dignum, De homicidio, Suscepimus, De homicidio, and Significasti, De homicidio.[58] The latter two decretals have already come up for consideration on this issue, though Panormitanus will understand them differently than his predecessors; Sicut dignum is met for the first time. This decretal of Alexander III establishes various penalties for different types of homicide and degrees of cooperation in these homicides. In the course of doing this, the decretal states as "a well-established fact" the severe penalty imposed upon clerics who arm themselves to kill.[59] Panormitanus interprets this law as not forbidding a cleric to kill to defend himself when that is an unavoidable necessity.[60] But it does not legitimate a cleric killing to defend others nor to defend goods; in these cases Panormitanus does not find "inevitable necessity." It is possible for the cleric to avoid the killing; so he must avoid it.[61]

The decretal Suscepimus (containing the incident involving the two monks) is understood by Panormitanus to require clerics to lose goods rather than to kill to retain them. He cites Hostiensis' teaching that clerics, who may call on the secular power, are not to take up arms themselves; but Panormitanus disagrees with this position. Beginning here and with further remarks on Significasti (where the goods in question are valuable Church property), he teaches that a cleric may arm himself and "moderately" defend property. He may strike, but he may not kill. As long as no lethal blow is struck, there is no punishment. The prohibition against killing remains, but in the case of defense of goods Panormitanus allows armed defense short of killing.[62]

There is possible from this position of Panormitanus a development which will become an element of our discussion in the next two chapters. If a cleric can strike a non-lethal blow in defense of property, it is likely that the criminal will strike back. When this occurs, the cleric may then repel the force brought against his person, to the extent of killing if that be necessary. What begins as a defense of property ends as a defense of life because of the violence involved. Because of the likelihood of personal defense occurring, and in spite of his insistence that the blows be non-lethal, it is perhaps best to view Panormitanus' opinion as one of the last attempts to restrict clerics in their right to defend goods.

The solution to the problem of clerics killing in defense of self or of property is found by Antoninus in *Si furiosus*.[63] With this law the irregularity formerly imposed upon clerics who killed was abolished, and clerics (as well as religious) are now to be viewed, he says, in the same light as the laity on this question. There is no sin and no irregularity in killing to defend self or goods when the killing is necessary and done with due moderation, for the natural law permits force to repel force.

Antoninus continues to forbid, however, any killing by a cleric in war.[64] In warfare, a cleric is limited to exhorting and strengthening those engaged in battle and to "throwing rocks" and other things which will not kill anyone. Both the *Decretum* and *Olim*, *De restitutione spoliatorum*[65] are given as sources of this teaching. It remains true, however, that if in the course of his legitimate activities a cleric's life is in danger, he may defend himself by killing. There is also demanded for the legitimate role of the cleric that he have been called to this role by the authority of the pope; he is to answer no one else's call to war, especially not that of "secular princes."[66]

Antoninus also legitimates clerics calling upon secular authority to engage in a war.[67] Like Raymund, he requires that those asked to fight be encouraged not to kill; when killing occurs it is not to be imputed to the ecclesiastics, though these would sin if they did not oppose the killing. (That the opposition is futile, that war always includes killing, do not seem to matter.)

It is likewise unlawful for clerics to act as agents of secular authority in imposing or executing the death penalty. Antoninus relies upon Aquinas for his reasons why a cleric should not kill,[68] and then in this context adds, "for they are prohibited from all shedding of blood."[69] This prohibition can only be understood to apply in the context in which it is used: imposing or executing the death penalty. It cannot be taken as a blanket prohibition.

Panormitanus and Antoninus carry on the teaching that makes licit self-defensive killing by a cleric and the calling upon secular powers to go to war; they also carry on the dispute over the legitimacy of a cleric killing to defend property. The principle of repelling force with force, used by Lignano to justify killing for property by clerics, is incorporated by Antoninus, who also understands Si furiosus to place the cleric in a position equivalent to that of the lay person. With the removal of the ecclesiastical penalty, there is nothing to prohibit a cleric from acting on the basis of what is viewed as the natural law of defense. Panormitanus disagrees, holding that Church law (Significasti and Suscepimus) still prohibits killing in defense of property.

Sixteenth to Eighteenth Centuries

Once the sixteenth century is reached, the question of clerical killing in defense of self or property is almost unanimously judged on the same basis as that of a lay person. Consequently, the issue becomes whether or not it is licit for anyone to kill in defense of property. Sylvester, Cajetan, Vitoria, Soto, Covarrubias, Molina in the sixteenth century; Lessius, Diana, and Busembaum in the seventeenth; Alphonsus in the eighteenth: all agree that Si furiosus lifts what was merely an ecclesiastical penalty from necessary killing in self-defense; with the exception of Covarrubias, they also agree that it is legitimate to kill in defense of property.[70]

The question of the right to kill in defense of property will be the specific subject of the next two chapters. At this point the issue remains the morality of a cleric killing in this case or in self-defense. The issue is resolved as stated in the previous paragraph; the specifics of the broader question into which the clerical issue is absorbed will be left to the next chapters. There is, however, the question of the sources upon which the theologians and canonists of these three centuries base their positions. We have been following a development toward allowing clerics to kill on the basis of both natural and ecclesiastical law, for the opposition to their killing had come to be viewed as merely Church law. The references to the Gospel and Divine law remained in the thirteenth century, with the exception of referrals to Thomas' notions of "unfittingness" by Antoninus, Cajetan, and Vitoria; but the incompatibility does nothing to affect their teaching beyond the prohibiting of the exercise of public authority in passing judgment or executing the death penalty.[71] In the period between 1500 and 1800, there is exclusive reliance upon natural and Church law to determine the morality of the cases under consideration.

The importance of the decretal *Si furiosus* has been evident for many pages. With the removal of the penalty of irregularity, the moral authorities of these centuries find no obstacle to a cleric exercising the right which natural law gives him: the right to repel force with force to defend his life. The ones to add any further foundation for this self-defense are Diana and Alphonsus Ligouri.[72] They cite *Significasti*, *De homicidio*,[73] which simply restates the natural law principle.

The legitimacy of clerics killing in defense of property brings before us three decretals which have already been used by our sources: *Olim*, *De restitutione spoliatorum*, *Suscepimus*, *De homicidio*, and *Interfecisti*, *De homicidio*.[74] The decretal *Olim* is understood by Sylvester, Molina, Lessius, and Diana to legitimate killing to defend property.[75] The law itself repeats the "repel force with force" principle in giving legitimation to a bishop's action of violently expelling the unjust possessors of Church property. Lignano had used this law to justify a cleric killing to defend his life;[76] now it is used to justify killing for property, a justification which is implicit in a law which permits violent expulsion but does not mention any deprivation of life. *Suscepimus* contains the case of the two monks, and we have already had this law cited by Lignano as argument (which he rejects) against a cleric being able to kill in self-defense and by Panormitanus to forbid killing by clerics for property.[77] In the centuries now under consideration, Covarrubias continues the teaching of Panormitanus, while Molina considers this Church law a *counsel*.[78] Molina remarks that everyone is encouraged to suffer the loss of "external goods" rather than to kill for them; he concludes that especially ecclesiastics should follow this counsel, as they "must be despisers of external things." The removal of this decretal from the category of obligatory law to that of counsel is based on the legitimacy conveyed by both *Olim* and the natural law principle of repelling force with force. Because of this legitimacy, the only explanation Molina could give *Suscepimus* would be that of a counsel: a better though non-obligatory manner of behavior. How Molina understands the condemnation of the killing by the monks is not explained. It would appear that the decretal is doing more than admonishing them for not doing the "better" thing. Further discussion of this decretal will be found in chapter three.[79]

Interfecisti, *De homicidio* has been used by Richard of Middleton as the root of his teaching that there is no guilt if a cleric kill in self-defense.[80] When this decretal is used by Sylvester, Cajetan, and Lessius,[81] it is said to also permit the killing of someone to defend property. *Interfecisti* decrees the punishment for killing a thief or robber without necessity. Then it says that if one kills out of necessity *te tuaque liberando*, there can be a voluntary fast undertaken "to be on the safe side"; or, if one is a priest, life-long penance is to be done. The key phrase in this decretal is *te tuaque liberando*; the use of the decree in self-defense cases by Richard and in property defense by Sylvester *et al*. exemplify the ways in which the phrase is understood. The dispute centers on whether *te tuaque* is to be understood *copulatively* or *disjunctively*. If copulatively, it means one may kill without sin to free oneself *and* one's goods, i.e., there must be a threat to life accompanying the threat to property. If the phrase is understood disjunctively, it is read "you _or_ your goods." Thus one can kill to defend property when there is no threat to life; one can kill for property alone. It is clear that _te tuaque_ literally means "you and yours," but dispute revolves around how literally the phrase is to be understood. In the next chapter we will pursue the debated meaning of the phrase.[82]

The status of the question of the morality of clerics killing in defense of property by the late seventeenth century is clearly shown by Busembaum, whom Alphonsus repeats a century later.[83] In a quite brief and unexpounded paragraph, Busembaum says that all laws which forbid this killing are to be understood as referring to situations in which due moderation is not observed. We can see in this statement the full absorption of the clerical issue into that of the basic human right to kill. Force may be repelled by force, with due moderation; this principle of natural law is universally applicable and the major determinant of morality in all cases of killing, whether in self-defense or in defense of property.

This example of the process whereby the moral legitimacy of clerics taking someone's life in defense of their own lives or of property has been a vehicle for viewing the manner in which the canonists and theologians perceived and used law to establish a moral teaching. The general line of development has been from a more restrictive to a more lenient position in matters of self-defense and of property, while there has been refusal to allow clerics themselves to function as public officials or agents in punishing a criminal with death. The trend to broader permissiveness was marked by a decided shift from reliance upon the _Decretum Gratiani_ to dependence upon the _Decretales_. In the ongoing interpretation of these decretals, an increasingly widespread reliance upon natural law was in evidence; it is this dependency that surfaces in more frequent references to particular decretals which incorporate the natural law principle of repelling force with force (e.g., _Olim_, _De restitutione spoliatorum_, _Significasti_, _De homicidio_).

In the example of the morality of killing a person

caught in adultery, there was evidenced a triumph of Church law over civil law: whatever civil law might allow, Church law forbade a private person to kill. But this, too, was influenced by natural law principles. (In the case of clerics, the move is more emphatically to natural law, which then determines the understanding of particular Church laws.) The presence of moral guilt should a private person kill an adulterous person was consistently affirmed. With the exception of Alexander, Bonaventure, and Scotus (and possibly Panormitanus), those whose teaching was examined based this guilt on ecclesiastical law alone.[84] In the case of clerics, after an initial consideration of guilt for self-defensive killing by Alexander, there is no guilt for killing in self-defense; the punishment is an irregularity, a Church penalty, and this itself is removed in the fourteenth century. Along with the removal of this penalty, an increased application of the law of repelling force with force leads to an elimination of any ecclesiastical prohibition to killing for property. The cleric is morally obligated to act with due moderation, as is the layman. From the fifteenth century on, Panormitanus and Covarrubias are alone in forbidding clerics to kill for property.

Where, then, is the difference between the case of adultery and that of clerics? Why does Church law recognize moral guilt when a private person kills one guilty of adultery, whether civil law sanctions the killing or not, yet sees no moral guilt in killing in self-defense or for property? The difference seems to rest in the understanding of natural law. The "repelling force" principle in a case of necessary defense is a "law of nature." To act in accord with natural law cannot be sinful. In the adultery case there is no defense, no "saving," involved; there is nothing perceived as "natural" in killing a person guilty of adultery. The understanding of the application of the natural law principle is the key to moral guilt, and Church law reflects and reinforces this understanding.

The most obvious elements in both these issues are the evidence of a hierarchy of law—Divine, natural, human— which aids in determining morality, and the apparent absence after the thirteenth century of any influence of the Bible, especially the Gospels, on the determination of moral behavior. The reason for this absence is the understanding of the relationship between Old and New Testament morality and, because of this relationship, the role of human reason in determining right and wrong. It is to these issues that we now turn.

Old and New Testament Morality: Decalogue and Sermon on the Mount

The question of the hierarchy of law as perceived by Scholastics needs no more than brief mention for our purpose here. The function of the remarks is simply to illuminate the place within the hierarchy held by Scriptural law, its relation to natural law, and to lead us into a discussion of the understanding of the applicability of the moral teaching of the two Testaments. In pursuing these tasks, reliance will be primarily upon the extensive treatise on law of Thomas Aquinas,[85] though there will also be some reference to Alexander, Bonaventure, and Scotus on particular points.

In establishing the hierarchy of law, Thomas considers four types: eternal, natural, Divine, and human. <u>Eternal law</u> is not a specific kind of law but the exemplar law, the ruling idea of things which exists in God and governs all things, directing all to their proper end.[86] The proper end of rational beings is the good, and man's apprehension of what are his natural goods (or ends), his sharing in the eternal law constitutes the <u>natural law</u> in him.[87] Men make their own "the Eternal Reason through which they have their natural aptitudes for their due activity and purpose."[88] The natural law is, according to Aquinas, more an inclination to a direction through which one may achieve the end appropriate to him than a specific set of laws. These general, basic principles are not, however, sufficient in themselves to rule man's conduct. In order that the principles be applicable to concrete living, there is need for further explanation and precision. This is the function of either <u>Divine</u> or <u>human law</u>.[89] Man has both a supernatural end and a natural end in community; Divine and human law guide to the achievement of these respective ends. Basically human law is a detailed application of natural law, made by secular or ecclesiastical governments and by local custom; it is changeable, different with different times and places.[90] The measure of the justness of human law will always be the natural law.[91] The Divine law is contained in the revelation made by God, and is divided into two parts: the Old and the New Laws, the former serving to prepare for and prefigure the latter. The supernatural end to which Divine law directs man was revealed imperfectly in the Old Law of the Jews and is now perfectly made known in the New Law of the Gospel.[92] The New Law is implanted in man through grace and consists in reason.[93] Secondarily, the New Law contains precepts regarding the reception of grace through the Sacraments[94] and also what are termed "moral precepts." These moral precepts are identical with the Decalogue of the Old Law, and the Decalogue, with the laws deduced from it, is identical with the natural law.[95] Thus the New Law reaffirms the precepts of the Old, and both renew the law of reason. Consequently, the natural law of reason and the Christian law are identified for all matters of morality outside the Sacraments.[96]

Given this hierarchy and the interdependence of the elements, it can be seen that what is involved is a process of participation and specification rooted in the governance of God and aimed at the achievement of man's supernatural end.[97] Divine law is one of the laws which further specifies the natural law. Its chief purpose is to establish a harmonious and loving relationship with God and a relationship between men that is in conformity with man's orientation toward God.[98] But Divine law has two parts: the Old and the New. It is in the relationship between these two parts that we are interested, with an eye to examining especially the issue of their specification of the natural law.

When one looks for the relationship between the Old Law and the New, there are found images such as child-adult, fear-love, temporal-eternal, carnal-spiritual. These are used to denote a development from Old to New, and a fullness residing in the New.[99] The precepts of the Old Law were perfect for the people of the Old Testament, but they were not absolutely nor perpetually perfect. The Old Law could be surpassed and was surpassed by the New Law, which is signified more by love than fear, governs more fully the inner acts of man, and fulfills the promise to which the Old Law pointed.

To say that the New Law fulfills or even replaces the Old is not to say that the Old Law is totally voided. Thomas divides the precepts of the Old Law into three categories: moral, ceremonial, judicial.[100] The moral precepts, the Decalogue, as restatements of natural law, need further specification. The first three commandments of the Decalogue, concerning worship of God, are specified by the ceremonial precepts; the final seven, regulating justice between men, by the judicial. Of these types, Aquinas states that the moral precepts, in that they embody natural law, remain binding in the New Law; the ceremonial precepts are voided;[101] the judicial precepts are left by Jesus to the discretion of those in authority, though he did explain some of the judicial precepts of the Old Law which had been misunderstood.[102]

It is at this point that the pivotal relationship between the Old and New Laws appears for our study. If the judicial precepts do not continue into the New Law, but only the general embodiment of justice in the last seven commandments of the Decalogue, will the understanding of these Decalogue precepts have to be influenced by the corrections of misunderstanding on the part of Jesus? Are the statements of Jesus, especially those of the Sermon on the Mount (Mt. 5-7), and particularly the "Antitheses" of Mt. 5:17-48, to be applied only to an internal state of mind which does not affect external actions? Do these antitheses provide a basis for an "elitist ethic" which does not apply to the common man, but only to the "perfect"? Does the Sermon on the Mount offer anything more than "counsels of perfection"?

Thomas teaches that the New Law is primarily the grace of the Holy Spirit.[103] Accordingly, this law contains certain things that dispose man to receive this grace and others which pertain to the use of that grace. It is in this secondary sense (use of grace) that the New Law is a written law; primarily the law is the inward bestowal of the grace of the Holy Spirit. This grace dwells in man more or less perfectly, though the state of the New Law in itself is the final and perfect state. Consequently, the "degree of perfection" in men will vary. Because of this variation, some will need external constraint to act virtuously, while others have what Thomas terms "love of virtue," by which they do the virtuous acts which are prescriptions of law.[104] These virtuous acts are dependent upon the prompting of grace, for as Aquinas says, "the end of every law is to make men righteous and virtuous."[105] The law in question here is primarily the New Law of grace; thus the acts to which this grace moves a person must be in accord with this grace in as much as this New Law surpasses the Old Law which it supplanted.

When Thomas turns to the issue of the right use of grace, he says that as far as actions are *essential* to virtue they are contained in the moral precepts (Ten Commandments), which were also a part of the Old Law. In this respect, "the New Law had nothing to add regarding external actions."[106] The basis of this statement is Thomas' view of the determination of these moral precepts by means of judicial precepts in the Old Law. Since these determinations are not necessarily connected with the inward grace which is the New Law, since they are not necessarily connected with "faith that works through love," they have been left by Jesus to the decision of man.[107] It is thus that Aquinas understands the statements of Jesus in Mt. 5: they are counsels, not precepts, directed to the preparation of the inner man.[108] For internal disposition, these statements are precepts; the states of mind are necessary for salvation. But that anyone should actually and promptly behave in this way is to be considered a matter of counsel, of option.[109]

Thomas' thinking, which continues the tradition of seeing Mt. 5 as prescriptions for internal disposition, is further exemplified in his interpretation of Mt. 5:38-42. The text is:

> You have heard the commandment, "An eye for an eye, a tooth for a tooth." But what I say to you is: offer no resistance to injury. When a person strikes you on the right cheek, turn and offer him the other. If anyone wants to go to law over your shirt, hand him your coat as well. Should anyone press you into service for one mile, go with him

two miles. Give to the man who begs from you. Do
not turn your back on the borrower.

Thomas uses this statement as indicative of what Jesus' approach to all the judicial precepts of the Old Law would be. He says that Jesus teaches in this passage that the intention of the law was "that retaliation should be sought out of love of justice, and not as a punishment out of revengeful spite, which he forbade, admonishing man to be ready to suffer yet greater insults, and this remains still in the New Law."[110]

This interpretation shows its linkage with Augustine and the common tradition. Does it correctly understand the text? It is obvious that Thomas' interpretation does not say precisely what the text says. What appears as a command to "offer no resistance to injury" is rephrased to mean "offer no revengeful resistance"; the text does not say retaliate out of love of justice, but rather "offer no resistance" and "when a person strikes you on the right cheek, turn and offer him the other." It says nothing about legitimate retaliation. How is the text to be understood?

We might begin to answer the question through Thomas himself. He teaches that the Sermon on the Mount contains "the whole process of forming the life of a Christian."[111] He also holds that what specified the Jewish people as the People of God (faith being presupposed) was the determination of the natural law by the ceremonial and judicial precepts. The ceremonial precepts of the Old Law have been replaced by the Sacraments. Is there no replacement for the judicial precepts? Is it enough to say that in his relations to his fellow man, no more is asked of the Christian than the observance of a general justice based on natural law (the Decalogue) as specified by the use of his reason? If the Sermon on the Mount is the plan for Christian life, would it not have to determine more than simply internal disposition? From internal attitudes external actions flow; the actions of a Christian are to flow from and conform to the inward grace.[112] If it would be such a determinant, would the Sermon then not be one aspect (Sacraments being another) of the constitutive element that distinguishes Christianity from Judaism? When Jesus "corrects" the misunderstanding of the

Old Law, is he speaking not only to internal attitude but also to the action which is to flow from that attitude?

The Sermon on the Mount has been the subject of much discussion throughout the history of Christianity.[113] We have been following through the teaching of Aquinas what is the dominant position in that history. But it seems that the dominant teaching is inadequate because incomplete. It is true that the Sermon on the Mount speaks to internal attitudes; but if it does not also speak to the action which is to flow from those attitudes, there is a drastic lacuna in the Gospel. When this is said, however, where are we? It would seem a mistake to move from commanding only internal attitudes to a demand that the Sermon be taken in absolute literalness, in which every statement is to be taken as applicable to every situation. What is needed is first of all to take the Sermon on the Mount in all seriousness; Jesus means what he says. What he says, however, is not in terms of "law," neither in the sense that one must do all these things in order to be blessed, nor in terms of "you ought to have done this; see what poor creatures you are."[114] What Jesus does is set forth the radical nature of God's demand, a demand that is preceded by the gift (grace) which enables one to accept and live the Gospel.[115] Although there seems to be no basis for considering the Sermon a "new code of law," it can be viewed as new guiding principles which impose a certain pattern of behavior as obligatory.[116] The major guiding principle is that of selfless love, a love which leads to the waiving of one's rights.[117] For example, Mt. 5:38-42, which we have seen interpreted by Thomas as forbidding <u>vengeful</u> retaliation, would be understood as establishing a principle of <u>non</u>-retaliation for injury.[118] But how is that possible? How can the Christian be expected to live up to such a demand? The demand placed upon him is one requiring that he pursue a <u>goal</u>; it is a norm which can be fulfilled only in the manner of perpetual conversion.[119] Jesus requires more than what men usually do, more than men consider themselves capable of doing; he refers to the power of God and lets the rigor of his words stand.

If one were to accept this more contemporary

teaching[120] of the Sermon on the Mount as obligatory in the sense of a direction toward a goal, the extreme difficulty of living according to the "direction" remains. Yet it is precisely the likelihood of failure which enables the Christian to rejoice that he is not saved by a perfect keeping of these "directions" but by grace. To say that Jesus demands that man live according to the Sermon on the Mount says nothing about how he treats or judges those who fail in the attempt.[121]

The role which the Sermon on the Mount must play in Christian morality may perhaps be stated in this way. The moral precepts (Decalogue) are considered essential to virtue and thus binding on all men.[122] By means of the Old Law, the Jewish people were specified as a morally distinct people because of the determination of these moral precepts by the ceremonial and judicial precepts. These precepts, though mediated through Moses and others, were considered of Divine origin. Likewise, the Christian people are constituted by the New Law, a law which is primarily internal and secondarily written. The correction of the Old Law's judicial precepts by Jesus are their fulfillment, the pointing out of the "true" or "fuller" meaning of the Old Law, adding to it where it was deficient. But the "new norms" for behavior established by Jesus are "goal norms," dynamic norms which demand a change of attitude that transforms an entire life, which transforms both thought and action. These "norms" are absolutely binding, not optional. It is not, as Thomas states,[123] a matter of counsel that a Christian love enemies when he is not bound to (he is bound in a case when the enemy is in "extreme necessity"); he is always so bound. It is not a matter of option that a Christian forgive injury when he might seek just vengeance. It is not sufficient that one may kill as long as there is no anger present. Killing may be a necessity in self-defense, and be guiltless, for example; but the Christian must take human life "with only the greatest remorse and reluctance."[124] However necessary the killing may be, it remains a violation of the demand of the Gospel which sought to remove not only the taking of life but the cause of killing. And what of the injury suffered through theft of property? The Christian is

held to forgive injury without retaliation. To make such
statements is not to deny the difficulty in carrying them out.
But to ignore the <u>command</u> to act in these ways is to ignore
the determination of natural law which specifically constitutes the Christian people.[125]

There is one further component in Thomas' understanding of law which indicates a need for at least something like
viewing the Sermon on the Mount as expressing binding "goal
norms." Thomas teaches that human law governs the outward
and observable acts of man by which he relates with others in
the community.[126] A constraining power is present in this
law, a power which through force and resultant fear of punishment can prevent evil to the community. Hopefully there will
also result an internalization of the type of behavior which
is the goal of the law. This progressive internalization is
the educative function of human law.[127]

The realization of this process of internalization
leads Thomas to apply to human law a variation in application.[128] The variation springs from the differing possibilities of action from a man who has a habit of virtue and one
who does not. Thus the law does not apply similarly to the
adult and the child, and certain things may be permitted to
the individual of mediocre morals that would not be to one
of higher morality. The crowd of imperfect men is not all at
once burdened with responsibilities which men of higher character assume. It is Aquinas' opinion that the majority of
people for whom human law is enacted have no high standard
of morality. Consequently, human law will forbid only those
grave vices which the average man can avoid, chiefly those
which do harm to others and must be stopped if human society
is to perdure.

This understanding of Thomas corresponds to his treatment of the "precepts" of the Sermon on the Mount and to their
traditional interpretation. A similar understanding of the
mediocrity of the common man's morals led to a dichotomous
vision of man: the perfect and the imperfect. Thomas
speaks of "permitting" particular behavior to people of
mediocre morals; he also speaks of leading them step by step
to better behavior.[129] If this "leading" is to be accomplished,

there needs to be an indication that one is required to be different than one is, to do other than one does. A present inability to conform to a particular norm can be understood, but if the norm is of importance there is need to lead to its internalization. If this is true of human law, it is at least as true of Divine law, which holds a higher place in Thomas' scheme. The inability to fulfill the "goal commandments" of Divine law can be understood and guilt perhaps entirely removed; but that is not "permitting" behavior contrary to the commands. It is recognizing an inability, but such recognition is not then the determinant of the moral principle. The "goal commands" serve an educative function, leading hopefully to the internalization of the values they embody and the performance required by the values.

Without some role for the Sermon on the Mount in determining the behavior of Christians, there is a definite lack in the teaching of Aquinas. He does not give us much by way of Divine law to which, in his scheme, human law must conform. We have seen that anything in the realm of "judicial precepts" in the New Law is considered by Thomas to be present only by way of the "essence of justice," not in any specific determination; and those of the Old Law have been abrogated.[130] This leaves only the Decalogue (with the Sacraments and what is "necessary to faith")[131] as a Divine-law source, a source which is then implemented for social living by human reason.

Conclusion

The understanding of New Testament morality exemplified especially in Thomas' vision and application of the Sermon on the Mount leaves Christian morality consisting in the Decalogue and what human reason judges to be just conclusions from the precepts of the Decalogue. There may be a "perfection" of this morality possible, but it is only possible, and therefore only obligatory, to those who freely choose to live in a "state of perfection," somehow removed from "the world."[132] It is this reason which stands as the ultimate determinant of morality, reason which can grasp the fundamental principles of natural law embodied in the

Decalogue. This reason understands "Do not kill" to mean <u>unjust</u> killing, and repelling force with force is not unjust.

The dominance of reason in determining morality is what overcomes an attempt on the part of Scotus (with some prior traces in Alexander and Bonaventure) to give greater weight to the teaching of Scripture. Scotus demands that there be an "exception" to Divine law by God (e.g., murderers are to be put to death; they are "excepted" from "Do not kill") is explicitly rejected by Cajetan on the basis of Jesus having left all to man's moral reason.[133] All man must do is to search out when killing is evil and when it is not. When killing is determined to be evil, then it is prohibited by God. Reason is the vehicle for judging the presence or absence of evil; the Gospel is not seen to have the possibility of demanding anything which man might reason to be "unreasonable."

It was on the basis of reason's grasp of natural law that the issue of a cleric's right to kill was finally resolved, both in the case of self-defense and that of property. The questions of killing on a broader scale (e.g., war) or acting as an agent of public authority was similarly resolved: natural law requires "necessity," and in these cases it is not necessary; someone else can do it. On such a basis both the initial imputation of guilt in self-defensive killing by Alexander and a more broadly held prohibition of killing for property were refuted.

Death for adultery was likewise resolved on the foundation of an understanding of natural law. Civil law can, for the common good, establish death as a punishment for adultery, but, since punishment requires a judicial process, the private person cannot be given the authority to kill a person caught in this crime. The influence of the Johannine text (Jn. 8:1-11) on this stance after Scotus (and possibly Panormitanus) is at best indirect. The Gospel is not viewed as containing such specific "laws."

In examining the varied and sometimes contradictory understandings of particular Church laws, it was again the natural law principle of repelling force with force which progressively determined the way particular laws were interpreted and the reliance upon specific laws for justification of particular positions (e.g., Olim, De restitutione spoliatorum; Significasti, De homicidio).

We have also touched upon the question of killing in defense of property, as the clerical issue merged with the broader question. It is to this specific question that the remainder of this work is devoted. The elements to both justify and limit killing in this case are broadly contained in the principle of repelling force with force, with due moderation. Curiously, in spite of the overwhelming declaration that the judicial precepts of the Old Testament have been abrogated, it is one of these precepts that provides the basis for the teaching on killing a thief. This precept will be the major consideration of the next chapter.

CHAPTER III

THE THIEF'S RIGHT TO LIFE

The previous chapters have been an exposition of the process whereby both the validity and limitation attached to taking human life were achieved. This study now turns to an analysis of the teaching on legitimate killing in defense of property. When may a thief be legitimately killed? We will look at the tradition under six headings: the distinction between theft and robbery; the text of Ex. 22:1-2; pertinent Roman laws; the transformation of the "day-night" concept; the decretals <u>Interfecisti</u>, <u>De homicidio</u> and <u>Suscepimus</u>, <u>De homicidio</u>; and finally what are termed "natural arguments."

Theft and Robbery

The basic distinction which appears in the tradition rests upon the <u>secrecy</u> of theft and the <u>openness</u> of robbery. Whether one consults the canonists[1] or the theologians,[2] the notion of deceit and hiddenness is contrasted to the manifest nature of robbery; in the latter the possessor of the property is aware of the criminal act, while in the former he is unknowing.

Because of the open nature of robbery, there is added to it as a distinguishing characteristic the presence of force. The most obvious application of force is by means of weapons, but Thomas, Scotus, and Panormitanus explicitly broaden the notion of force to include the presence of any kind of attack or pressure.[3]

If this distinction between theft and robbery is accepted, it has a bearing of importance upon the question of killing to defend property. First of all, theft is a secret act done without the knowledge of the owner of the goods or of anyone else who might protest the usurpation. Consequently, the issue of depriving the thief of his life could only come to the fore in the question of post-factum punishment of a captured thief or on the occasion of a thief being discovered either in the process of his crime or as he makes his escape with or without the property one seeks to defend. Secondly, the force that is characteristic of robbery (manifest theft) must be force brought against the person who possesses or seeks to defend property. The force cannot be considered as being brought simply against the goods themselves, as that violence is also present in theft. There is involved in robbery, therefore, a certain self-defense, personal defense, and not solely a defense of goods. Both of these implications arising out of the theft-robbery distinction play an important role in the on-going debate over killing within the Roman Catholic tradition.[4]

From the previous chapters it is clear that in a case of robbery killing would be legitimate if that were necessary to defend one's life. But what of the thief? Can force be used to repel force, even to the extent of killing, if the force is only brought against goods? We have already seen that killing is legitimate when the evil prevented is sufficiently grave to bring about a benefit which exceeds the evil of killing.[5] What evil is considered sufficient is determined by law. Is theft such an evil, and does law (and what law) so determine it? There has been evidence throughout the material we have examined that human life is highly valued. If life is to be taken, there must be a forfeiture of the fundamental right to life by some wrongdoing. There is a conflict which arises between the innocent and the guilty, and in the conflict the rights of the innocent are to prevail.[6] But how does one compare rights? What is the relationship between the right to property and the right to life?

Certainly part of the attitude toward the guilty person is rooted in the acceptance of his conduct as sinful. The major figure in the Catholic theological and moral tradition is Thomas Aquinas. He teaches (and his teaching is repeated almost verbatim two centuries later by Antoninus) that by sinning man departs from the order of reason, and thus "falls away from the dignity of his manhood."[7] Therefore, it may be good to kill a man who has sinned, Thomas says, even as it is good to kill a beast. Then, with reference to Aristotle,[8] Thomas says that a sinful man is worse than a beast and more harmful. The starkness of this statement is qualified by Thomas,[9] as he points out that sin does not make the bad man distinct "in nature" from the good man; he may be worse than a beast but he does not become one. The sinner does not become liable to indiscriminate killing as wild beasts are; there is required the legitimation of law before one may kill a sinner. Yet by the fact of his sin the evil man has lessened his dignity and fallen into a state in which he forfeits at least some of his rights. Harm has been done to himself, to the common good, and perhaps to others; if that harm is serious enough, he will have forfeited even his right to life. It is clear that Thomas,[10] following the Judaeo-Christian tradition, considers theft a sin and the thief liable to the punishment established for sinners.

The attitude indicated in Aquinas' teaching is further exemplified in much of the tradition through its teaching on the penance to be done for unnecessary and necessary killing. The unnecessary killing of a thief or robber is the specific situation envisioned. Such killing is considered homicide and there is to be a penance imposed. Beginning with Gratian,[11] the penance, when specified, includes forty days exclusion from the church, a fast of like length (on bread and water) and the wearing of sackcloth and ashes. But this same tradition in a case where killing the criminal is considered necessary simply invites the one who kills to do penance if he wishes; the penance is to be done _ad_ _cautelam_, i.e., in case there was an excessive use of force.

The important element in the necessary or unnecessary cases is that the determining factor in the thief's right to life is not his life itself but the victim's ability to stop the crime. The criminal's right to life increases in proportion to the victim's ability to stop the crime. The criminal's right to life increases in proportion to the victim's capacity to prevent the crime by some means other than killing. The "due moderation" principle is, of course, applicable, as are other factors, such as the nature of the crime to be prevented (as, for example, the crime of theft and the value of the goods threatened), but the thief's right to life, given the other criteria (to be seen in both this and the following chapter), depends on the ability of the victim to defend his own rights. The controversy which will engage us for the remainder of this study pivots around the "rights" which the victim may legitimately defend by killing. The major problem will be whether property can be valuable enough to legitimate killing to defend it. The right to life can be forfeited through sufficiently grave harm to the common good.[12] Thus if the thief is thought to have lost his right to life, this can only be because his theft fulfills the conditions for grave harm to the common good.

Among the conditions for grave harm to the common good, the singly most important circumstance for the determination of gravity in crimes against property is the presence or absence of a threat to life accompanying the threat to goods. It is the presence of this threat to life which constitutes robbery as distinct from theft, and Aquinas determines the specific sinfulness of robbery on the basis of its presence.[13] To examine the presence or absence of this threat, we will consider the use and interpretation of the text of Ex. 22:1-2. These verses make a distinction between a daytime and nocturnal thief, and on the basis of this distinction the moral tradition under examination interjects the issue of the concurrent threat to the life of the victim. We will proceed to the examination of the role played by this passage by first examining the text itself, then the similar teaching in Roman law, and finally the use and interpretation of the content of these Exodus verses by the authors being used in this study. The Roman law on this issue is interjected between the discussions of the Exodus text because of the influence it has on the interpretation of the Biblical passage.

The Text of Exodus 22:1-2

Among the judicial laws of the Old Testament there is a law which deals with the liceity of killing a thief. Ex. 22:1-2 states: "If a thief is caught in the act of housebreaking and beaten to death, there is no bloodguilt involved. But if after sunrise he is thus beaten, there is bloodguilt."[14] To understand the meaning of this text we will first look at the interpretation given in the <u>Babylonian Talmud</u>.[15]

The <u>Babylonian Talmud</u> does not understand these verses of Exodus literally; it directs its attention not to day-night as a time distinction, but to a symbolic understanding which focuses on the ability of the victim to discern the intention of the thief.[16] Considering this law of Exodus to be clarified by Job 24:14—"The murderer rises with the night, he kills the poor and needy, and in the night he is as a thief"[17]—a <u>Baraitha</u> in the tractate <u>Pesahim</u> says:[18]

> If the matter is as clear as light to you that he /the thief/ comes /even/ to take life, he is a murderer, and he /the victim/ may be saved at the cost of his /the thief's/ life; but if you are doubtful about it, like /the darkness of/ the night, you must regard him /only/ as a thief, and he /the victim/ must not be saved at the cost of his life.

The victim is required by this passage to be certain of the thief's intention before he may kill the intruder. But another text teaches that if "it is doubtful whether he has come to take money or life, . . . yet it is lawful to save oneself at the cost of his life."[19] The contradiction involved in these texts on the legitimacy of killing when in doubt is solved by <u>Sanhedrin</u> 72a-b, which declares the cases envisioned to be different.[20] The first, that in doubt one may not kill, refers to a father robbing his son: the son is to presume his father would not kill him, unless the opposite is clear. The opposite case concerns a son robbing his father: the father may presume his son would kill him.[21]

The Talmudic interpretation thus concentrates upon the intention of the thief: he is to be considered willing to kill if he is opposed.[22] Day and night in the text have been understood to refer to the clarity of knowledge regarding the thief's intention, without concern for whether he comes at night or by day.[23] The effect of this understanding is to destroy the notion that only at night may one presume the intention of killing and thus have guilt automatically removed if one kills. It also removes the automatic presumption of guilt if the killing is during the day. Rabbi Ishmael accomplished these effects in the following passages.

> . . . But does the sun rise upon him alone? Does it not rise upon the whole world? It simply means this: What does the sun signify to the world? Peace. So, then if it is known that this burglar had peaceful intentions toward the owner and yet the latter kills him, he is guilty of murder.[24]

> . . . Behold it says: "If a thief be found breaking in" etc. Now of what case does the law speak? Of a case where there is doubt whether the burglar came merely to steal or even to kill.[25]

The first quotation forestalls an automatic presumption of intention, while the second permits either a daytime or a nocturnal thief to be killed if there is doubt about his intention. The determining factors are thus the intention of the thief and the defender's ability to determine that intention. Yet the right to kill is not taken to be absolute. Even if the thief's intention to murder is evident, he is not to be killed if help is available that could prevent him from killing. An analogy with the case of rape is made to indicate this "due moderation" notion.

> And just as there if the girl had someone to protect her from the attack of the pursuer and she nevertheless kills him, she is guilty of murder, so also here if the owner of the house had someone to protect him from an attack by the burglar and the owner nevertheless kills him, he is guilty.[26]

The Rabbinic understanding of Ex.22:1-2 is thus seen to legitimate the killing of an intruder only when he is a threat to life, actual or presumed; there is no reference to deprivation of life solely for the sake of property. The use of day and night is recognized as a vehicle for transmitting teaching about the presence or absence of a threat to innocent life; there is a realization that such a threat is as likely to be present during the day as it is at night.

Roman Law

The distinction between a daytime and nocturnal thief as linked with a threat to life is also present in the Roman law, as codified by Justinian in the sixth century A.D. The issue is dealt with in a manner similar to that of the Babylonian Talmud, which dates from about the same decade, the second, of that century. The Roman law provides what seems to be further foundation for the subsequent Roman Catholic tradition.

The law <u>Furem nocturnum</u>, <u>Ad Legem Corneliam de sicariis</u>,[27] states that the only legitimate killing of a nocturnal thief occurs when the thief cannot be spared without danger to the victim himself. Clearly the case is one of a threat to the victim's life, and it is this threat which justifies killing the thief. But there is a thirteenth-century gloss of Accursius on this law which introduces an entirely new element.[28] After exemplifying the threat as resistance with a sword, the gloss adds: "and a reason can be that if he [the thief] leaves with the goods, they cannot be recovered afterwards; it is otherwise in the daytime, as one can be accused and thus is not to be killed easily." Besides the threat to life this gloss recognizes the impossibility of recovering the stolen goods as reason for taking the thief's life. And it is on this basis, recovery through ability to recognize and accuse the thief, that a more stringent practice is demanded in the case of daytime theft; but killing during the day when the goods would otherwise be unrecoverable is not ruled out.

The law <u>Furem nocturnum</u> and its gloss thus make very clear the issue which will be debated for centuries. Does the thief forfeit his right to life only when he threatens the victim's life, or is it sufficient that the goods he steals be unrecoverable, with no threat to the owner's life? The Rabbinic interpretation of the Exodus law restricted killing to cases in which there was threat to life; this particular Roman law does the same, but the gloss extends legitimate killing to cases in which recovery of property is otherwise impossible.

Another law in the <u>Digest</u>, <u>Si pignore</u>, deals with the case of daylight theft.[29] This law refers to the <u>Law of the Twelve Tables</u>[30] as having permitted the killing of a diurnal thief "if he cannot otherwise be seized, if he defends himself with a spear." Then the law goes on to say that "spear" is to be understood to include a club, sword, or whatever may cause harm. Once again threat to life is what legitimates killing. But this law also has a gloss by Accursius.[31] The gloss states that "spear" is included in the text of the law because "a nocturnal thief can be killed even when he does not have a spear." The basis upon which this killing may be legitimate is not given by the gloss. Does it mean the obviously unarmed can be killed, or does it mean that the nocturnal thief is always to be presumed to be ready to kill if he is opposed? If the latter is the case, there is a likeness to the Rabbinic teaching that unless a nocturnal thief is clearly not going to kill, the victim may presume the intention to kill to be present and act accordingly. <u>Si pignore</u> does, however, make clear that the daytime thief is only to be killed if he defends himself by means of force.

    The same teaching on the daytime thief and the apparent blanket justification for killing the nighttime thief is also established by the law <u>Itaque</u>, <u>Ad Legem Aquiliam</u>.[32] Since the <u>Lex Aquilia</u> is some two centuries earlier than the <u>Lex Cornelia</u>, we might view the teaching of <u>Furem nocturnum</u>, <u>Ad Legem Corneliam</u>, as an attempt to clarify the teaching of <u>Itaque</u>, <u>Ad Legem Aquiliam</u>, on the issue of the nocturnal thief by restricting the killing of such a thief to cases where it is necessary for self-defense. The law <u>Si pignore</u> of the <u>Digest</u> would, then, simply repeat the teaching of <u>Itaque</u> regarding the daytime thief.

    There is one more law that needs to be mentioned: <u>Unde vi</u> of the <u>Codex</u>.[33] This law established that "if one possesses [property] rightly [i.e., legally], he can with due moderation licitly repel force." Due moderation is again insisted upon, but there is no reference to killing's relationship to that moderation. The laws from the <u>Digest</u> which have been referred to would have to be employed to reach that decision. That the <u>Codex</u> was cognizant of the day-night consideration is exemplified in the law <u>Sunt casus</u>.[34] A twofold case is presented: a nocturnal despoiler of fields and a nocturnal attacker of travelers. The law states that both of these criminals may be subjected to "immediate worthy punishment" and "receive the death" which was threatened and intended, for it is better to retaliate at the moment than to take revenge later. Judicial punishment is seen to come too late. There is in the law a presumption that the acts of these criminals involve an intended deprivation of life. The presumption is obvious in the case of attack upon travelers, but what of the destruction of crops? Is it, like the case of travelers, a matter of not being sure what the attacker will do if opposed, and so being able to presume intent? Or is there, perhaps, a connecting of the attack on the fields with an attack on life? The fields provide livelihood, perhaps direct sustenance of life; thus an attempt to destroy crops could be an indirect attack upon the life of those who need the crops to live. Whatever the thought behind this law, it allows the criminals mentioned to be killed because they threaten life. Whether the connection with threatened life is through the "opposition" or the "sustenance" notions in regard to the fields cannot be said. We will find both notions present in subsequent centuries.

Like the Rabbinic understanding of the Exodus verses, Roman law also concentrates on threat to life as the justification for killing a thief, whether the act of theft occurs at night or during the day. The texts of the laws themselves demand some sort of forceful defense during the daytime before killing is justified. It is the thirteenth-century gloss on <u>Furem nocturnum</u>, <u>Ad Legem Corneliam de sicariis</u>, which opens the possibility of killing if the goods are otherwise unrecoverable. At the same time, the law <u>Unde vi</u> of the <u>Codex</u> speaks simply of the legitimacy of repelling force with due moderation in defense of property. This law does not rule out killing as an act expressive of due moderation, but it would demand criteria for determining that moderation. The other laws cited here would offer the day-night distinction as criterion, while the gloss on <u>Furem nocturnum</u> would contribute "recoverability" as a criterion which would eliminate the day-night distinction except for the notion of relative ease of recoverability at night or during the day.

The Roman law transmitted to the Scholastics thus contains both the unspecified notion of due moderation and the

gloss on the ability to recover property which take it beyond
the understanding of the Exodus text by the Rabbis. The discussion on the morality of killing a thief from the thirteenth
to the eighteenth century will revolve around the issues raised
by these sources: threat to life, recoverability, and the
principle of due moderation. The starting point is the text
of Exodus and the establishment of the criteria upon which
killing the thief is legitimate.

The Acceptance and Transformation of "Day-Night"

Thirteenth Century

The Church legislation which speaks most directly to
the content of Ex. 22:1-2 is the decretal Si perfodiens, De
homicidio.[35] This law, making reference to Augustine, super
Exodum, quotes verses 1-2, and goes on to say that the nighttime thief can be killed because one cannot tell if he has
come to kill or just to steal. The daytime thief's intention
can be determined; so he is to be killed only when he defends
himself with a sword. The decretal also refers to "ancient
secular law" (Roman) as teaching the same, and remarks that in
both the case of the nocturnal thief and the daytime thief who
defends himself with a sword there is a case of the criminal
being "more than" a thief. The threat to the victim's life,
presumed at night and actual in the case of the armed daytime
thief, adds the circumstance which legitimates killing. The
simple threat to property is not given as a legitimating
cause for deprivation of life.

Among the thirteenth-century authors incorporated in
this study, Innocent IV, Hostiensis, and Raymund of Pennaforte explicitly refer to Si perfodiens, De homicidio for
their teaching on the thief's right to life.[36] Innocent and
Raymund just repeat the content of the decretal, while
Hostiensis adds one important element. He says that the daytime thief who is armed may be presumed to have the intention
of killing, and thus may be killed. What this statement of
Hostiensis appears to do is to remove the necessity of some
actual attack or action to indicate intention; the thief's
being armed is sufficient indication of his intention to use

his weapon. The decretal teaches that the thief can be killed if he defends himself with his weapon; Hostiensis says that being armed is in itself sufficient to indicate his intention. There is no need to wait to see what he does with the weapon (though due moderation would still be required). The importance of this statement by Hostiensis seems to be more in the realm of clarification of the decretal than of change.

Alexander of Hales, while not referring to the decretal, is in agreement with it in his citing of Ex. 22: 1-2.[37] The daytime thief is not to be killed when it can be discerned that his intention is only to steal. The ability to determine intention remains the criterion for legitimate killing. Alexander emphasizes, however, the distinction between this teaching of Exodus and what he calls "human law."[38] He says that while human laws allow a thief to be killed when that is necessary to save temporal goods, the Divine law makes the day-night distinction which requires a discerning of the thief's intention. Such determination is not possible, he says, at night; so the thief can be killed. The daylight theft is otherwise. What "human laws" he has in mind, Alexander does not say; but it can be presumed that he was familiar with the Roman law and the gloss on **Furem nocturnum** which we have already cited. In this case, Alexander teaches that the Exodus law is to overrule the human law in determining the morality of killing a thief. The reason is that these verses are **Divine law**. Unlike Thomas, Alexander does not consider the judicial precepts of the Old Law to have been abrogated;[39] they have been "fulfilled," but he does not say they have been nullified completely. Consequently, he can view these Exodus verses as a statement of Divine law which remains binding under the New Law. Christian morality thus demands a discerning of intention to kill, actual or presumed, on the part of the thief before he can be killed; the killing is, consequently, a matter of **self-defense**, not of protecting one's property. Furthermore, Alexander points to this distinction between human and Divine law in response to an objection that it is never licit to destroy a higher good for the sake of conserving a lower good. Thus, holds the objection, it would not be licit to kill any thief, whether he comes at night or during the day. Alexander's answer shows that while human law would violate that principle of comparative value, the Divine law would not, as the attack on life (even presumed) would constitute a situation in which equally valuable "goods" would be involved: life-vs-life.

It would seem that the human law would have to be considered in conflict with Divine law, and thus invalid. Alexander, however, does not draw this conclusion explicitly. In fact, he teaches further on another situation in which the killing of a thief would be morally licit.[40] Besides the nocturnal thief or a daytime thief who comes armed to defend himself, a thief may be killed for "obstinancy," i.e., for repeated conviction of theft. According to Alexander, thieves are "marked and branded" the first and second times they are caught; the third time they are hung. The justification for this punishment is found in Deut. 17:2: "Any man who has the insolence to refuse to listen to . . . the judge, shall die." This verse is considered to be Divine law, as were the Exodus verses. Yet in this case the obstinancy is punished by the public authority, by the judicial process. The private individual cannot kill a thief unless there is a threat to life. As Alexander says, "/Other than for obstinancy/ a thief is not punished by death unless he is presumed to be a robber."[41] This statement applies not only to judicial punishment, the context within which Alexander makes it, but also to the individual who is defending against the thief. There is need for a threat to life, real or assumed, before killing a thief is morally irreprehensible for the private person, i.e., it must be a case of robbery.

The position of Thomas Aquinas on this question appears to break with the Exodus-rooted teaching and tend more in the direction found in the gloss on <u>Furem nocturnum</u>. Thomas deals with the case of killing a thief almost incidently,[42] which in itself is somewhat curious given the explicit consideration of the issue by his contemporaries. He quotes Ex. 22:1 as allowing killing in defense of property, and then concludes that killing in self-defense must therefore be allowed; if the lesser is legitimate, the greater is legitimate. Thomas uses the verse without elaboration and for the purpose of justifying killing to save one's own life. Yet his use of the verse shows that he accepts it as justifying killing in defense of property (and later authors will cite him in this way).[43] There is significance in Aquinas quoting only the first of the two verses usually linked together when this Exodus text is cited. By leaving out the "but if after sunrise" etc., of Ex. 22:2, the text reads simply: "If a thief is caught in the act of housebreaking and beaten to death, there is no bloodguilt involved." The text would then appear to legitimate killing in all cases of theft; for the day-night distinction and its possible implications have been omitted.

If we leave aside for the moment the later understanding of Thomas, we can ask if such an overall legitimation of killing for property was what he wanted to teach. In citing the text Thomas remarks that it allows killing in defense of one's "house." Is it possible that such "housebreaking" is understood by Thomas to be a nocturnal occurrence? Would he thus imply the common distinction and the common understanding? Does his quoting of only the first verse necessarily exclude the second? Certainly, there is nothing like an "etc." in his text; but would he presuppose a knowledge of the full passage, quoted once again in its most common context? There is no way for these questions to be answered. For whatever cause, Thomas does not deal separately with the problem of killing in defense of property. This brief reference is all he says. And what he says is "how much more licit to defend one's own life than one's house." The first verse of Ex. 22 says only that one breaking in can be killed.

However, if we conclude, as subsequent generations of scholars concluded, that Thomas is without qualification (except perhaps for the due moderation requirement) legitimating killing in defense of property, we are left with four important questions. If Thomas is here breaking dramatically with the Church's theological and legal tradition, would he do so in such an offhanded, indirect way? Would not such a departure demand an expanded presentation, perhaps including some reference to sources such as Roman law? How does the deprivation of life for property coincide with his teaching that the private person can only kill with the "intention" (end) of self-defense in mind? He cannot intend the death of the other. It is in the same article that the Exodus text is quoted that Thomas puts forth his "double effect" teaching as the solution to the issue of self-defense. If the lesser (property) legitimates the greater (life) as an object of protection, can the lesser require anything but at least as stringent a criterion? Where is the indirect intention based upon self-preservation in the bold statement on property? Again, how does Thomas simply accept the judicial precept of Exodus as legitimating moral law when he teaches that these judicial precepts have been abrogated? At least he would have to engage in some argumentation to show that the conclusion drawn is in line with the process of human reasoning. Finally, if Thomas is departing from the tradition, why does he do so? What might have led him to do it? Perhaps his acceptance of Roman law (in terms of the gloss which has been referred to) could have done it. Thomas could have recognized this law as an exercise of human reason leading to a "reasonable" moral position. Perhaps his reading of Aristotle brought to his attention the role which property (wealth) could play in respect to virtue.[44] Hence man would have the right to defend that property. It may be possible that Thomas is here giving expression to his opposition to the glorification of poverty and the condemnation of wealth on the part of thirteenth-century Franciscan Spirituals.[45] The climate of the mid-thirteenth century was against stern renunciation; the growing burgher class was gaining power and influence as it strove for increased material possessions through the development of the emerging capitalist economy. There was in the thirteenth century a new respect and even a justification for private gain; the economic activity of individuals was beginning to be appreciated.[46] These factors might have been influential in forming the teaching of Thomas, but even if they were only indirectly involved we could expect Thomas to engage in some lengthier presentation of his novel position. But he does not deal with this question as a separate crime.

There is one aspect of Thomas' teaching that might lead to an acceptance of killing in defense of property. Thomas teaches that vengeance is at times lawful, and when lawful it is a virtue.[47] He finds justification for the possible lawfulness of vengeance in the text of Lk. 18:7, which says: "will not God revenge His elect. . . ."[48] Since God can do only what is good and lawful, vengeance cannot be essentially evil and unlawful. Thomas declares vengeance lawful when the avenger's intention is directed chiefly to some good to be obtained by means of the punishment of the person who has sinned. He then gives as examples of the good to be obtained the amendment of the sinner, "or at least that he may be restrained and others be not disturbed"; justice is thus upheld and God is honored.[49] The points which Thomas wants to emphasize are the removal of harm done or the resistance of harm by defense.[50] Although Thomas initially writes of man "defending himself" against wrongs, he removes the possibility of being understood to mean only corporal harm by stating that the virtue of vengeance is concerned with defending the "rights of individuals."[51] Thomas views vengeance as both lawful and virtuous because it tends to the prevention of evil. To restrain sin, he says, man should be deprived of what he loves most: life, bodily safety, freedom, external goods.[52] But death is to be inflicted only for sins which are conducive to the "grave undoing of others."[53]

Thomas does not apply his teaching on vengeance to any particular cases, but it certainly would be possible for someone to apply it to the defense of property.[54] Such defense would be either resistance to or removal of harm, a defense of what came to be seen as a "right" to private property, and the possibility of being killed could serve as a deterrent to potential thieves. The gravity of theft would also contribute to such an interpretation. But again it must be asked why, if Thomas intended this teaching to be so applied, he did not somewhere in the <u>Summa</u> deal with the issue of killing to defend property. The later understanding of his teaching would tell us nothing of what he himself would have taught, regardless of how his teaching on a different subject was applied through the later understanding.

With these questions posed, we are still left with the simple statement of Thomas that one may kill to defend property. Subsequent tradition will take the statement at its face value, but the acceptance seems to leave too many unanswered questions. Although Thomas will have a significant role to play as a supporter of killing in defense of property, it does not seem that the statement in itself can be taken as an unequivocal legitimation of killing in defense of property. Such an offhanded, indirect reference does not seem to be the way that Thomas would interject a radical, tradition-flaunting teaching. He usually takes pains to express his reasons.

Perhaps the manner in which we can (and the post-Thomas authors should have) understand Thomas is indicated in the teaching of Richard of Middleton.[55] Richard wants to justify killing in self-defense, and he uses the argument that if the "less licit" is justifiable, the "more licit" is also justifiable. One example he gives is that of the thief. He says that Ex. 22 allows a thief to be killed; so killing in self-defense can be licit. He then goes on to give the criteria (inevitable necessity and due moderation) which justify self-defensive killing. He also goes on to give the criterion to justify killing a thief; he uses the day-night distinction as referring to the ability to discern the thief's intention. One can tell the daytime thief's intention: if he comes to kill he can be killed. Richard thus agrees with the tradition: a thief can only be killed when he also threatens life.

We have seen that Thomas' purpose in using Ex. 22 is the same as that of Richard: to legitimate self-defensive killing. Both cite Ex. 22 in a broad fashion (though Thomas quotes the first verse of the chapter while Richard quotes no verses): it is legitimate to kill a thief. Richard then proceeds to establish criteria for self-defensive killing and includes the killing of a thief under that category: only as an act of self-defense may someone kill a thief; there must be a concurrent threat to life accompanying the danger of loss of property. This is the step missing in Thomas. Except for the inclusion of theft under "self-defense" when a threat to life is present, Thomas agrees with Richard's form of argument. There are tendencies in Richard which speak of reliance upon Thomas;[56] could we then consider Richard to follow Thomas in this case? He uses the same basic argumentation, but then adds further clarifying specification. Does he specify what Thomas presumes? Such presumption would answer the problem of Thomas having omitted any real consideration of our question. The ecclesiastical tradition was quite clear that a thief only forfeited his life when he himself threatened life. Thomas' citation of Ex. 22:1 might have been merely a general statement of the possibility of a thief being killed which presumed the criterion of a threat to life.

The requirement that there be danger to the victim's life is also affirmed by Scotus.[57] He views Ex. 22 as clearly teaching that a man cannot be killed for theft alone. The reason a nighttime thief can be killed is because he is presumed to be prepared to kill a person who resists him. Consequently, the nocturnal thief fulfills the requirement of Scotus that only the thief who is also an "attacker" may be killed. Presumably, the deception, the ability to go unrecognized at night, and the inability of the victim to discern the thief's intention are what lead to the presumption that the nocturnal thief will kill if resisted. The only remark Scotus makes about the daytime thief is to say that such a thief is not presumed to be ready to kill. This statement is consistent with the requirement that the daytime thief only be killed when he defends himself with a weapon. Such defense gives actual information; there is no need for presumption. Scotus thus adds nothing new to our discussion: only a threat to life—presumed at night, actual during the day when intention can be recognized—legitimates the deprivation of a thief's life, i.e., only a "robber," actual or presumed, may be killed.

While Thomas' teaching remains problematic, the other thirteenth-century authors display a consistent interpretation of Ex. 22:1-2. In requiring a threat to life, presumed at night, actual during the day, before a thief may be killed, they agree with the Rabbinic understanding of these verses. Alexander makes direct reference to human (Roman) law and rejects its legitimation of killing merely to prevent loss of goods. At the end of the thirteenth century (with the possible exception of Thomas) this statement of Scotus could sum up the moral teaching: "I do not see any law justly established which enables a man to be killed for theft alone."[58] For these teachers, Ex. 22 made this conclusion clear, and it was reaffirmed in Church legislation by Si perfodiens, De homicidio. The position of Thomas, which has been considered here at least ambiguous, will be accepted in subsequent centuries as supportive of killing for "theft alone."

Fourteenth Century

A continuation of the previous-century canonists' understanding of Si perfodiens, De homicidio is found in the work of Joannes Andreae.[59] He reaffirms the notions of "day and night" to mean "intention," and specifies the decretal's mention of "ancient secular law" to be the Twelve Tables, which permitted the killing of a thief at night if he could not be spared without danger to the victim.[60] The thief's right to life remains dependent upon his intention and the ability of the victim to discern that intention. Andreae adds nothing new; he simply allows Si perfodiens to interpret Ex. 22:1-2.

A definite and radical change in the teaching on killing a thief appears in the work of two fourteenth-century lawyers, Bartolus de Sassoferrato and Joannes de Lignano. Both rely heavily and almost exclusively on Roman law as the basis for a radical departure from a tradition that neither mentions.

Bartolus de Sassoferrato was one of the leading jurists of the fourteenth century (b.1313-d.1357). He studied at Pisa first, then at Perugia, where he taught until his death.[61] His most famous work is his commentary on the Roman law codified by Justinian.[62] His comments on Furem nocturnum, Ad Legem Corneliam de sicariis are quite unequivocal: a nocturnal thief and a daytime thief can be killed to protect one's life or one's property, if that is the only way to save life or property.[63] Bartolus' focus in regard to property is the recovery of the property, and the basis for his position is the principle of repelling force with force. The threat to life along with the threat to property is not included as a requirement for justifiable killing.[64] Since force can be repelled with force, property can be defended even to killing when that is necessary to save it, to repel the force. He cuts through the day-night distinction by teaching that if the property can be recovered later because the victim recognizes the thief, the victim of the theft cannot kill the thief. If the recognition is present at night or during the day, one cannot kill; if there is no recognition either at night or during the day, one may kill. The criterion is clearly the possibility of recovery and not the presence of danger to the victim's life.

This teaching of Bartolus is obviously quite different from that of the theologians and canonists of the thirteenth century, as well as that of his contemporary Andreae. How might the change be accounted for? Already in the twelfth century a capitalist economy had emerged in Italy, but, as is to be expected, thought lagged behind practice. There was reluctance to recognize capitalist activity and acquisition as worthwhile. The thirteenth century began to appreciate the economic activity of individuals, and the appreciation was aided by Roman law's concept of the community being best served when each individual takes care of his own interests.[65] By the fourteenth century businessmen were rationalistic, and materialism and thirst for profit were becoming increasingly accepted by the broader society. The notion that riches may contribute to moral growth, evident in the thirteenth century, increased among the fourteenth-century Scholastics, who were perhaps reflecting the ideas of the humanist authors who expressed the spirit of the age.[66]

The greatest among the humanist authors is the Florentine merchant-moralist Paolo da Certaldo, who came to adulthood during the first half of the fourteenth century. He wrote a work entitled *Il Libro di bouoni costumi*, which was a collection of traditional maxims.[67] Paolo extols the amassing of riches for the future, the value of work and business acumen, and emphasizes the need for the merchant to remain as independent as possible.[68] He writes of the individual's obligation to guard his possessions, and even advises that one not lend weapons to others in case they be needed by oneself.[69] But Paolo is a "transitional" person. He repeats the teaching of the Gospel and remains faithful to the economic morality of the Church; yet he makes a large place for profit and individual success. There are contradictions in his work: e.g., vengeance is considered one of the great human satisfactions, "the first joy of life";[70] yet he advocates that one not take vengeance.[71] Certaldo's position is one in which theory and practice are divorced; it is intermediate between a Christian and a merchant ethic, though on the side of the merchant ethic.[72]

Paolo wrote at a time of economic crisis and recession, and he reflects the merchant desire to be both more sure of profits and more desirous of retaining what is gained: these are the means for dominating the future. The Florence in which and from which he wrote was in process of becoming dominated and governed by the bourgeoisie, who emerged on the twin props of money and intellect. The basis of power was rapidly becoming the possession of money, of productive capital; consequently, acquisition outstripped consumption as a goal.[73] There was an enterprising spirit, an assertive self-consciousness which rejected limitation on the "free individual." This new man" was free to dispose of his property, material or intellectual; the entrepreneur could exercise unlimited property rights over the means of production.[74] Consequently, it is not difficult to recognize in this setting an environment conducive to the shift in theory evident in Bartolus. But the likelihood of Bartolus being influenced by the domination of the bourgeois environment of especially northern Italy, does not say why Andreae was not so influenced.

Joannes Andreae worked with the <u>Decretales</u>, Bartolus with Roman law. Andreae shows a reliance upon Roman law, while Bartolus makes no reference to Church law. Do we have here a case of Church law-vs-civil law? Does Andreae acknowledge an influence from civil law, while Bartolus exercises an independence from Church law? That would seem to be the case. Bartolus bases his legitimation of killing for property on the natural law principle of repelling force with force. The principle has been present all along, but Bartolus is the first we

have seen who directly extends its application to property
and not just to self-defense. The principle was present;
Bartolus views it as more broadly applicable than his predecessors. Why he saw it this way is possibly answered by
the remarks made above on the general social situation in relation to wealth, profit, and the rising bourgeoisie. The
social environment was conducive to the changed teaching.
There is also need to consider something of the intellectual
environment in regard to the theory of private property.

At a time of growing materialism and individualism,
and of increased value being placed on wealth, the fourteenth-century merchant-writers rediscovered Cicero.[75] In Cicero
they could read that the state was founded principally to
protect the property of the individual.[76] Cicero makes this
statement even though he also teaches that private property is
not from natural law but from civil law.[77] The first statement of Cicero implies that private property is "natural,"
while the second seems to involve the notion that common
possession was the "natural state," private ownership a
necessity because of the corruption of human nature.[78] The
ambiguity found in Cicero had also become a part of the Roman
law so heavily relied upon by our fourteenth-century authors.
The individual was seen to have title to private property on
the basis of both natural and civil law: some property was
considered owned on the basis of natural law, some on the
foundation of civil law.[79]

When Roman law had come to be studied again in the
twelfth century, it was the theory of property as an institution of the law of nature which began to regain popularity.[80]
With the aid of Roman law, canon lawyers grasped private
property as natural; since the texts of the law were ambiguous it was possible for the thirteenth-century lawyers to
read them in a sense that fitted their optimistic view of the
world and gave a firmer foundation to the status quo. The
theologians achieved the same result through consideration of
private property as natural given the corruption of human
nature by the Fall.[81] The movement toward accepting private
property as based on natural law was also aided by the recovery of the works of Aristotle in the thirteenth century.

In his *Politics* the scholars could read that it was natural and good for men to own things privately.[82] And this is precisely what Thomas taught.[83] Thomas makes no mention of private property being an institution necessited by sin. For him private ownership is the more perfected form of ownership.[84]

With this background, the disputes over Church property with the kings and princes were entered by the fourteenth-century Churchmen.[85] This was also the century of the heated dispute over the poverty of the Franciscans, a dispute used by those in favor of the secular power as a weapon to justify royal control over clerical property.[86] One of the major controversialists in the poverty dispute was the Franciscan William of Ockham (d.1347). In response to John XXIII's *Quia vir reprobus*, which was a long declaration on poverty, especially that of Jesus and the Apostles, Ockham wrote the *Opus nonaginta dierum*.[87] In the course of defending the Franciscan ideas on poverty and the distinction between ownership and use of property, Ockham states that a man has a "natural right to property," the natural right to own and use it, or to resist it being taken.[88] This "right" to property is a legitimate power which is anterior to human convention; right reason demands the institution of private property as a remedy for man's moral condition after the Fall.[89] This teaching of Ockham would have received a wide audience as his influence spread to certain key universities in the second half of the fourteenth century.[90]

Between the twelfth and fourteenth centuries, then, there was both the development of a social order which accentuated the importance and value of property and the rediscovery of a theory of property which considered private ownership an institution of natural law, even, in the case of Ockham, a "natural right." The context was ripe for a change in a teaching predicated on a theory which viewed common ownership as the original ideal, the institution in accord with nature. The actual lived-situation by the fourteenth century also would contribute to an increased value for privately owned property. Bartolus makes the change. He attributes it to Roman law (though we have seen it to be not the law but glosses on the law) and bases it upon what was grasped all along as a principle of natural law. Joannes de Lignano will make the same shift in his teaching, but he will attempt to give as a reason for the change the linkage between a person and his property.

Joannes de Lignano, also using Roman law as his basis, reaches the same conclusion on killing in defense of property as Bartolus does.[91] But, unlike Bartolus, he attempts to do more than give "repel force with force" as the reason for his teaching. Relying on the laws <u>Unde vi</u> and <u>Scientiam, qui cum aliter</u>, <u>Ad Legem Aquiliam</u>,[92] Lignano teaches that one may licitly kill or mutilate in defending property with due moderation.[93] Both of these laws incorporate the principle of repelling force with force, though only <u>Unde vi</u> explicitly speaks of property: "if one possesses rightly, he can with due moderation licitly repel force." <u>Scientiam, qui cum aliter</u>, refers to the saving of oneself, not to property. Lignano links the two laws by stating that "one can kill for goods because the person is atoned for by means of the goods."[94] Defense of property thus becomes equated with defense of persons, and the requirement of due moderation remains.[95] Lignano indicates by his stated reason a linking of a person and his property to the extent that an "injury" accrues to the person when his property is threatened. To prevent the violation of property and thus a personal injury, a person may take the necessary action to forestall the thief. It is as if a person's property is an extension of himself. This teaching of Lignano fits well with the Aristotelian notion, incorporated by Thomas, that wealth—money, property, or goods—is advantageous to virtue, that property is not a necessary evil but is rather natural and good.[96] The institutions of the "world" were increasingly the institutions of the Church. Civilization and its institutions, including private property, were already being sacralized in the thirteenth century; Lignano's position is a logical step in conformity to the "goodness" of private property and the evil of unjustly taking it, and the position finds support in the Roman law which exercised ever-increasing influence.

To further specify his position regarding killing in

defense of property, Lignano cites <u>Furem nocturnum</u>, <u>Ad Legem Corneliam de sicariis</u>.[97] In referring to this law, Lignano says that it allows the killing of a thief when he cannot be recognized and when the goods cannot be recovered through the legal process. We have seen that this position is not the content of the law itself (which legitimates killing a nocturnal thief when he cannot be spared without danger to oneself), but it is the teaching of Bartolus and Accursius' gloss on the law. The danger to oneself, required by the text of the law, is perhaps considered present by Lignano through his uniting of danger to the person to every threat to property. The "nocturnal" element has no bearing on his teaching. Lignano's only concern, his only broadly significant criteria for killing in defense of property, are the possibility of recovery and the necessity for due moderation.[98] Once again Lignano is a source for a new position; once again the debate is not concluded, but the outcome is evident in the teaching of Joannes de Lignano.[99] He and Bartolus show the importance of Roman law as a "rational" determiner of valid moral behavior. For them a thief forfeits his life even if he endangers only a person's property.

Fifteenth Century

Despite the unequivocal teaching of Bartolus and Lignano, the fifteenth century continues to evidence considerable vacillation. The idea of recovery is present, but somewhat ambiguously. There is no complete agreement on the criteria for killing a thief.

The only reference to Ex. 22:1-2 found in Jean Gerson's writing on killing is a statement of an "error" taught in relation to the precept "You shall not kill."[100] The error is given as follows:

> That a nocturnal thief, that layer-in-wait, heretic and soothsayer, is meritoriously killed by anyone even if he can be led to judgment, nor is there a certain danger of death threatening the killer, on account of which he must repel force with force by killing.

The condemnation of this teaching seems to be an attempt by Gerson to reaffirm the need for a danger to one's life before one is permitted to kill a nighttime thief. The mere occurrence of the theft at night is not sufficient grounds. If there is the possibility of capturing the thief without killing him, it is then forbidden to kill him. Gerson here seems to deny any automatic presumption of a threat to life simply because it is night: there is to be "a certain danger of death." There is to be "certain danger"; Gerson does not say there must be some sort of attack on the person, just that there be "danger of death." His teaching would thus seem to demand of the victim some attempt to capture without killing, or at least some founded judgment that the danger to himself exists.

Gerson does not cite any other authors or laws in making his condemnation. His position is, however, in accord with <u>Si perfodiens</u>, which legitimated killing at night when the thief could not be spared without endangering oneself. If that danger to one's own life is absent, even the nocturnal thief cannot be killed. It would seem that an inability to determine the intention of the nocturnal thief would constitute a danger of death, and in that sense the danger would be "certain." On the other hand, Gerson's use of "certain" may be an attempt on his part to demand of the victim some effort short of killing which would then determine the extent of the force necessary to repel force. He would in this way be re-emphasizing the concept of "due moderation." What is clearly condemned is the unnecessary killing of a nocturnal thief; consequently, the victim would be bound to some effort at prevention short of killing.

The teaching of Panormitanus on our question poses a problem.[101] He acknowledges that <u>Si perfodiens</u> offers Augustine's understanding of Ex. 22:1-2 as required: the daytime thief is not to be killed, while the nocturnal thief may be killed. Implied, though not mentioned by Panormitanus, are the statements about threat to life. Panormitanus then notes that it is more difficult to confront nocturnal thieves than those who act in the daylight; but daytime thieves are also difficult to accost. In conjunction with these ideas, he makes reference to an opinion which held killing a nocturnal thief legitimate even when the thief did not defend himself.

(This is perhaps the same notion as that condemned by Gerson.) Panormitanus answers this opinion by saying it is to be understood as meaning a situation in which a nocturnal thief cannot be captured without killing him. It is this use of "capture" here that creates the difficulty. Does Panormitanus here legitimate killing to capture the thief, to perhaps recover the property, whether the thief threatens his victim's life or not? In making his statement, Panormitanus gives as the source of it the Roman law Furem nocturnum, Ad Legem Corneliam de sicariis. But in his reference, Panormitanus refers not simply to the law, but to the commentator Bartolus on the law. It would appear, therefore, that Panormitanus would agree with Bartolus and not require a threat to life. However, he also makes reference to what had been taught in his previous section on the decretal Interfecisti, De homicidio.[102] In his remarks on this decretal Panormitanus also makes reference to Si perfodiens. He teaches that a thief or a robber who can be captured is not to be killed, while one who cannot be captured may be killed. He understands "capture," however, as not meaning only immediate detention. If the thief can be later identified and the property recovered through the judicial process, he is not to be killed. "A nocturnal thief who is known is to be treated as a daytime thief and not killed." The mere circumstance of nocturnal crime is not sufficient reason to deprive the thief of his life. Thus far Panormitanus still seems to use as his criterion for killing the notion of "capture," of identification, which would or would not lead to the recovery of the stolen property. But two elements of his teaching lead us in the opposite direction.

In making his statement that a thief or robber who can be captured cannot be killed, Panormitanus refers to Itaque, Ad Legem Aquiliam,[103] which cites the Twelve Tables as legitimating the killing of a nocturnal thief, and also a daytime thief who defends himself with a sword. There is also Panormitanus' statement that "to free goods alone it is not licit to kill a thief, even a nocturnal one." If we take these two references seriously, Panormitanus cannot be teaching that recovery of property through capture is the criterion for killing the thief. If it is not allowed to kill only for property, "capture" must refer to something beyond the goods themselves. There must be some threat to life involved, as both *Itaque* and *Si perfodiens* teach regarding the daytime thief. So when Panormitanus speaks of the "capture" of the nocturnal thief could he have in mind a situation in which the attempt to prevent the theft can only be successful if the thief is killed inasmuch as the thief would kill his victim rather than be captured by him? The teaching would then consist of a demand that a threat to life be present either at night or during the day before the thief could be killed. In both cases, day or night, the victim may initiate defensive action, and if he is resisted by a threat to himself he may kill if that is necessary to remove the danger. Panormitanus apparently is concerned to remove any "automatic presumption" of the nocturnal thief's willingness to kill. At no point does Panormitanus indicate any specific rejection of the *Si perfodiens*-Augustinian understanding; he rather attempts to tighten-up the nighttime circumstance by legitimating killing only when other means of prevention are not possible and there is a danger to life. Because of the difficulty in recognizing the nocturnal thief and thus being able to accuse him later, it remains more likely that killing would become a legitimate option at night. If Panormitanus is read as agreeing with Bartolus, he then flatly contradicts himself. The key to Panormitanus' position, despite the citation of Bartolus on *Furem nocturnum*, is his demand that he be understood in accordance with what he had written on the decretal *Interfecisti*, *De homicidio*. When that is done, the teaching cannot be taken as legitimating the killing of a thief to defend only property.[104]

    The examination of the teaching of Antoninus is going to involve us in the same sort of difficulty that Panormitanus presented. With Antoninus a conclusion will be even more difficult to reach.

    Antoninus teaches that a nighttime thief can be killed if one cannot tell whether he has come to steal or to kill, nor is he able to be apprehended in another way. The daytime thief can only be killed when he defends himself with a sword, for, says Antoninus, this case is more than just theft.[105] The problem with this teaching is twofold, yet the parts are interrelated. The phrase which I have given as "nor is he able to be apprehended in another way" reads in Latin: nec alias poterat deprehendi.[106] The question which this phrase raises is: Does Antoninus here simply reinforce the due moderation principle—the nocturnal thief can be killed when his intention cannot be discerned and there is no way short of killing to protect oneself—or is he saying that the inability to apprehend is a distinct criterion which legitimates killing?

To support his teaching, Antoninus refers to the decretal Si perfodiens, De homicidio, and to a law titled in the text as Fures, De furtis. There is a law with this title in the Decretales,[107] but all it says is that thieves and robbers are not to be prayed for if they are killed in the act of theft or plunder; they may be given Communion if they confess. All this law seems to indicate is the serious sinfulness of the act; it says nothing of the legitimacy of killing such a sinner. There is, however, the law Furem nocturnum, Ad Legem Corneliam de sicariis, which is in the section De furtis; so it is quite possible that Fures is a misprint. If Furem nocturnum is the reference here, the content of that law agrees with Si perfodiens: the nocturnal thief can only be killed when he is a danger to oneself. It would then seem that the phrase "nor is he able to be apprehended in another way" would be just emphasizing due moderation. But when Antoninus' position on due moderation is examined, this conclusion does not fit. On the question of due moderation Antoninus cites Furem nocturnum and states that a thief may be killed when he is unable to be recognized and the goods cannot be provided for through the judicial process.[108] Due moderation excludes killing when the property is recoverable. Antoninus cites only the law, no commentator, no gloss; yet we have seen that the law in itself does not allow killing simply to protect property. He must, therefore, have more than the law in mind. In the context of due moderation, Antoninus speaks of the principle of repelling force with force as both natural and positive law; he may be referring to Bartolus' commentary. But how are we to understand what appears to be a contradiction in Antoninus' teaching? The discrepancy can be reconciled if we understand "nor is he able to be apprehended in another way" as a separate criterion. If not, we must simply accept Antoninus as contradicting himself, requiring a threat to life at one point, and simply the saving of property at another before the thief is legitimately deprived of his life. Both positions have predecessors. If we attempt to use subsequent authors as an aid to understanding, Antoninus would have to be taken as legitimating killing to save property alone.[109]

In chapter one[110] we noted the opinion of Antoninus that one is not to kill in order to avoid evil of less magnitude than the evil of taking another's life. His concern involved a situation in which fear of consent to sin was present. If one cannot kill to avoid a lesser evil than killing, what of the case of theft? There is no sin to be avoided on the part of the victim. Is the loss of property a "greater evil" than the loss of life? In the previous discussion of this principle of Antoninus it was stated that law may be the determiner of what is the greater evil. That is the case with the issue of theft. Antoninus uses Roman law as the justifying basis for his teaching, and, if the understanding of the "apprehend" clause is correct, he does this in defiance of ecclesiastical law. He makes no attempt to show how the loss through theft is a greater evil than the loss of the thief's life. Force may repel force inasmuch as that is necessary: such seems to be the extent of the rationale. Antoninus does not make any reference to his principle of "greater evil"; somehow he presumes the greater evil to lie on the side of lost property.

Antoninus' concern for "lost property" is exemplified in his opposition to usury. He is uncompromisingly against usury because of the social evil he saw in the practice. However, he did justify the making of a profit when money is loaned in such a way that the owner is deprived of the opportunity to benefit from the use of his money. The issue involves capital, and money intended to be "kept in a chest." Thus, profit is legitimated in cases of forced government loans. Antoninus' position is that the owner has a right to the profit he could have made if allowed to use his property productively; by the loan "productive opportunity" has been lost. Theft would also be a deprivation of the opportunity to gain from the use of what was one's own.[111]

The disparate positions and ambiguity of these fifteenth-century authors reflects well the relative newness of legitimate killing to defend property. Gerson's position is unequivocally in line with the more limited tradition; Panormitanus and Antoninus reflect an awareness of the criterion of "apprehension" ("recoverability"), but they differ on its meaning. Antoninus' *Summa* is said to give the best picture of his century's morality;[112] he also wrote the work while Archbishop of Florence.[113] Florence was the mercantile and capitalistic center; it had also received an influx of Byzantine scholars after the fall of Constantinople (1453). These scholars helped the noblemen and the bourgeoisie to find justification for a practical life athirst for pleasure and beauty.[114] It was a time of heavy expenditure, of wealth as a criterion for social status and a necessity for virtue.[115] The widespread study and appreciation of Aristotle's *Nicomedian Ethics* informed this association of wealth and virtue.[116] There was also a developing concern, arising from experience of varying fortune, to simply preserve wealth, to want security above all. Religious and moral values were subordinated to economic, intellectual, and aesthetic ones.[117] In this Florentine environment, it would not be surprising if Antoninus were to accept and promulgate the rational application of the principle of repelling force with force. Panormitanus, on the other hand, was located in Palermo, on backward Sicily. He was a compiler, unoriginal, never responding to the pressures of his times.[118] He would be most likely to continue the traditional position.

The fifteenth century thus continues the requirement of a threat to life as well as legitimates killing for property alone. The fourteenth-century change has begun to take hold; it will dominate from this time forward.

Sixteenth Century

The sixteenth century marks the firm takeover of the position that legitimates killing in defense of property. This opinion began to be upheld by prominent authors in the fourteenth century and received further impetus from Antoninus in the fifteenth. It is interesting that the major economic problem for the moralists of these centuries, usury, was at the same time in the throes of a decisive change. The pivotal years for the liberalization of usury theory were 1450-1550, the very years in which killing to defend property was gaining wide acceptance.[119] It was during these years that the Scholastics began to accept the view that money should be compensated for when it was put out to loan. The compensation was to cover the gain which could have come through investment in partnerships, annuities, and foreign exchange. With that change come greater signs of sensitivity among the moralists to the uses of property and the rights of property owners.[120]

The century of the Reformation brought with it serious problems of heresy and toleration, and those afraid of the rigor of heresy laws moved strongly in the defense of the rights of individuals. By the second half of the century absolute value was being attached to liberty and to possessions, and the individual was broadly considered a radically self-subsisting unit.[121] While much of the working out of these problems took place in the political realm, there were also economic ramifications, most evident in the case of usury, but also possibly crucial for the question at hand here.[122] Even prior to the Reformation, as has been indicated, the mercantile classes were pursuing a policy in which lay life, the lay calling, was sanctified and wealth was free for capitalistic enterprise.[123] These elements were intensified in the sixteenth century, given impetus from the energy released by the relocation of many of the mercantile class. The age was one of continual strife and warfare. As a consequence, it was routine procedure to have town gates closed at dusk and curfews imposed; travellers and merchants were forced to journey in armed convoys. As the century wore on, there was an increased link between war and delinquency, and of both with brigandage.[124] The population changes also contributed to this atmosphere of unrest: as populations moved and density increased more bandits and vagabonds lived on the fringes of society and the law; their numbers were augmented by masses of people on the verge of subsistence as a result of inflation, depression, lagging wage-rates and rising prices, crop failures, and the inability of production to meet the demands of mass consumption.[125] In this environment, there was no move to improve police protection.[126]

The conditions of the sixteenth century did nothing to hinder the dissemination of the teaching that a thief may be killed in defense of property alone. Sylvester, Cajetan, Navarrus, and Molina all support this position;[127] Covarrubias is a lonely voice in opposition.[128]

Sylvester begins his discussion of killing in defense of property by distinguishing what is permitted to be done by civil law without punishment and what can be done on private authority without sin.[129] He says that much civil legislation allows killing to defend goods which cannot otherwise be recovered; *Si perfodiens*, *De homicidio*, is declared to be both recognized by civil law and to excuse from sin those who kill on the basis of its night-day distinction and the threat to life. The possibility that he might be understood to be declaring killing on the basis of inability to recover justified only by civil law and thus to be a matter of sin according to ecclesiastical (moral) law is avoided by Sylvester in another place.[130] He teaches that killing is just whenever it is done to resist an unjust attack on goods: the natural law of repelling force with force, observing due moderation, applies. "Due moderation" is considered present when by the omission of an action injury to property could not be repelled. Further justification for killing when property is otherwise unrecoverable is found in *Furem nocturnum*, *Ad Legem Corneliam de sicariis*. Sylvester does not refer to anything but the law itself; this law has already been seen to justify killing a thief only when there is a danger to the person being victimized. Sylvester's use of it need not include the interpretation of commentators because he agrees with Lignano that repelling for goods is licit in the same way that repelling to save persons is: property and person are linked. The key for Sylvester is recoverability of the goods and the consequent violence necessary to prevent the loss of otherwise unrecoverable property.

Cajetan likewise relies upon the notion of recoverability and says that the law *Furem nocturnum* concedes the liceity of killing in defense of property that cannot otherwise be recovered.[131] The major thrust of Cajetan's position is rooted in arguments from reason; these will be considered later in this chapter.[132]

Among the legitimate reasons for killing another person Navarrus lists the protection of property which cannot otherwise be saved.[133] He finds authority for this position in the writings of Antoninus, Sylvester, and Cajetan, the Church law *Olim*, *De restitutione spoliatorum*, the Roman laws *Scientiam*, *qui cum aliter*, *Ad Legem Aquiliam*, and *Unde vi*, and the glosses on these Roman laws. The ecclesiastical and Roman laws are given as examples of the legitimacy of repelling force with force. The "due moderation" requirement is understood as fulfilled by Navarrus when "that is done without which injury could not be avoided." Navarrus also uses *Si perfodiens*, *De homicidio*.[134] He acknowledges that according to this decretal a person sins mortally who kills either a nocturnal or a daytime thief who could be apprehended without being killed. He also says that the day-night distinction remains important in the "external forum," but has no meaning for the "internal forum." The reason given for the unimportance of the distinction for conscience is that in this "forum" the presumption goes to the person who would kill the thief. What Navarrus seems to be saying here is that it is the person's recognition of the situation which determines (for himself) the morality of killing in the concrete circumstance. The automatic presumption that the nocturnal thief is willing to kill and the daytime thief is not is rejected. The way that Navarrus deals with this decretal shows that he understands it to be confined to a case in which there is a threat to life. Even though the decretal speaks only to this case, it is not considered by Navarrus to outlaw killing just for property; he has sufficient backing to legitimate such defensive killing. *Si perfodiens* appears to be grasped as principally concerned with insuring that killing not take place unless it is a necessity. While the decretal deals only with a threat-to-life situation, "necessity" may also be present when deprivation of life is the only means to protect property.

Of the authors whose positions we have expounded here, Louis Molina has the most organized presentation of the material.[135] Among the arguments against killing for property alone, Molina cites *Si perfodiens* and "civil laws" which teach the same: the day-night distinction revolves around the ability to discern the thief's intention and killing is only permissible when there is at least a presumed threat to life.[136] Molina responds to this understanding by teaching that what the decretal and such civil laws as *Itaque, Ad Legem Aquiliam*[137] intend to say is that "when a person defends his own things, regularly he defends at the same time his own person, which he exposes to danger for the defense of his goods." So a person can, with due moderation, kill to defend possessions. The interpretation of Augustine in *Si perfodiens* is said by Molina to have presumed that the thief would not resist opposition and that the killing would have no relation to the defense of the goods threatened. Molina is here saying that a person can kill to defend property because when he tries to stop the thief he will be resisted; he is also saying that killing is legitimate when it is necessary to defend goods. He says that when there is no other way to prevent the theft or there is danger that the property be lost, it is "without doubt lawful" to kill. In support of his position, Molina refers to *Furem nocturnum, Ad Legem Corneliam de sicariis*[138] with its gloss. The gloss is said to explain the "danger" of which the law speaks: danger to one's own person *or* danger of loss of one's goods. By his understanding of a threat to one's life being "regularly" present in defense of goods and his agreement with the gloss on *Furem nocturnum*, Molina seems to cover the possibilities: whether the threat to life is or is not present, property may be defended by killing. He goes so far as to say that if one can apprehend a thief yet prefers to kill him, there is "more cause" in that he has done the injury.[139] The phrase "more cause" may be an indication that Molina does not totally excuse what seems to be blatantly unnecessary killing; yet he uses this teaching as supportive of the gloss on *Furem nocturnum*. The mere incurring of injury gives at least partial justification for killing. Property appears here to have achieved something of an absolute value: its mere violation approaches being sufficient for deprivation of life; the thief appears to somewhat forfeit his life simply by threatening the property. The thief's intention regarding killing is irrelevant.

Covarrubias takes under consideration the elements which have been met in Molina and others.[140] He agrees with Molina that often one's attempt to defend goods results in the thief attacking his person; killing when necessary in this circumstance is a legitimate act of self-defense.[141] When self-defense is not the circumstance, when only protection of property is the goal, Covarrubias teaches that a person cannot kill. He cites *Si perfodiens*' day-night dichotomy to refer to discernment of intention; *Si pignore*, *Itaque*, *Ad Legem Aquiliam*, and *Furem nocturnum*, *Ad Legem Corneliam de sicariis*[142] are read strictly, without glosses, to demand danger to life before killing is allowed.

It is obvious that the disparate positions on killing for property alone have fallen into a definite pattern. If the glosses on Roman law are accepted as authoritative, killing is legitimate; if the law is accepted literally, it is not. If the threat to life is considered the point of *Si perfodiens*, a negative is given to killing for property alone; if recovery is accepted as the determining factor, the danger to life is not required. There are other arguments, other sources whose interpretations fall into similar patterns. These will be met in the later sections of this chapter.

Seventeenth and Eighteenth Centuries

The Catholic moral teaching of the seventeenth-eighteenth centuries is solidly on the side of killing to defend property even when there is no threat to life. The seventeenth century was the era in which the "modern theory of natural law, the theory of individual rights, was perfected."[143] The teaching of Lessius, Diana, the school at Salamanca, Busembaum, and Alphonsus reflects the emphasis on a person's right to his property and justifies the deprivation of a thief's life in order to prevent property's loss.[144] It is the notion of recovery that dominates. The text of Ex. 22:1-2 is understood by Lessius, the Salamancans, Busembaum, and Alphonsus as allowing killing when the goods are not otherwise recoverable.[145] The Roman law Furem nocturnum, Ad Legem Corneliam de sicariis is directly cited by Lessius, indirectly by Busembaum and Alphonsus, to the same effect.[146] Lessius also refers to Itaque, Ad Legem Aquiliam for support. None of these men makes any mention of the discrepancy between the texts of these laws and the broader legitimation given killing by the glosses.

The only new addition to the argument approving killing for property alone is a decretal of Innocent IV, Dilecto, De sententia excommunicationis.[147] Lessius, the Salamancans, and Alphonsus use this decretal in support of their positions.[148] Dilecto repeats the "repel force with force" principle and concludes that a deacon's action in defending himself when his mundane goods were wrongfully and violently taken from him was legitimate. This decretal was not incorporated into the teaching of earlier authors because it is not that clearly speaking of justifiable killing for property alone. We have seen that Innocent IV upholds a literal understanding of Si perfodiens;[149] there he demands a threat to life before a thief may be killed. Dilecto speaks of wrongful and violent theft and the deacon saving himself. It would then be just another statement of already well-established teaching. By the seventeenth century, the opposite teaching is dominant. It is now possible to understand Dilecto in a different way: oneself and one's property have been linked, clerics and laity have been linked, and the natural law principle has been firmly extended to include property under defensive killing. Consequently, Lessius, et al. can look at the decretal as giving them further weight for their positions.

The previous pages have shown us a drastic shift in

the understanding of "day-night": from a threat to life to
the possibility of recovery as justifying cause for killing
a thief. In following the shift we have seen the important
role played by Roman law and particular glosses upon it.
There has also been evidence of changing social and intellectual environments which provided an atmosphere conducive to
the new teaching. But there are also other arguments, other
laws which contribute to the newer moral position. It is to
these we turn now. First we will look at the changing interpretation of two significant decretals: Suscepimus, De
homicidio, and Interfecisti, De homicidio. Then we will examine some crucial arguments from reason which were used to
support killing for property alone.

Interfecisti, De Homicidio, and Suscepimus, De Homicidio

Interfecisti, De Homicidio[150]

This decretal establishes punishment for unnecessary
and necessary killing of a thief or robber. If the killing
was not necessary, the punishment is exclusion from the Church
and its Sacraments, as well as a mandatory period of fasting;
necessary killing done without hatred requires life-long penance for a priest (though he is not deposed from office),
while the laity have the option of undertaking a voluntary
fast just in case they violated due moderation. It is in the
statement on necessary killing that the key phrase te tuaque
liberando occurs. The text is: Si autem sine odii meditatione
te tuaque liberando huiusmodi diaboli membra interfecisti—
"If without thoughts of hatred you have killed members of this
kind of devil in freeing yourself and your goods." The translation just made of te tuaque liberando—"yourself and your
goods" is disputed: should it be understood as an "or," or
should it be considered an "and"? If the "and" is accepted,
killing is only legitimate when a threat to life accompanies
the threat to property; if "or" is the interpretation, one may
kill for property alone. It is this disputed understanding
that we will trace here.

The teaching of Hostiensis on this decretal is not
perfectly clear.[151] In quoting the te tuaque he remarks that

defense is permitted not only for persons but also for things. (Note that he speaks of <u>defense</u> and not explicitly of killing.) He then refers to his remarks on <u>Suscepimus</u>, <u>De homicidio</u>,[152] where he says that <u>Interfecisti</u>'s use of <u>tuaque</u> and not <u>vel tua</u> is to be understood as referring to the particular case in that decretal, because goods alone can be defended with arms by both clerics and laity. In reference to clerics, Hostiensis writes that what he says here in <u>Suscepimus</u> is to be read in terms of what <u>Dilecto</u>, <u>De sententia excommunicationis</u>[153] says: clerics can call in the secular arm to defend property; they cannot do this themselves. He reinforces this teaching with a reference to his comments on <u>Significasti</u>, <u>De homicidio</u>,[154] where he says that clerics cannot kill for the sake of property, but they can call on others. He concludes by saying that if goods are attacked, the force may be forcefully repelled if one acts immediately.

In his comments Hostiensis clearly states that clerics cannot kill in defense of property. They are to call on the "secular arm," they are to call on "others." He also says that "defense" is permitted for goods; force brought against them can be repelled. Does this mean that <u>killing</u> in "defense" is permitted? Are the "others" whom clerics can call on to be understood as laity in general, or are they just those who would be part of the "secular arm," i.e., public authority? At no point does Hostiensis explicitly say that <u>killing</u> in defense of property is permissible. In dealing with <u>Interfecisti</u> under the title <u>Suscepimus</u>, he says that the killing considered in <u>Interfecisti</u> is licit because of <u>se suaque</u> (<u>sic</u>). Is he restricting the linkage of person and things to just this case, or is he saying that they must always be linked? Goods can be defended, and defended with arms; Hostiensis does not say that the arms can be used for killing. Is it possible that he had in mind defense short of killing? We have seen such a teaching in Panormitanus on the question of clerics and property.[155] It is also possible that for Hostiensis defense included legitimate, necessary killing. His concluding remark that force may repel force for property is supported by reference to two Roman laws: <u>Unde vi</u> and <u>Scientiam</u>, <u>qui cum aliter</u>, <u>Ad Legem Aquiliam</u>.[156]

Unde vi says what Hostiensis has just said: for property force can be used to repel force. Scientiam says that one may repel force with force to save oneself. Neither law helps to clarify the teaching of Hostiensis. This lack of clarity is further compounded when we recall his position on Si perfodiens, De homicidio.[157] There he legitimated killing not only on the traditional basis of day-night, which required the daytime thief to defend himself with a sword before he could be licitly killed, but merely on the daytime thief's being armed. It was the bearing of arms, the threat to life, which legitimated killing. When Hostiensis speaks of "defending property" against "force," is he assuming the threat to life which he required under Si perfodiens? The ambiguity of Hostiensis' position is an appropriate starting point for our look at a subsequent tradition which will first require the threat to life and later separate the te tuaque into te vel tua, legitimating killing for the defense of property alone.

Beginning with Hostiensis' contemporaries Raymund and Richard of Middleton in the late thirteenth century through Joannes Andreae in the fourteenth and Panormitanus in the fifteenth, there is among these authors a consistent interpretation of Interfecisti.[158] These are, significantly, the only men from this period (among those used for this study) who refer to the te tuaque of this decretal.[159] (This means that Joannes de Lignano, whose teaching has appeared to be of such importance, does not take Interfecisti specifically under consideration.) The understanding passed on by these four authors is that this decretal demands a threat to life along with the danger of loss of property for killing a thief to be legitimate. Raymund and Richard quote the decretal in full, and then in paraphrasing it both use et ("and") between te and tua. Andreae and Panormitanus both state that the text does not say te vel tua, but te tuaque; therefore it is not permitted to kill for goods alone.[160]

It would seem that the interest shown in the te tuaque phrase by these men indicates its importance for them in rejecting what we have already seen to be a growing theory and practice which would justify killing to defend property alone. Panormitanus specifically rejects the notion that because civil law allows one to kill to save property, it is therefore morally permissible.

The solidity of sixteenth-century authors, with the exception of Covarrubias, on the legitimacy of killing to defend property has been examined.[161] The understanding of *Interfecisti* follows the same pattern, though the paths of Sylvester, Cajetan, and Molina will differ on the way to the same conclusion.[162] Sylvester understands *te tuaque* as meaning "or"; Cajetan accepts the "and." They agree that the text does not expressly say that one cannot kill for goods alone when there is no other way to save them. Both authors focus on the notion of "no other means available," and Sylvester specifies this notion by saying that the decretal is considering that there will be another way available or the thief will attack with weapons. Molina teaches that *te tuaque* is to be understood as "or." His reason is that it is legitimate to kill in defense of oneself when there is no concurrent threat to property; thus the opposite is also true. (This reasoning totally avoids consideration of comparative value, an issue to be discussed in the next chapter.) Molina also says that the case with which the decretal is dealing involved the simultaneous threats; so it had to be put the way it was. Simultaneous threats to life and property are considered by Molina most often the situation, as the threat to life arises when the person attempts to defend his property. But, since both are not required, Molina legitimates killing to avoid either danger.

Covarrubias argues in much the same way that Panormitanus does: though civil law may allow killing for defense of goods, it is not licit "in conscience."[163] He adds that because such killing is immoral, the civil law is itself invalid. The reason for the condemnation is the *te tuaque*: it forbids killing solely for property. Covarrubias will not accept capture of the thief or recovery of property as legitimating criteria for killing; the opposition does.

Lessius, Diana, and the Salamancans in the seventeenth and eighteenth centuries continue the interpretation of *te tuaque* as meaning "or."[164] Lessius simply quotes the

key sentence and says it justifies killing in defense of
property; Diana repeats Molina's idea that if the phrase is
not disjunctive, a person could not kill to defend himself
alone; the Salamancans acknowledge the literalness of "and,"
but that is because of the specific case at hand; te tuaque
is to be understood disjunctively, as "or."

One cannot avoid concluding from this brief survey of
the interpretation of te tuaque that the change in understanding
took place post-factum. Given the influence of Roman law,
especially the glosses, and the turbulent and increasingly-
capitalistic environment, there was a need to deal with a
Church law which apparently required a threat to life before a
person could kill. With the possible exception of Hostiensis,
the pre-sixteenth-century authors used here relied upon Interfecisti to uphold the tradition against killing for property.
With the sixteenth century (except for Covarrubias) the
decretal's opposition crumbles under an interpretation which
brings it in conformity with a line of thought that had been
gaining proponents since at least the fourteenth century.

Suscepimus, De Homicidio[165]

The case contained in this decretal is that of two
monks who killed a robber whom they had already captured.
They are condemned for the killing, both because the robber
was already subdued and because they should have let the robber have the clothes he wanted rather than kill him for "such
vile things." (The latter cause is hypothetical in the actual
circumstance: the robber had been captured.) The grasp of
the significance of this decretal will roughly follow the
same pattern as that of Interfecisti.

In the two hundred years covered by Hostiensis,
Andreae, and Panormitanus, the understanding of Suscepimus is
basically the same. These three canonists agree that the
monks were guilty of homicide: there was no need to kill because the robber was in custody, and the monks should have
let him have the clothes.[166] But whereas the later men,
Andreae and Panormitanus, explicitly regard this decretal as
forbidding killing for property alone, Hostiensis concentrates on the violation of due moderation by the monks. His

major emphasis is that the killing could have been avoided. Whether this interpretation of Hostiensis is to be read as a justification for killing for property in unavoidable circumstances is clouded by the ambiguity witnessed in the remarks on Interfecisti.

The positions of Covarrubias, Sylvester, and Molina in the sixteenth century are consistent with what we have seen in them before.[167] Covarrubias accepts the condemnation of the monks and adds: "the life of man is more precious than things." Sylvester simply rejects Panormitanus' understanding of the decretal on his way to his own positions; he does not deal with the case outright. Molina accepts Suscepimus as a counsel, especially for clerics, but also for the laity: "suffer the loss of external goods rather than kill for them." He does not explain how the monks could be condemned for homicide through the violation of a counsel. How can one be guilty of violating that which he has the option of imposing upon himself? Molina does condemn the killing on the basis of the small value of the goods in question and the absence of any need to kill the robber.

The Salamancans and Alphonsus Ligouri agree on the rightness of the monks' condemnation; they also agree with Molina on the reason: the goods in question (clothes) were not of sufficiently great value to legitimate deprivation of life in their defense.[168] (The question of what constitutes sufficient value will be a part of the next chapter.) The Salamancans also agree with Molina in condemning the killing in Suscepimus because it was an excessive use of force.

The varied implications and causes for condemnation seen in the decretal Suscepimus lead us into considerations of comparative and sufficient value, as well as bring home the persistent emphasis on the necessity of due moderation. The notion of value which was here mentioned by Molina, the Salamancans, and Alphonsus is a major justifying criterion from the sixteenth century. Before pursuing that issue, we will look at some "arguments from reason" which were employed from the sixteenth century.

Some Arguments from Reason

By the sixteenth century the taking of a thief's life simply to prevent him from stealing one's property was quite firmly established as legitimate. Particular criteria were put forth and argued about, criteria which sought to prevent the owner of the threatened property from killing for all property and in all circumstances. It is the criteria of value and recovery-possibility that will be the principal subject matter of the next chapter. Along with the development of these norms, the authors of the sixteenth-eighteenth centuries employed three arguments which they considered to be based upon reason. The use of the term "reason" seems to be an indication that the process of reasoning employed is not one that is based directly or strictly upon a legal foundation, whether that be natural, civil, or ecclesiastical law. The three arguments which we will explore here are the following: the "higher good" argument; the "practice of princes" argument; the "deterrent to crime" argument. The precise meaning of each of these will surface as we discuss them; the titles are given merely as points of reference.

The "Higher Good" Argument

We have had occasion to mention the presence of a hierarchy of "goods," of values, in the tradition.[169] It is held that the spiritual is superior to the corporal, that one's own life is higher on the scale than another's life, that life is to be preferred to temporal goods (property). It is the requirement that life is to be preferred to property that gives rise to the need to justify the preference given property when legitimation is given to killing a thief solely to protect property.

Among our sources, the objection raised by the hierarchy-of-values principle is first answered by Sylvester Prieras.[170] He says that preference must be given to a neighbor's life over one's own property only when the other person's life is "in necessity," i.e., when he is in danger of death. Sylvester holds that if the person puts himself in the danger of death, that is his own fault and need not be the concern of the person who is protecting his property. With this point Sylvester is saying that the "necessity" required for preferring life over property is not present when the person has put himself into the circumstance of danger of death.

The teaching of Sylvester is repeated, with some variation, by Cajetan, Vitoria, Navarrus, Molina, Lessius, the Salamancans, and Alphonsus: from the sixteenth to the eighteenth centuries.[171] Only Covarrubias rejects it, holding that just as one must prefer his own life to that of a neighbor, the neighbor must be preferred to property.[172] He notes that he is rejecting the positions of both Sylvester and Cajetan. The lonely stance of Covarrubias is not unfamiliar to this study; he is a consistent opponent of killing for property alone.

Having seen the argument of Sylvester and the others, we might, before looking at variation, ask where it comes from. Was it created for this specific use, or was it present in the tradition? I believe the source of the teaching can be found in Thomas Aquinas' position on the question of almsgiving.[173]

Thomas teaches that almsgiving is a matter of precept: since love of neighbor is a precept, whatever is a necessary condition to the love of neighbor is also a matter of precept. But, according to Thomas, right reason must come into play in considering what is required of both giver and receiver. The giver is to give of his surplus, after caring for himself and those for whom he is responsible. The receiver must be in need. Since it is not possible for any person to relieve the needs of all,

> we are not bound to relieve all who are in need, but only those who could not be succored if we did not succor them . . . accordingly we are bound to give alms of our surplus, as also to give alms to <u>one whose need is extreme</u>: otherwise almsgiving, like any other greater good is a matter of counsel.[174]

According to this teaching of Aquinas a person is required to give alms only when someone's need is urgent and he is not likely to receive help from another source. The emphasis is on the urgency of the need, the extreme nature of it: a matter of life or death.

If this position is looked at from the side of the giver, he is seen to be required to give up his goods only when the other is in extreme need; only extreme necessity demands that one "lose" his property. When the post-fifteenth-century authors considered this teaching it would have been a simple step from a requirement that one give alms only in extreme necessity to one is held to "give" (lose) property only in the same need. All were aware that the only legitimation for stealing someone else's property was a person's extreme need and the absence of any other means to relieve it.[175] If a man cannot take except for extreme need, a person is not required to lose except in that same case of need. Consequently, in order to legitimate killing to protect property all that would be necessary would be to show that the thief was not in extreme need. Putting oneself in such a position leaves the responsibility to yourself; others need not worry about it. A person has a "right" to another's property only in extreme need; extreme need is not applicable when one creates the need himself.

If we look at the variations on the "necessity" principle, we will not find anything that changes the content of Sylvester's statement. Cajetan, for example, speaks of the obligation every person has to care for his property, especially as it is an aid to virtue.[176] This obligation is constantly with each person, whereas the care of another person's life obliges only in cases of necessity. Cajetan then repeats the idea of necessity being absent when the person freely puts himself in the situation.

However, with Molina (and after him Diana, the Salamancans, and Alphonsus) a new case is joined to the one we have been considering.[177] The case involves extreme need in conjunction with a person's spiritual life. Can one kill when there is extreme spiritual harm likely to result (damnation because of serious sin)? The answer given by Molina and the others is a result of the same thought process as that regarding life and property: extreme need imposes no obligation on others when it was freely created by the one in it.

This argument from reason which we have been viewing

is a major basis for the justification of killing in defense of property. Alphonsus Ligouri, for example, considers it the strongest proof for the justifiable killing.[178] It is the one which "entirely cuts down" the arguments which forbid killing a thief because life is preferable to property. Yet the key to the argument seems to be the self-exposure to a situation in which death is likely. If there were not such free exposure it would be necessary to defend the higher good (life) in preference to the lower good (property). This argumentation appears to beg the question. The danger-of-death situation is precisely what is being proven. Just because a person puts himself in a situation where someone might kill him cannot by itself justify the killing. It seems, however, that this is just what is used by these authors as the foundation upon which their proof is based.[179] The moral teaching has moved a long way from requiring a threat to life by a thief before the one threatened can kill him. On the basis of this principle a person can kill because the thief has put himself in a situation where that person might kill him.[180]

The "Practice of Princes" Argument

A further argument is given by Sylvester in the sixteenth century, passed on by Molina, rejected by the Salamancans in the seventeenth-eighteenth centuries, and finally is used by Alphonsus in the late eighteenth century through quoting Sylvester.[181] The argument is that princes constantly wage war in behalf of property, and in doing so kill many people. Sylvester says that this would "not be possible" if it were against the law of God; and the others follow him. This argument is clearly conditioned by the turbulent times in which these men lived. But it avoids all obvious need to distinguish between public and private authority, as well as omitting any consideration of the conditions for a "**just** war." Nothing need be said about the danger of determining morality on the basis of the practice of princes. As early as the thirteenth century Scotus had said of them: "It is clear what princes look at, for they look more to temporal convenience than to the honor of God."[182]

The "Deterrent to Crime" Argument

The final argument to be proffered here is the "deterrent to crime" argument. Molina, Lessius, and the Salamancans incorporate it.[183] All these people consider killing a necessity in preventing rampant theft; what else could constrain thieves? The argument by itself is dangerous: it canonizes an "end-justifies-the-means" attitude. These men, however, do not use it alone; it is simply a statement which attempts to say something to the issue of "necessity"; the basis for killing is otherwise firmly established in their teaching. The next chapter deals with the notion of comparative value implied in this argument.

This "deterrent to crime" argument is ultimately a "utilitarian" approach. It is perhaps significant that Molina and Lessius approach a particular issue in the realm of usury from a similar utilitarian stance.[184] The case is that of a "triple contract": a person enters a partnership from which he has capital guaranteed and from which he hopes to profit. Molina and Lessius teach that it is legitimate to further insure one's capital with a third party. Both men support their position by saying that the third-party contract is useful, necessary, expedient, and widespread. Expediency is not their only argument; it is merely supportive, as is the deterrent to crime argument in the case of killing to defend property.

Conclusion

The thief's right to life has been the subject of this chapter. We have seen the moral teaching of the thirteenth century require a threat to life (at least presumed) before a thief may be killed. With the increased influence of the Roman law and its commentators, this position began to be supplanted in the fourteenth century. Antoninus and Panormitanus witness to some ambiguity in the next century, and each appears to conclude on a different side of the question. From the sixteenth century to the eighteenth, Covarrubias is the only author who opposes killing for property when there is no concurrent threat to life. There are other authors, men of lesser stature and influence, who are cited in all the post-Tridentine manuals as agreeing with the likes of Panormitanus and Covarrubias. But these people provide little more than opportunity for the dominant opinion, the "common opinion," to express itself.

We have also had the opportunity to see the compatibility between the "property alone" justification and the growth of the power of the middle class, with its increased value placed on property and the individual's right to it. Practice more than likely preceded the theoretical formulation in the manuals.[185] With the growing mercantile economy, goods became more available; yet they were still out of the reach of the vast majority of people: theft was a grave problem.[186]

In this social and intellectual environment the teaching changed. From a threat to life the criterion became the property itself: its recovery became the determining factor. Yet even with the change there was an endeavor to keep some limitation on the possessor's right to kill. What property could one kill to defend? How much value must it have? What does "recovery" involve as a criterion? To these questions we now turn. Property might be important enough to cause a thief to forfeit his life, but there was still concern that human life be not totally stripped of its value by an absolute equation of property and life.

CHAPTER IV

THE VALUE OF PROPERTY

The change of the basis upon which a thief may forfeit his life has been seen to begin with the Roman law commentators' establishment of <u>recovery</u> as a criterion.[1] Certain fourteenth and fifteenth century authors used "recovery" as an unqualified concept;[2] so with the sixteenth century there came an effort to further specify the notion, as well as the beginning of an attempt to create some specific criteria for the determination of the <u>value</u> which property must have before it may be defended by killing.

The concentration on the recovery and the value of the goods stolen involves a profound value change. In the prior teaching a threat to life makes lawful the deprivation of life. The issue is the defense of innocent life against unjust attack. The lives which come into conflict are abstractly of equal value, but the innocence of one gives it a higher value in the concrete situation of unjust attack. The later teaching, by focusing on the value and recovery of goods, makes a comparison between the value of the thief's life and the value of the goods threatened. The conflict is between values which are not self-evidently equal. Consequently, an effort is made to link property with life so that property can be equated with life.

The relationship between person and property to the degree that an injury to property is understood as a personal injury was found in the teaching of Joannes de Lignano.[3] This explicit teaching in the fourteenth century has its roots in earlier statements by Alexander of Hales and Thomas Aquinas.[4] Both comment on the crime of killing an ox belonging to another. They teach that the killing is a crime of theft; for the harm is not done to the owner directly, but rather he suffers injury _in_ his property. There is in this teaching a connection made between the person and his property; the owner is harmed through the injury to what is his. The development of this manner of thinking is not difficult to grasp. Once the link between harm to property and harm to person is stated, the gravity of injury to property becomes the gravity of injury to the person; "serious" harm in property becomes the equivalent of "serious" harm to the person. Thus the owner may react to property injury in the same way that he may respond to personal injury. This is the position of Lignano. Those who follow him in the fifteenth and sixteenth centuries are at first satisfied to repeat the broad criterion of recovery as legitimating killing for property. But there came in the sixteenth century a recognition that there was need for a more specific determination of "serious" harm in regard to property.

It is the task of determining serious harm that is the subject of this chapter. We will first examine the question of the value which property must have before its loss constitutes serious harm. Once the value is determined, it will be possible to further specify the recovery-criterion in its application to the situation of a fleeing thief or of a thief who has already fled, as well as the case in which the possibility of recovery is in doubt. When these issues have been explored, the development of the teaching on killing in defense of property will have been demonstrated. It will then be possible to evaluate the teaching and point to the crucial omission of an element that had been part of the tradition for over a thousand years.

Value

While the sixteenth century marks the beginning of the quest to determine a specific value for property before it may be defended by killing, not all of our sources from that century engage in the quest. Sylvester, Cajetan, and Navarrus content themselves with the general statement that one can kill when the threatened property would otherwise be lost.[5] Because of the possibility of applying this teaching to any and all property, it is not surprising that initially Vitoria

and Soto, then more elaborately Molina begin a process of
limitation. What these moralists begin will be continued in
two directions: a required monetary value and a relative
value which is to be established from the consideration of
particular circumstances. The common ground of these approaches is the requirement that the property be <u>of great
value</u> before killing is allowed; the common search is for a
definition of great value.

Specific Norm
==

Sixteenth century.—Vitoria, Soto, and Molina determine the value of property in terms of its money-value.[6] Each
of them gives a specific sum which he judges to be "great value" and thus capable of being defended by killing. For
Vitoria the amount is ten or twenty gold pieces; for Soto it
is four ducats;[7] Molina gives two separate sums, depending on
whose property one is defending.[8]

In discussing a case in which the property is not one's
own, nor does one have direct responsibility for it, and the
thief is in the process of fleeing, Molina declares that if
the property is worth six ducats, the fleeing thief may be
killed. But when the case is one of the owner or his guard
resisting the attack of a thief, it is legitimate for them to
kill to protect property valued at one gold piece "or of still
less value." In this case there appears to be no restriction
in killing for property. The key to Molina's variant mini-
mums appears to be the status of the defenders: if the
threatened property is one's own or one's responsibility,
lesser value need be involved than if it were a neighbor's
property. The "fleeing" criterion does not seem terribly
significant in that the value of the goods in question remains
constant. There is no indication that these monetary values
would change if the "present-fleeing" circumstance changed.
The basis for such a distinction seems to be simply the
direct and consistent responsibility of the owner or guard;
one is held to have less concern for others' property than
one's own.[9]

What is accomplished by these positions of Vitoria,
Soto, and Molina is the establishment of an "absolute norm,"

a monetary value for which any person may kill. The term "absolute" is not used by these authorities (it will not be found in our sources until the eighteenth century), but whenever a specific sum is given the effect is to create a norm which is absolute. Such a norm is based solely on monetary value, without any reference to the person suffering the attack on his property. That the "injury" suffered by a rich or a poor man who loses five gold pieces is potentially quite different is not taken into account. The only element which matters is the monetary value.

At the beginning of the use of money-value for property-value the arbitrary nature of the valuation is evident. Three moralists give three significantly different criteria for evaluating the property which can be defended by a legitimate deprivation of life. None of the authors gives any criteria by which his norm was chosen; each one simply states the amount he considers to constitute great value. Vitoria, whose norm is the highest, teaches that to kill for a value of less than ten gold pieces would be a show of contempt for life. Soto and Molina would no doubt also condemn contempt for life, but they find this contempt at a different monetary level. The lack of criteria for judging great value and thus eliminating contempt for life is a lacuna which later centuries attempt to fill, but ultimately the norms offered will retain their arbitrary characteristic.

Seventeenth and eighteenth centuries.—The major contribution on specific value in these centuries is the condemnation by Innocent XI (1679) of the opinion which stated that a person could "regularly kill to conserve one gold piece."[10] Full ecclesiastical authority was thus placed behind the establishment of a minimal criterion. Subsequent seventeenth and eighteenth-century authors will cite this proscription as abrogating any contrary teaching, which would include that of Molina.[11] But it can be seen that Innocent's condemnation does not really solve the problem. One gold piece does not regularly constitute great value; does that mean that two gold pieces would? To say what is not sufficient does not indicate clearly what is sufficient.

Consequently, the effort to give a specific sum receives some further attention. Busembaum gives three or four ducats as sufficient value, while the Salamancans hold that it is a "probable opinion" that a value of three ducats makes property defensible by killing.[12]

Innocent condemned an opinion which used the term "regularly": a person cannot "regularly" kill to save one gold piece. This usage seems to leave an opening for an exceptional circumstance in which one could kill to save the gold piece. Such a situation would occur because of particular factors pertaining to the person whose money is threatened. There is here a recognition of a "relative norm," one which depends upon the potential harm to the victim, regardless of the specific value of that which is threatened. It is the discussion of a "relative norm" which dominates in the seventeenth and eighteenth centuries. Informing the discussion is the concern expressed by the Salamancans that to inflict the most grave penalty (death) for light injury is barbarous.[13]

The final statement of a particular amount among our sources is by Benjamin Elbel. He is the first among the authorities used in this study to use the term "absolute norm."[14] The norm which he gives is four hundred silver pieces. Regardless of the disparate value gold and silver pieces might have had, it is obvious that Elbel's absolute norm is enormously higher than any of the previous authors. The reason for the great discrepancy is Elbel's use of a relative norm in conjunction with his absolute norm. He has a different purpose for his absolute sum than did his predecessors. We will return to this purpose in our examination of Elbel's principle of relative value.

Relative Norm

Relativity of value demands a consideration of persons and circumstances; this is the way Lessius, Diana, the Salamancans, Elbel, and Alphonsus proceed. In the case of the Salamancans, the relative approach is what is preferred; yet they acknowledge the legitimacy of following a contrary opinion, an "absolute norm." We will see that Elbel's concept of "absolute" is much more compatible with the relativity of value than is that of the Salamancans. Lessius, Diana, and Alphonsus stay strictly within the framework of relative value.

Seventeenth century.—Lessius is the first of our moralists to deal with our question from a perspective of relativity. He teaches that a person may kill to save goods "necessary for life."[15] He then tells us what he means by this statement: not only goods that are "precisely necessary" to sustain life, but those which enable one to live "decently." It is clear that such a norm will vary; it is also clear that a broad interpretation is possible of what constitutes the decent life of which Lessius speaks.

The teaching of Lessius that a person may kill to defend property which is necessary for a decent life establishes a quite different basis of judgment than does, for example, Vitoria's ten gold pieces. Lessius establishes a principle which must be applied to specific persons. A loss which would deprive one man of the "decent life" would not necessarily do the same to another. Property loss inflicts a relative injury, an injury which must be evaluated in each case.

Lessius has broken with the teaching of his immediate predecessors. He has denied the validity of fixing a specific sum as being in all cases "of great value," and he has made an attempt to put some limiting framework on those who simply taught that a person could kill to save otherwise unrecoverable property. Are there any sources from which he might have drawn his position?[16]

Lessius developed the teaching in De Justitia et Jure at the turn of the seventeenth century.[17] The time was one of profound economic transformation and intense moral crises in the Low Countries. With the input of metals from the colonies, the value of money increased, as did speculation and international exchange. There was a developing desire for gain, with a taste for consumption and luxury. (For some, of course, the primary necessities of life were priced beyond their reach.)[18] There was, at the same time, because of inflation and high taxes, a chronic shortage of the working capital needed to take advantage of the expanding trade possibilities. The thrifty merchants of Amsterdam were beginning to supplant those of Antwerp as the commercial leaders of Europe.[19] In this context, Lessius addressed himself to economic questions. He went to the merchants and bankers of Antwerp, listened, learned, and became an expert adviser.[20]

One of the areas to which Lessius devoted his attention was that of the "just price." The Scholastics had considered the just price to be that "established by genuine consumer or commercial demand and available supply."[21] The just price is thus a product of a human act, the determination of value, based on the estimation of something's usefulness in fulfilling human needs. Because of the abuses of his day, Lessius required a consideration of products which were indispensible and necessary to everyone; these should be made available to all. He also emphasized the need to incorporate the notions of the abundance or rarity of the product and the resources of the purchaser. Finally, following the teaching of Aquinas,[22] he says that the product's ability to satisfy collective human needs and desires must be taken into consideration.[23] The usefulness of a product in fulfilling human needs and desires helps to determine its value, its price; products which are necessary to live a decent life (thus fulfilling a human need or desire to live such a life) are judged by Lessius to be sufficiently valuable to legitimate killing in their defense.

While there may be some connection between Lessius' ideas on just price, his association with the commercial community in Antwerp, and his principle for determining great value which then sanctions killing, there is another source which may have likewise influenced his position. Lessius introduced the *Summa* of Thomas as a replacement for Lombard's *Sentences* at the University of Louvain.[24] In Thomas he could read of a man's responsibility to retain not only what he needs to remain alive, but also what he needs to live in keeping with his social station.[25] Just as Thomas would consider a failure to hold on to what was thus needed an "inordinate" act, so, in our context, would Lessius judge the effort to keep from losing such necessities legitimate. Lessius implies that a man has a right to live "decently"; Thomas says that "no man ought to live unbecomingly."[26]

There is also reference to this idea of valuing property, and thus legitimating killing in defense of it, in terms of its use in living a decent life in Sylvester, Cajetan, and Soto. These men do not, however, apply the point to killing. Sylvester and Soto speak of property as the means to an honest life, the means of sustaining not only life but status and honor.[27] Cajetan holds that a man has a right to improve his condition; so wealth which enables him to do that is necessary for him.[28] The raw material for Lessius' teaching was, perhaps, contained in the writings of these predecessors.

There may also be significance in the turbulence which reigned in the war-torn Netherlands in the second half of the sixteenth century. While upheaval is rather constant in history and thus not a primary cause, the presence of such conditions as marauding bands of soldiers and brigands, the consequences of battles which lead to destruction and appropriation, which deprive people of what is needed not only to go on in a "decent" life but also to begin again, all tend to intensify the need to protect property. Given the other changes which had taken place by the sixteenth century, these circumstances would help to emphasize the "right to kill." Lessius himself was forced to flee a destructive advance on Louvain.[29]

We have, then, Lessius offering as his principle of evaluating property to be defensible by killing the statement: when the property is necessary to living life decently. There is no more precise rule given. What is "the decent life"? Is it to be judged in terms of each person's particular condition alone? Or is there to be some notion of decency interjected? Is each person to judge for himself what he considers necessary? The just price requirements demand an incorporation of collective notions of human needs and desires. Are these to be considered? If so, how are such notions to be determined? It is certain that Lessius wants to move legitimate killing beyond defense of those goods which are necessary for the sheer preservation of life. He also rejects, perhaps as too arbitrary, perhaps as too lax because

of the variety of wealth possessed by different people, the
attempts to fix a particular money-value to property defensible by killing. He likewise appears to recognize a need to
somehow limit the capacity of a defender to kill with moral
impunity. Despite his intention, the principle he offers remains quite vague and seemingly open to not only relative application on the basis of what wealth a person may possess,
but also to application on the arbitrary judgment of a person
as to what he needs to live in a manner he considers decent.
Lessius' principle legitimates killing relative to what is
necessary for living life decently; but the notion of decent
life is itself extremely relative.[30]

Diana offers as a guiding principle a statement that
is even less helpful than that of Lessius. After reminding
his readers to take care that the loss being prevented is
compared to the loss which would come from killing, he says
that "to kill the property must be of great value of itself,
or in its price, or its consequence."[31] This principle, without specifying a price, acknowledges that there can be a
price-level at which great value is achieved. It also says
that a certain item can be intrinsically of great value (e.g.,
a work of art) or worth a great deal because of the consequence which would follow its loss (e.g., a poor man with just
enough food to keep himself alive). Diana's statement of
price opens the door to an absolute norm, but he gives no
indication of what that norm might be. His intrinsic and
consequent norms are relative concepts, relative to the person who would suffer from a loss. But what has Diana really
taught? His "great value equals great price" does not tell
us the price he has in mind; nor would a rephrasing in terms
of a price which would cause great loss to one who would
have to replace the stolen items help us: we are given no
price. The other two elements of the principle, intrinsic
and consequent value, are also unspecified statements; and
the point of consequence can only be saying that something
is of great value when the consequence of losing it would inflict grave harm. But what does "grave harm" mean? Diana
does not help clarify the notion of "great value"; "grave
harm" is simply the "loss-side" of great value.

Lessius and Diana have given us their rejection of attempts to specify a particular price-level as always determining great value. (Diana does, however, indicate the possibility of such a price being established.) They have also made an effort to establish a relative principle: necessary for the decent life by Lessius, grave because of the consequence of loss for Diana. But neither Lessius nor Diana have given any criteria for determining the decent or the grave. A relative principle will no doubt have to retain a certain ambiguity; decency and gravity will vary with persons and circumstances. But would it not be possible to offer some guidance as to the content of "gravity"? It is to this task that the eighteenth-century moralists direct their attention. They were hardly more successful than Lessius and Diana.

Eighteenth century.—Although the Salamancans declare it morally permissible to kill for property worth three ducats, they prefer that a relative principle be followed. Their stance is that one can kill to defend only "something notable with respect to the person from whom it is taken, so that from its loss the person suffers notable harm."[32] This principle clearly focuses upon the harm that would come through loss; the criterion is not the property itself, but the harm its loss would inflict on the possessor. The relativity of such a position is clear in that the harm has to be judged according to circumstances of time, place, and person. Again, however, nothing is mentioned which would help in the determination of what constitutes "notable harm."

Benjamin Elbel denies the possibility of establishing a universal rule by which great value is determined.[33] He accepts as a working concept the determination of great value in a particular case on the basis of "prudent judgment." Elbel recognizes, however, that this norm of prudence still leaves people with a very great difficulty: even the most prudent men may make greatly different judgments. Because of this difficulty, Elbel refers approvingly to the distinction between absolutely and relatively great value. The amount of four hundred silver pieces is accepted as an absolute norm, while "truly grave detriment" is the relative. Elbel gives

as an example (and thus not exclusive) of relatively grave
detriment, goods which are "necessary for sustenance," regardless of their value in themselves. This example, obviously
a case of grave harm (the loss would presumably result in
death), does not seem to rule out the legitimacy of killing to
defend goods of less than sustenance-value. Thus Elbel would
be in agreement with Lessius, Diana, and the Salamancans:
great harm is not necessarily linked to sustenance of life.

Elbel tries to solve the "prudent judgment" difficulty with the absolute-relative distinction. His citation of
four hundred silver pieces as being in all cases an absolute
norm for which one may kill achieves a different purpose, however, from that of earlier authors who considered three, five,
ten, or some such sum as always defensible by killing. Whereas the smaller amounts are given without any reference to a
relative norm, Elbel's high figure is used in conjunction with
relatively grave harm. The smaller amounts leave no room for
the possibility of a situation developing in which the loss of
something of less value than that stated sum would have a very
serious effect on the possessor (e.g., Diana's "consequent"
norm would allow a small amount of food necessary for life to
be defended by killing, as would Elbel's "relatively grave
harm"). Nor do the lesser specific sums take into consideration the harm-factor: only the amount is weighed, not the
resultant injury to the loser. Three, ten, or whatever amount
could be lost by a person and actually inflict little injury.
Elbel's use of both an absolute and a relative norm proposes
to overcome these weaknesses in the earlier positions. The
relative principle is based solely on the notion of injury
inflicted, regardless of objective value; it is the personal
harm threatened that determines the morally permissible behavior. At the same time Elbel recognizes an objective value
which, evidently on the basis of a common prudential judgment, can be considered in all cases "great value." This
objective norm is given without reference to persons. Could
not one speculate that Elbel recognized that the relative
norm with its emphasis on person-related harm would be oper-
able in most cases, while at the same time realizing that
such a relative norm would be inapplicable except in most

extreme cases if a very wealthy person were the victim of an attempted theft? The amount threatened would have to be very considerable before "grave harm" were done. Consequently, we can view Elbel's absolute norm as a principle aimed at the protection of the wealthy.[34]

Although Elbel offers the absolute and relative norms as legitimate guides for moral behavior, he gives evidence of his own uncomfortableness with the teaching.[35] In discussing the practical level of the sacrament of penance, he says that the prudent confessor is always to advise the gentler act before the fact: "bear the loss of temporal goods rather than stain [your] hands with human blood." After the fact, the confessor must determine how great the injury would have been from the loss of what was protected and "from what deliberation and dictates of conscience the homicide proceeded." In these statements Elbel shows interest not only in the determination of guilt after a thief has been killed, but also in the inequality between loss of goods and loss of life. He does not forbid killing to defend property of great value, but he seems cognizant of man's propensity to overevaluate what is his (precisely because he has a right to what is his) and to underevaluate that which threatens what is his own. Elbel seems to demand a close look at a particular circumstance ahead of time (when possible) in order to calmly evaluate the harm that would truly follow if something were lost.

Elbel does justify killing in defense of property. The absolute-relative distinction he accepts as valid basis for judgment does not, however, entirely solve the "prudent judgment" problem. The absolute norm establishes a clear criterion, but it is applicable only in what are considered extreme cases. The norm is also the result of the judgment of particular moralists. If we view Elbel's sum together with the earlier sums, the judgments give evidence of arbitrariness. If we view the four hundred silver pieces by itself, we might still ask how it was chosen. Whether alone or with its predecessors, the norm is rooted solely in monetary gravity and in terms of property in isolation of persons. The relative norm still demands judgment as to what is "truly grave detriment" (or "necessary to the decent life," or "great in its consequence," or "notable harm"). Elbel gives sustenance as an example, but as an example it is not meant to be an exclusive criterion. The need to form prudent judgments remains, as does the lack of any very helpful guidelines in making those judgments.

The seventeenth and early eighteenth-century moralists wrote in a war-ravaged, famine and plague-stricken age when population shifts led to overcrowding in the cities and increased problems of unemployment, poverty, and poor relief.[36] The need to maintain public order against mobs and riots, vagrants and bandits, was constant and acute. While religious charity was certainly involved, it was this need to avoid potential chaos that led to the establishment of workhouses throughout Europe.[37] In an age in which the individual right to property was considered absolute and inviolable,[38] the crises of the time and the seemingly relative inability of government to guarantee that right would help to focus the attention of moralists on the individual's capacity for morally legitimate defense of his property.

The seventeenth and eighteenth centuries were also the arena for continual debates over the resolution of doubtful moral situations. How is a person to solve the problem of the goodness or evil of an action when he is in doubt of that goodness or evil? For an action to be good and thus sinless some sort of certainty as to goodness is necessary. The effort to supply this certainty led to the formulation of particular moral systems: probabilism, rigorism, laxism, which varied on the degree of certainty required before a specific opinion could be accepted and followed in conscience.[39] We have already mentioned the seventeenth-century condemnation of a number of opinions judged to be overly lax;[40] in the same century the rigorism of the Jansenists (which demanded direct certainty, so that not even the most probable opinion on the side of liberty might be followed) was condemned.[41] In the midst of this search for a viable approach to the moral crisis, the system called "equiprobabilism" was devised in the eighteenth century. This system differs from probabiliorism by allowing an opinion for liberty to be followed when it is as probable as the opinion for law; it disagrees with probabilism by forbidding the following of an opinion less probable than the opinion for law. (The "probability" of an opinion depends upon the cogency of the arguments used to support it.) The best known proponent of equiprobabilism was Alphonsus Ligouri. He strove to find some "truly certain" opinions amid the maze of more probable, less probable, certain, more certain, rigorist, and laxist opinions. It is to his effort to determine "great value" out of the confusion we have been tracing that we now turn.

Ligouri is of the opinion that no definite sum can be pre-established as "of great value";[42] the gravity of loss depends upon the person who loses. Alphonsus thus separates himself from the teaching of Vitoria, Soto, Molina, Busembaum, the Salamancans, and Elbel.[43] Having rejected the attempt to specify a monetary criterion for great value, Alphonsus tries to determine the meaning of great value in terms of the effect the loss would have on the loser. He cites, among others, Elbel as teaching that to be of great value the item threatened would have to deprive someone of <u>sustenance</u> for himself and his own.[44] He also approves the norm: <u>notable harm</u>.[45] When he gives his own position, Ligouri uses the term <u>enormous harm</u> as his criterion for the constitution of great value. All of these terms—enormous harm, notable harm, sustenance—are to be evaluated according to the person who would suffer the loss.

Alphonsus tried in this way to establish a norm which would avoid both rigorism and laxism. He wanted an opinion which could, because of the reasons for it, be safely followed in conscience. But his effort was as unsuccessful as that of his predecessors. What remains unclear in Ligouri's teaching is the relationship between the terms he approves as declaring the presence of great value. Does he mean to define "enormous" and "notable" in terms of "sustenance"?[46] If so, then only goods necessary for sustaining life would be sufficiently valuable to justify killing in their defense. If this is not his teaching, he leaves us a situation of confusion. Every loss of goods necessary to sustain life is grave, but not every loss that would be considered grave ("enormous," "notable") is a loss of sustenance. "Sustenance" is concerned with the very basis of life's continuance. If Alphonsus is separating "enormous" and "notable" from "sustenance," he is then teaching that one may kill to defend not only what is necessary for life to continue, but also to kill for what causes "grave harm." But he does not establish any criteria to determine gravity. Alphonsus is content to state the relativity of gravity; he does not give any guidelines which could help one to judge gravity.

The attempts of the seventeenth and eighteenth-century moralists to create a relative norm for the determination of great value end up telling us little. All agree that if one is to be allowed to kill to defend material goods, these goods must be "of great value." They also agree that "great value" is to be judged in terms of the harm which would come to the person should he lose his property. But none of them give us any clear indication of how gravity of harm is to be judged. Lessius' "necessary for decent life," Diana's "great value in itself, its price, or its consequence," the Salamancans' "notable harm," Elbel's "truly grave detriment," Alphonsus' "enormous harm": all of these positions simply repeat the notion of grave harm directly or they turn "great value" around to get "great harm." The consequence of a loss of great value is great harm: these moral opinions enlighten us no more than that.

The notion of sustenance lurks in the teaching of Elbel and Alphonsus, but neither of them require sustenance for the determination of great value. The other authors clearly do not demand sustenance, i.e., preservation of life, before killing is legitimated. In this way these authors continue the trend since the fourteenth-fifteenth centuries to not require defense of life to validate deprivation of life.

Although the purpose of the relative norm was to supplant the specification of a monetary sum, it is evident that money-value remains a dominant element in the judgment of grave harm. When the moralists write of grave harm in terms of the person who loses, two possibilities come to mind. The first is the injury which would follow when something is of itself worth little but its loss would have serious consequences. An example would be a small portion of food necessary to sustain someone. The other possibility is that harm suffered because of the "value" of the thing—its value, but in relation to the person. This second possibility requires some evaluation of the thing itself so that it can be valued in relation to someone. How would the moralists make such an evaluation? It would seem that they would do so in monetary terms. The use of money is the easiest and most common form of evaluation. The loss of a particular thing would then cause "harm" to the individual inasmuch as a certain amount of money would be required to replace it. Thus a "notable" or "enormous" amount of money would be required to live or have those things necessary to live a "decent" life. A hint of this underlying notion is present in Alphonsus' statement that the amount of five ducats cannot be established as sufficient to permit killing, because "the process of time increases the abundance of money and the price of things."[47] Price and the availability of money are the determining factors. The result of focus on price is the necessity to understand what is truly being said by those who advocate a relative norm to determine great value. The relativity is in conjection with persons and circumstances, but the relative gravity to a person is determined on the basis of money-value. Ten gold pieces can be a grave loss to one person, not to another; but the gravity or its lack is in terms of the ten gold pieces. The difference between the moralists who propose a relative norm and those who give a specific sum is simply the refusal of the former to specify a particular amount as always sufficiently valuable to justify killing. Both groups of moralists use a monetary base for at least part of their determination of gravity; both groups equate property and personal injury; both groups determine the thief's right to life according to a monetary norm.

   A serious difficulty with equating property and personal injury is that regardless of the gravity of the crime against property, the personal injury suffered remains an <u>indirect</u> injury. (This is true even in the most extreme case, that in which the loss of something material would result in death.) When the consequences of an act are indirect, the situation is very different from one in which there are direct consequences. If an individual's life is directly attacked, the result of this act will most probably be death if no adequate defense is undertaken. The same cannot be said of a serious attack on property. The result of such an attack has the probability of death only in an extreme sort of situation. In most cases, the possibility of some intervention changing the outcome of an attack on property remains. Options for sustaining life will most likely be present, as will avenues through which the deprivation might be rectified. The inevitability of the consequence is not present as it is in a direct attack on one's person. Thus it is invalid to simply equate injury to property with injury to the person. Such equation is what was done almost unanimously by the moralists we have examined since the sixteenth century, as well as by certain earlier theologians and lawyers. Given this equation and the understanding of due moderation and great value, the only factor which can spare the thief is the possibility that the property he steals might be recovered.

Recovery

The possibility of recovery of stolen goods is an important issue for the moralists because of the need to remain true to the principle of due moderation: killing must be a last resort. We have already had occasion to note the shift in the understanding of due moderation that took place in the sixteenth century: from attention to the equality of the violence which occurs and the evils resulting from the two-sided use of violence, interest focused upon the injury to be avoided.[48] At the same time, the injury was considered primarily in relation to the property being threatened.[49] The possibility of recovering the stolen goods becomes crucial, so crucial that Sylvester, Cajetan, and Navarrus say nothing more than that one may kill to defend otherwise unrecoverable property.[50] But beginning in the same sixteenth century we have seen the efforts to somehow determine the value of goods whose inability to be recovered would justify killing. The notion of recoverability is an issue because of the variability in the possibility of recovery. The issues to be discussed here are the case of doubt regarding recoverability, and the situation in which the thief is fleeing or has already fled.

Doubt

Sixteenth century.—The first moralist in this study to deal directly with the question of doubtful recovery is Dominic Soto.[51] His statement is brief and to the point: if there is doubt of recovery, a person can kill to prevent loss; the hope of recovery must be a certain hope before killing is forbidden. Soto requires assurance of recovery before it would be wrong to kill. His position is a logical conclusion from a stance which regards the saving of property as the primary consideration. If a person is not sure he can recover his goods without killing, he can make recovery certain by killing the thief.

Seventeenth and eighteenth centuries.—The situation of doubt is referred to by Lessius through his teaching that killing is forbidden if there is <u>probable</u> hope of recovery.[52] Probability is on the "sure side" of doubtfulness, being more sure than possibility. Thus, if there is less than probability, Lessius would permit killing. Yet probability is not certainty; there remains some uncertainty, some reasonable fear that one's judgment may be erroneous. By forbidding killing when there is probable hope of recovery, Lessius is teaching that less than certainty of recovery prohibits killing; one need not, as Soto taught, have absolute assurance of recovery before he is forbidden to kill. But when this is said, the norm being offered is neither very precise nor helpful. What circumstances constitute probability? How does one judge probability from possibility? Is "some good chance" of recovery or just the availability of channels for recovery enough? Do some clues to the thief's identity and/or location suffice for probability? Lessius' principle leaves the wronged person with the need to make a rapid judgment that may determine the life or death of a thief, but it gives little aid in the making of the decision.

Busembaum, whom Alphonsus follows quite strictly, teaches that in the case of doubt of recovery one may kill.[53] Both moralists refer to Diana's opinion that "one need not suffer the loss of his goods" as a justification of their position.[54] Nothing else is offered to clarify the concept of doubt. The opinion of Busembaum and Alphonsus would thus allow anything less than certainty to justify killing.

The Salamancans treat doubt only by way of an example.[55] They say that killing is justified when property "cannot otherwise be easily recovered, as when there is a doubt." The doubt of which they speak refers to recovery: if there is doubt as to the ease of recovery; they also concern themselves with the expense of recovery, allowing killing when "great expense" would be required to recover the property. In the teaching of the Salamancans, doubt is considered a characteristic which automatically makes recovery difficult. The "ease" with which the victim might recover his goods appears to determine the thief's right to life. It almost appears that if any effort would be required of the victim, the thief may be killed.

A precedent for the Salamancans' concern with ease of recovery is perhaps found in Thomas' teaching on almsgiving. The possible connection between the requirements of almsgiving and the defense of property has been seen in relation to the "need" of the person who accepts or appropriates one's property.[56] In the case at hand, there is a possible connection through the notion of "ease." Thomas teaches that one is required to give to another who is in need, even when the giving would deprive one of what is required to meet the ordinary occurrences of life, if what is lost can be easily recovered.[57] Thomas' criterion is the avoidance of "extreme inconvenience" (as well as the great need of the person who would receive the alms). Given what appears to be an influence of this almsgiving-teaching on the question of defense of property, it would seem possible that Thomas' "ease of recovery" might have influenced the Salamancans. Where there is no requirement to give if recovery would be difficult, there would not be a requirement to suffer loss.

The conclusion of these authors, who span the sixteenth to eighteenth centuries, is that in the case of doubt of recovery killing is permitted. The difficulty with this consensus is the same as was the case with Lessius' "probability": how does one determine doubt? Is doubt to be judged on the statistical probability of capture? And if so, at what percentile does doubt cease? Would this percentile be based on crimes in general, or on specific types of crime? It would seem that without specific identification of the thief or his location, doubt would always be present in the crime of theft.

Fleeing Thief

The post-Tridentine teaching on defense against a fleeing thief has roots in the entire tradition which opposed post-factum killing as revenge and not defense, and in the teaching of Hostiensis, Lignano, and Antoninus.[58] These men, representative of the thirteenth, fourteenth, and fifteenth centuries, employ the concept of "interval" as the key to defensive-vs-revengeful action. "Interval" is understood to mean that if defensive action is not taken immediately, action against the thief is illicit. Hostiensis illustrates his meaning by forbidding the offended person to wait, collect his friends, and then act. Lignano and Antoninus emphasize the illicitness of acting after an interval by teaching that the thief may resist the rightful owner's attempt to recover his goods after the interval. The reason given by these authorities is that "no one recovers lacking proper authority." The right of recovery belongs to the public authority, not to the individual.

The intent of this teaching on the "interval" is to avoid revengeful action as well as the possibility of anarchy through the private usurpation of law enforcement. But it must be noted that the situation envisioned by Hostiensis, Lignano, and Antoninus is one in which the location, if not the identity, of the thief is known. Consequently, the direct application of their teaching can only be made to the circumstance in which the thief <u>has already fled</u>, not when he is still in the process of fleeing. This latter situation would perhaps be indicated by the legitimation of repelling force "immediately"; there is no interval. It is the notion of "force" which is the key to the teaching of the post-Tridentine moralists.

Sixteenth century.—The remarks of Sylvester addressed to our question repeat the ideas of his predecessors: resistance is legitimate as long as no interval occurs; and as long as that interval is absent, a thief cannot resist the effort to regain property.[59] But present throughout Sylvester's discussion of killing in defense of property is the notion of the presence of force. It is this concept, perduring force, that is the subject of some debate in the sixteenth century.

Soto and Covarrubias hold opposite positions on killing the fleeing thief. Soto teaches that because the force brought against the stolen property lasts, a thief who flees can be killed.[60] Covarrubias disagrees. In line with his persistent opposition to killing for property, Covarrubias declares that since the fleeing thief is neither a nighttime thief who may be a threat to life, nor a daytime thief who is defending himself by attacking anyone, nor a direct attacker of another person, he may not be killed.[61] As we have come to expect, Covarrubias stands alone on issues related to property.

The teaching of Soto is reaffirmed by Molina: as long as the act of theft continues, i.e., the stolen property has not been safely put somewhere, the force continues; the fleeing thief can be killed.[62] But Molina demands that the thief be first admonished that unless he gives up the property he will be killed. Some warning is required lest the wrong person be killed. From the demand that the stolen property be given up and the lack of any request that the thief allow himself to be captured, the emphasis of Molina (and others) on recovery of property is made very clear.

Seventeenth century.—Lessius, Diana, and Busembaum perpetuate the concept of the force involved in the act of theft continuing even though the thief flees.[63] Lessius and

Diana, moreover, add two further considerations. They make a
distinction on the basis of whether the goods being taken away
are otherwise recoverable or not. Since recoverability of
property is the basic criterion in determining legitimate killing, it would seem that the distinction is an unnecessary one.
Lessius, however, teaches that while it seems "more right" to
not kill the fleeing thief when the goods are recoverable,
there remains the right to defend one's possessions, a
right which is kept "as long as the thief is in sight."
Therefore, Lessius concludes, one may kill a thief fleeing
with property that is otherwise recoverable.[64] He goes on
to say that while one can kill in this case, the killing
would be against charity; charity demands that goods be saved
with minimal evil to one's neighbor. There seems to be a
contradiction here: one may kill, yet the killing would be
against charity. Is Lessius teaching that the killing is in
accord with justice (one's right to what is his own) yet
contrary to charity? Is he saying that the violation of
charity is not sufficiently grave to demand avoidance? When
Diana discusses this point, he mentions the right one has to
not only recover property but also to prevent its being
stolen. Is this idea not the same as Lessius' "right to defend property as long as the thief is in sight"? Diana does
not take a stand on this point; he mentions the opinion which
would agree with Lessius and says: "You think about it."
Lessius does take a position: he legitimates killing even
though it is against charity, even though the goods could
be recovered without killing.

     What Lessius means by his legitimating something
which he sees to be against charity may have roots in the
teaching of Aquinas on charity. Thomas teaches that charity
requires a person to love enemies in general and inwardly;
it also requires that one be ready inwardly to love an individual enemy if a case of necessity occurs. It is only in
such an urgent situation that charity demands one to show any
signs or effects of love (the inward disposition) to an enemy.
Any action beyond this is "of the perfection" of charity, and
no one is required to do that which belongs to charity's perfection.[65] When Lessius declares killing a fleeing thief to

be against charity, could his use of "more right" to not kill
be an indication that he means it is against the perfection
of charity? The urgency of the situation would be removed because of the thief having placed himself in the "urgent" circumstance.[66] Lessius says, however, that charity requires that
only minimal evil be done to an enemy. It does not seem that
this obligation is of the perfection of charity. In fact, it
would be a matter of justice, not of charity at all. That
minimum evil be done to save goods is a statement of the due
moderation principle. A violation of this principle is a
violation of justice. To justify killing for property which
could be recovered without killing goes far beyond anything
we have seen in the moral tradition; and there does not seem
to be any way that such unnecessary killing could be justified. The deprivation of property for a time (until it is
recovered) cannot be considered an evil of such magnitude that
the thief responsible for the deprivation could be killed.

The second consideration added to the notion of force
is applied only to the case of a thief fleeing with what would
be unrecoverable property. Both Lessius and Diana write of
the need to keep thieves from having "free reign."[67] They see
this "freedom" present if the fleeing thief is safe from being
killed: safety in flight would render all defense almost inapplicable. All the thief would have to do is hurriedly flee
and he would be safe. Given the legitimation of killing in
defense of property otherwise unrecoverable, it follows that
recoverability and not fleeing would be the criterion. The
threatened loss of property is what determines the legitimacy
of killing. On the other hand, this argument is similar to
the "deterrent to crime" proposition. The aim of both arguments is to legitimate action deemed necessary to prevent an
unjust, sinful act. The gravity of the injustice has been
established according to the various norms we have seen.
Once that degree of gravity is reached which legitimates killing, then recoverability becomes the goal, killing the means
to it.

Eighteenth century.—The Salamancans and Alphonsus
agree with their predecessors that the attack perdures even

when the thief flees; so the thief may be killed.[68] They reject, however, the opinion of Lessius that the fleeing thief can be killed even though the property can be recovered without killing. Recovery is the goal; for the Salamancans and Alphonsus it is not legitimate to use unnecessary force or inflict unnecessary harm to achieve that goal. The requirement of Molina that the thief be warned before being killed is reaffirmed by the Salamancans, while Alphonsus acknowledges that such forewarning is not always possible.[69]

The simple reiteration of the fundamental position on a fleeing thief by Alphonsus and the Salamancans shows the broad acceptance of this position in the eighteenth century. Except for Covarrubias, the position was acceptable to the moralists from the sixteenth century. It is significant that the major element of the pro-killing argument is the threat or force which remains in relation to the goods stolen, while the anti-killing position of Covarrubias is based upon the absence of any threat to the person being present. Covarrubias consistently refuses to equate property and person, as the others do. Those in favor of killing a fleeing thief have simply followed out the logic required of a position which legitimates killing not only in defense of persons but also in defense of property.

Although by the eighteenth century moralists agreed on the legitimacy of killing a fleeing thief to save one's property, there was in the teaching of Elbel a set of criteria that might have deserved the attention of Alphonsus but did not. Elbel offers criteria to be followed by public officials who are commanded to caputre someone.[70] The requirements for killing such a person who attempts to escape would appear to be applicable to a private individual who wants to capture a thief and thus recover his property.

The criteria established by Elbel are five: (a) if the ones to be captured resist with arms; (b) if the crime committed is terrible and capital; (c) if there is no other way to capture; (d) if grave evil is feared if the escape is successful; (e) if the ones to be captured are sufficiently defamed of crime. Elbel declares that if any one of these conditions is missing, it is not licit to kill the person who is escaping. It appears evident that condition "a"—resistance with arms—is not present in the case of a fleeing thief. The personal danger that comes with armed resistance could occur as a result of the attempt to capture (the thief seeks to prevent his capture), but it is not present automatically in the circumstance of flight. Consequently, on the basis of this criterion, it would have to be said that a fleeing thief could not be killed—even if all the other criteria were fulfilled. Elbel, however, does not apply these criteria to the fleeing thief. He teaches that a public official cannot kill one who flees simply to capture him; yet he allows a person (presumably public official or private individual) to kill a thief to stop him from taking property. It seems strange that the criteria would not apply to this case of theft. Even if one were to grant the "grave evil" criterion ("d") and presume theft to be a capital crime ("b"), the resistance with arms is at least possibly lacking in a situation of flight. Yet if one transposes this attack with arms into threat to life, the ignoring of these criteria fits the general pattern. If the loss of goods of great value is regarded as equivalent to life, then theft of these goods would legitimate the taking of life. But even when that is said, is it not puzzling that a murderer, for example, who does not resist with arms, but simply runs away, must be allowed to escape rather than be killed, while a thief who does the same can be killed? Elbel's criteria are based upon a demand that there be a threat to the life of those who seek to capture before they may kill. He harkens back to an opinion popular for the last time in the fifteenth century. Yet in his (and others') way of thinking the loss of goods of great value constitutes just such a threat to life. The question that has still not been answered is whether "great value," expressed in terms of "decent life" or "enormous or notable harm," is really equivalent to life.

Fled Thief

The question of what a person may do to save or recover his property once the thief has fled will be answered rather consistently in the opposite manner from the question of a fleeing thief. Once the thief has retreated to safety, there is no longer considered to be any "force" present. Consequently, when the location of the thief is known, other channels are to be followed to achieve recovery of the property. To go where a thief is keeping one's stolen property to recover it is considered revenge and an action done without proper authority, for recovery of such property is the sphere of public authority.

The position just stated is explicitly or implicitly the teaching of Hostiensis, Lignano, Sylvester, Soto, Molina, Lessius, Diana, Busembaum, the Salamancans, and Alphonsus.[71] There is a unanimity here from the thirteenth to the eighteenth century. The agreement on this issue is easy to understand. If killing is justified only when no other means of prevention or recovery are available, the case of a fled thief does not meet this requirement. Once a thief has fled and the question of killing him rises, the situation has to be one in which the identity and/or location of that thief is known. When it is known who and/or where he is, the task of recovery belongs to the public officials; defense is no longer a part of the circumstance. The one question that is discussed is the course of action morally open when public authority is difficult to call on or it is unavailable.

The use of the concept "public authority" is found as early as the writing of Lignano and Sylvester,[72] but the lack of availability of this authority is not discussed until Lessius takes up the question in the seventeenth century. The disrupted and war-torn atmosphere of his age no doubt made the ordinary processes of justice difficult to follow.[73] Lessius acknowledges the possibility of "a judge" not being present whose assistance can be obtained to regain one's property.[74] In such a case, he allows a person to go after his property on his own. But Lessius demands that one take into consideration the possibility that greater disorder might follow the act than comes from the loss of goods. If greater disorder is feared, a private person is not to go after his stolen property. By his concern for order Lessius appears to be making a plea for the avoidance of the anarchy which comes from taking the law into one's own hands. He also denies that a person may use the resistance of the thief to his attempt to regain his property as an excuse to repel force with force. Once the property is "safely and quietly" in the possession of the thief, Lessius refuses to admit any continuation of force on the part of the thief. It would thus seem that Lessius would require at least a postponement of recovery until public officials could be obtained to regain the property. If the circumstance is such that even a delayed presence of these authorities is not possible, he would require a judgment as to the disorder which would result from a wronged person attempting to regain his stolen property. Lessius does not, however, give any specifics on the content of disorder. Is the possible death of the thief, or of oneself, or of those who help you an example of disorder? Is the effect of acting on one's own in this case, action which would require planning of sorts and the likelihood of intentions of revenge, itself a cause of disorder? Is the danger of greater disorder always present? Lessius does not answer these questions; he simply calls attention to the possibility. When a thief has escaped, force ceases and defense is no longer the issue. To go after one's stolen property is an initiation of force on the owner's part. If such initiation is too easily legitimated, the door opens to too much violence on the part of "wronged" persons. Maybe this fear colors Lessius' warning about "greater disorder."

The moralists who come after Lessius take up the issue which he left in some doubt. Diana, Busembaum, the Salamancans, and Alphonsus address themselves to the question; they do not entirely agree on the resolution of the problem.

Diana, Busembaum, and Alphonsus agree that if there is no public authority available, the individual may go after his stolen property; if the thief resists the attempt to regain the property, the owner may kill if that is necessary to repossess the goods.[75] None of these men makes any reference to Lessius' interest in avoiding greater disorder. In fact, Diana allows the attempt to recover and the possibility of killing not only when public authority is not present, but also if the request for the assistance of that authority would invllve "great expense or trouble." This teaching would be able to be interpreted in such a way that a delay in a legal process might be considered greatly "expensive," through the loss of the property's availability; and what is "great trouble"? Is the legal process and the effort of turning to any but immediately available authority "trouble"?

The Salamancans follow the stricter line present in Lessius' teaching.[76] They teach that an owner simply cannot take his property back by force. Two reasons are given for this position. The Salamancans say that if one were allowed to retake his property by force, the "disruption of the republic" would follow. As with Lessius, the taking of the law into one's own hands is forbidden. The recognition that force has ceased is also involved in the Salamancans' decision. For them, once the thief is "peacefully at home" he is no longer an "attacker"; he is, rather, an "evil retainer" of property. He holds on to something unjustly, but he is not using force any longer.

The context in which the Salamancans declare their teaching on this point is one in which "there is not certain hope of recovery by legal means."[77] This statement rules out the need for certainty of recovery before an attempt at recovery is illegitimate. Does it deal with the situation in which there is certainty that legal means are <u>not</u> available? Perhaps not. But it seems likely that the Salamancans' requirement that less than certainty of recovery does not allow personal action was made to include the concept of delayed and uncertain recovery. Given the knowledge of where the property is and the existence of public officials, perhaps the Salamancans could not envision a situation in which civil authority would be totally lacking. Once a thief becomes a "retainer," only public authority has the right to take that property away and restore it to the owner. The reason for this is found by the Salamancans in the teaching of Aquinas (even though Thomas is dealing with restealing what was stolen, and not with overt attack).[78] Thomas gives to a thief a <u>secundum quid</u>, or relative, ownership over what he has stolen; it is his not simply but as regards the custody of the property. Because of this "relative ownership," Thomas holds that an owner who would try to recover his goods by stealth would be sinning against general justice through disregard for the order of justice and would usurp judgment to himself. What Thomas applied to "restealing" what is one's own, the Salamancans use as applicable to even an overt attempt to regain stolen property. Their interest is to avoid a breakdown in the orderly process of justice.

It is interesting that in conjunction with this teaching the Salamancans do not mention their teaching that one may kill if recovery of the property is not otherwise easy, as in a case of doubt.[79] It would appear that a doubt as to the ability of legal authority to recover one's property would fulfill this requirement for killing. The basic difference between the two cases appears to be the presence or absence of "force." While the force is present, while the property is being stolen or the the thief is still in flight, one may kill; but when force ceases, public authority must take over the attempt to regain the property. The private individual's right to kill is strictly determined by the "repel force with force" principle.

The efforts of the moralists to judge the morality of killing a thief who has completed his flight do not result in agreement. Many simply say that one cannot kill in this case (Hostiensis, Lignano, Sylvester, Soto, Molina); others agree that the case is primarily one for public officials to handle, but they allow the individual to act when these officials are unavailable (Diana, Busembaum, Alphonsus): recovery remains the primary goal. Lessius requires a consideration of social disorder before any action be taken on one's own, but he is unclear as to the possibility of that disorder ever being absent. The Salamancans also focus on the effect on society. They, however, do not seem to see any possibility of civil authority being so totally ineffectual that the disruption caused by individual action would be justified. What Lessius and the Salamancans have done is to reintroduce an idea last seen in Antoninus: lesser evil is not to be avoided by greater evil.[80] There is, according to Lessius and the Salamancans, a value which can outweigh the value of property: social order, social peace. Is it possible that killing thieves needs to be examined as possibly causing "social disorder" by demeaning the value of human life through its consideration as less valuable than property?

The variations and sometimes contradictions in the teaching of the moralists on the questions of fleeing and already fled thieves are a result of different understandings of the perdurance of force, the inclusion or exclusion of the notion of resultant social disruption. But these issues are academic (even for the moralists used here) without the more fundamental question of great value. Property's value is what justifies killing in whatever circumstance one might imagine. We have seen property-value joined with life-value, though there has not been a consistent norm of comparison. Great loss, loss of that necessary to life and the decent life, are not equivalent concepts. The tendency that surfaces in the post-Tridentine moralists is to equate "great" monetary value, whether specified or relative, with "necessary for life" and thus with life itself, thereby justifying the taking of a thief's life. The focal point in all this process of justification is property: its value, its loss, its recovery. Just what property are our authors talking about? How do they view this property in their effort to evaluate it? Is their evaluation process the right one for a Christian morality?

The Evaluation of Property

In the discussion of theft and the right to kill to prevent it, the authors relied upon for this study do not engage in any analysis of what kind of property they are talking about. The pre-Trent sources go no further than the statement that the property in question in theft is mobile and corporal.[81] From the sixteenth century, the moralists simply assume this definition.[82] The consequence of this generic approach to property is the lack of any distinction between different types of property beyond mobile-immobile, a distinction that merely says that something can be carried away.

Since the legitimacy of killing in defense of property did not become widely accepted until the sixteenth century (though it was legitimated by certain authors prior to that), the failure to make any further specification earlier than that does not really matter for this study. But with the efforts beginning in the sixteenth century to establish specific norms to determine the value of property that would make it defensible by killing, the vision of property as an undifferentiated whole would appear to be significant. Before looking at the significance, there will be an attempt to explore why no distinctions were made.

The understanding of private property as rooted in natural law by twelfth and thirteenth-century theologians and lawyers has already been noted.[83] But at the same time the disputes between Pope and King led to a view of property as a natural institution determined by human law under the jurisdiction of secular, not ecclesiastical, authorities.[84] The purpose of this position was to justify attacks on Church wealth and to remove the power of the clergy to deprive people of their secular rights. However, this concentration on the secular power was itself in process of modification. The dispute was basically over who had dominion over property, the Pope or the King. The theory of dominion posited a hierarchy of rights and power (with the accompanying potential privileges) over the same objects; it was not a matter of complete supremacy by anyone, but a hierarchy of superior and inferior power. To whom had God, the lord and owner of the world, given earthly dominion? Was the Pope or the King the supreme feudal lord? Whether the Pope or the King was accepted as feudal lord, those below the lord in the hierarchy were viewed as having only a <u>conditional</u> right to use property. If the conditions were not met, the lord could revoke the right of use.

The consequence of this dispute over feudal lordship was conditioned by the progress of the middle class.[85] It was not to their interest that even the secular power have dominion over their property. What came after the Reformation to be seen as a right to property independent of the use made of it was prefigured by the view of private property as rooted in nature and by the triumph of the Roman concept of ownership. The feudal theory of ownership as a conditional right to use property was gradually replaced in the fifteenth century by the Roman notion of absolute ownership: an exclusive owner could use, dispose, or destroy his property as he pleased.[86] These were the root theories which led through a host of hypotheses to the classical formulations of the seventeenth-eighteenth centuries.[87]

The ever-present difficulty for the ascending middle class in its attacks on vested wealth, whether ecclesiastical or secular, was the reliance upon "inappropriate use" as justification for transferring property to new owners. In order to protect themselves from subsequent attacks based on the same principle of wrongful use, they had to defend property as a "natural right" and ownership as absolute. Otherwise, they would themselves be open to confiscation.[88] No property owner, feudal lord or newly-prosperous merchant, was willing to give any authority the right to judge "right use" of property, though they would use that notion to benefit themselves.

Two significant points are contained in the above comments on property. The notion of "right use" as a legitimating condition of ownership was replaced by an "absolute right" of ownership once it had served the purpose of the middle class. The history of the triumph of "absolute right" runs from the thirteenth to the seventeenth century, but it was not until the fourteenth century that the natural law concept began to be applied specifically to individuals and not just to the generic idea of private ownership.[89] Secondly, there is in the course of the discussion on property little that indicates what type of property is being discussed. It would seem that in the category of "mobile" property, the concern would be for goods of production, not for consumer goods.[90] Productive capital was the source of wealth and power for the middle class. Surplus wealth was the foundation of the economic system, the impetus for productive expansion. Consumer goods would, of course, be a consequence of increased production and their acquisition a consequence of increased wealth. But when efforts were made in the sixteenth through eighteenth centuries to establish norms of value, not even this distinction between productive and consumer goods was made. The efforts of the age in which they lived, as well as of the preceding two or three centuries, were directed to establishing the fundamental natural right to absolute ownership (not conditional). The energy was not used to distinguish types of property and the possible relationship of absolute ownership to these types.

The post-Tridentine moralists on the whole accepted the legitimacy of killing to defend property. The task they undertook was the determination of the value property must have before it would be defensible by taking human life. Property and life were not absolutely equated; the value attached to human life and the grave and irreparable nature of killing demanded some effort to establish a norm of value for property which would put it on some level of equality with life.[91] We have seen the efforts at work: insufficient minimum, absolute monetary sums, relative harm inflicted upon the victim of theft.[92] Every attempt to create an absolute monetary norm as constituting great value and every creation of a relative norm, once the circumstance was other than the direct preservation of life, were based on the monetary value of the property. This has been evident when a specific amount was given; it was also present in the case of the relative norms. That was the manner in which property was evaluated. If the property threatened would cause "great" financial loss to a particular person, it could be defended by killing. It was the harm to be avoided that determined the fulfillment or violation of due moderation.

The changing focus of the due moderation principle has been expounded.[93] From attention to avoiding excessive defensive violence and judging the relative evil which would or would not occur, interest was directed to the injury to be prevented. Prevention of injury then led to the legitimation of the means necessary to prevent the injury. The moralists from the sixteenth century onward tended to do just that. They did not completely capitulate to an "end justifies the means" position—the demand for "great value," however determined, shows this—but they did engage in an effort to legitimate the avoidance of injury by killing. They determined the gravity of injury in terms of monetary value, absolute or relative. These moralists were aware, however,

that the long tradition which preceded them (at least up to
the fourteenth century) had justified killing by a private
person only in a case of self-defense. When property became
defensible by killing it was because property and the person
possessing it were joined together; property was a "necessity
of life." However, they seem to have shown clearly that they
recognized that while property as a general reality might be
necessary for life, not all specific property, not every item
of property, was so necessary. Consequently, the post-
Tridentine moralists tried to determine just *what* property was
such a necessity. But because of the changed perspective on
due moderation, the concept of absolute ownership, and the
common practice of evaluating property in terms of money,
they looked at the injury to be prevented in terms of the
monetary loss which would be incurred. They lost sight of the
notion of "necessary for life." Because of their focus on
injury, they did not look to the relationship between specific
property and that property's relationship to life, but rather
to the injury to be prevented. Even when the notion of giving
a fixed sum as always being gravely harmful was rejected in
favor of a relative norm, the relationship was with injury and
monetary value; it was not between injury and life.

The clearest example of attention to injury and omission of consideration of the relationship of injury to life is
found in the "deterrent to crime" argument proposed by Molina,
Lessius, and the Salamancans.[94] These moralists justified
killing as a necessity for the prevention of theft. The norms
for great value and the absence of lesser means of prevention
were, of course, still a part of their teaching. But these
men saw killing as a way of discouraging theft, of avoiding
the loss of property. Killing was judged a "necessary means"
to a "good end"; it was therefore justified. As with all the
arguments offered to legitimate killing in defense of property,
there were only the ambiguous, relative-value norms, the overly
lax specific sums (e.g., Molina), and the absence of other
ways of prevention to serve as determinants. The method of
evaluation involved the consideration of "grave harm" to be
equivalent to the life of the thief, for the thief's life had
somehow depreciated in value by his crime. But that depriva-

tion was initially viewed in terms of <u>innocent life</u>, not in terms of property; it was a case of innocent life-vs-guilty life. In this case, involving property, there was no direct consideration of the value of the thief's life. How could even "grave harm," suffered indirectly through the loss of property, compare to the direct and irreparable "harm" which comes to the thief? Does the killing of the thief truly meet the requirements of the principle that lesser evil not be prevented by means of greater evil?[95] Is the harm done the thief equal to or greater than the harm which would follow if certain property were lost? Is it legitimate to create a norm of "great value," or "grave harm," or some like concept, and make that automatically equivalent to the great value attached to human life? Can the grave harm of deprivation of life, final as it is, be equated to the "grave harm" which comes from theft, a harm that is not necessarily final nor incapable of being rectified?

Perhaps all these questions can be approached from a different viewpoint. If the teaching of the post-Tridentine moralists as it concluded with acceptance of a relative norm of gravity is not accepted, what sort of norm could be employed to protect the individual's right to his property?

The moralists and lawyers whose teaching we have examined wrote and taught during a time when property was becoming increasingly important and the right to possess it considered both absolute and natural for the individual. Property was increasingly available and the benefits accruing from possession increasingly appreciated. Wealth, even relative wealth, had become a possibility for many more people than ever before in history.

The morality of wealth, of being wealthy, had been a concern of Christian thinkers for many centuries. Clement of Alexandria, John Chrysostom, Augustine, Aquinas, Cajetan: these authors from the third to the sixteenth century addressed themselves to the problem. The early Fathers of the Church, Clement, Chrysostom, and Augustine, determine the morality of being wealthy on the basis of the use made of wealth, of property.[96] Augustine and Thomas, some one thousand years apart, consider possession of more than a person needs to be evil.[97] Thomas explains himself this way:

> . . . man seeks . . . to have external riches in so far as they are necessary for him to live in keeping with his condition of life. Wherefore it will be a sin for him to exceed this measure, by wishing to acquire or keep them immoderately.[98]

This statement of Thomas' would appear to ratify the status quo and deprive man of the right to change his condition in life; it is a teaching quite expressive of the static, hierarchial society of the thirteenth century. Cajetan, however, lived in the sixteenth century, a time of changing social status as the merchant class made its way up the social scale. He takes up the teaching of Thomas to clarify its meaning and remove what he considers the absurdity of an overly literal reading.

It is Cajetan's teaching that man may desire to the degree necessary to achieve his end.[99] The proper end of each person, according to which rules are reasonable, is the proper life of each (and those who depend on him) according to his condition. By "life" Cajetan understands "all opportune conveniences."[100] Outside of this end, right reason would not allow desire for or the having of possessions except for the sake of generosity to others. However, according to Cajetan, the "proper life of each" does not preclude a change of condition. According to human nature, happiness in the present life is a capacity of each person; so it is according to reason for man to be able to try to achieve this for himself and his own. Riches can thus be acquired in order to realize one's potential. Riches are needed to reach this potential, though, Cajetan says, not in huge quantities.

Despite the differences in these opinions which span some thirteen hundred years, one thing remains constant: the morality of possessions is judged in terms of their _use_. The purpose of wealth is to be a means to an end. Would it not follow that the _value_ of wealth, or property, would have to be formulated in terms of its end, its purpose, and not simply in terms of itself?[101] The end of which these authors speak is related to persons; it is not a matter of property looked at just in itself. The formulation of any "absolute norm" to determine the value of property would thus appear erroneous. If property's value is in terms of the ends of persons, value could not be judged without reference to persons. Even the varied reference points of Augustine and Aquinas lead to the same conclusion. Augustine's "need" and Thomas' "condition of life" are not necessarily the same. The "need" which Augustine required could be read as "needed to keep condition" or as "needed for life's perdurance." Thomas' "condition of life" could be read as a simple ratification of the status quo. It is to this point that Cajetan addresses himself, in terms of social advancement. He argues that it is legitimate to have more than a bare minimum or what is needed to continue in one's present social condition. Man may enjoy the goods of life which bring happiness and so advance the realization of his potential. The possession of what is needed for moderate happiness and the possession of what is needed to achieve the capacity to be of benefit to others are both legitimate according to Cajetan. This teaching would also rule out an absolute norm, as what would deprive an individual of either end (being moderately happy or beneficial to others) would be relative to the person's whole economic and social condition.

The general tendency in the seventeenth and eighteenth centuries, while not unchallenged, was to rule out any absolute norm for judging the value of property.[102] To this extent, the moralists were in agreement with what is the consequence of the above teaching on the morality of wealth. But they did not accept the idea of evaluating property in terms of its purpose or end, the use made of property. Seemingly influenced by the movement led by the middle class from the fourteenth century onward, the moralists who tried to give norms for justifiable killing in defense of property worked within the framework of an absolute right to ownership. Property belonged to its owner by natural law, natural right; he could use that property as he saw fit. The moralists, however, stopped short of total acceptance of this absolute right to one's property. To kill, the property had to be of great value; so it could be defended by killing. Because of the strife and violence which had been connected with the idea of judging rightful possession on the basis of proper use, that idea was rejected. Property was valued according to the harm its loss would inflict, and that harm was judged most often according to the monetary value of the property.

If the teaching of the early Fathers, Aquinas, and Cajetan is looked at closely, does its notion of "use" have to be aligned with the idea both fostered and rejected during the ascendency of the middle class? The middle-class concern in rejecting what had been for them a profitable idea was to forestall an attack on their right to possess property if it were not properly used. The teaching of Aquinas and the others is also aimed at rightful possession and right use; even Cajetan, whose opinion is the most favorable to acquiring wealth, limits rightful possession. But there is another element in this teaching which appears important. If property is a means to an end, the end or purpose to which property is put has to be involved in its evaluation. Property gains its value from its usefulness in filling human needs and human desires.[103] But needs are more basic than desires, and needs themselves vary. The variation in needs is not just from person to person, it is also in terms of more or less essential. That property which would fulfill the most essential needs would be the most valuable to man. The clearest example would be some material thing which would sustain a person's life. It would be the most useful, fulfilling that need which if not met would make all other needs superfluous.

If the purpose of property is used in the process of evaluation there would be demanded a categorizing of property. The divisions employed would not be necessarily in terms of money-value (the criterion employed by most moralists from the sixteenth century onward), but would rather be in terms of the needs which the property fulfills. On the basis of what has been said here of the teaching of the early Fathers, Aquinas, and Cajetan, it would seem that property could be divided into three categories: essential property, goods useful for moderate happiness, and luxury property. It is such a mode of distinction that is lacking in the moral teaching examined here. The division of property into these three categories would make monetary value, so crucial in the undifferentiated scheme, largely irrelevant. The irrelevancy is due to the necessity of evaluating more highly that which is essential to life, while realizing that in terms of money other goods usually carry a higher price.

The process of determining the property which would classify in the categories essential, for moderate happiness, and luxury would not be an entirely easy one. Man has a tendency to make necessary what he becomes accustomed to, and needful for his ordinary happiness that which is luxurious—what makes him "happy" is often that which is somewhat beyond his ordinary means.

The establishment of these property-types according to purpose would then demand the determination of which types could be legitimately defended by killing. If one were to follow the teaching that dominated the pre-Trent period, it would be clear that only essential property could be so defended. That teaching demanded a concurrent threat to life as justification for taking life; the loss of property essential for life would be a threat to life. The post-Trent authors, however, almost unanimously linked a person and his property, and taught that property was necessary for life. What they did not do was ask: "Necessary in what way?" Necessary for sustaining life? Necessary for moderate happiness? Necessary for the enjoyment of a luxurious life? It is not correct to simply link property and life; distinctions need to be made. The moralists from the sixteenth century made an effort at distinction through the concept of "great value," and they tried to relate that value to persons. But they did not relate the value to the purposes which varying types of property fulfill. In the process of judging whether a thief can be killed, the value of the human life involved has to be viewed in terms of the threat involved. Is the threat a threat to life, or is it a threat to a moderately happy or luxurious life? Can one person's need or desire or "right" to moderate happiness or luxury override another person's right to life? Can a right to what is most essential give way to avoid a loss which is not necessarily irreparable (of that which provides moderate happiness or luxury) or in any way connected to the preservation of life?

These questions would have to be answered in the negative if there is to be any consideration of equality of value. A man cannot be judged to forfeit his right to life just because he makes life more inconvenient or more difficult for someone else. Throughout the five hundred years covered by this study, self-defense has been the justifying basis for taking human life. If there is to be true self-defense in the defense of property that can only occur when the property defended is essential to life (or there is a concurrent, overt threat to life).

If the distinction of property types according to the need they fulfill is accepted, the problem of protecting property remains. Theft does create social disorder and anxiety; it is wrong to steal. But just because an act is wrong, just because it creates a problem for society, does not mean that the person who does the act can be killed. There is need to evaluate the evils involved in both the crime and the punishment or remedy. When the evaluation results in a judgment that the evil to be prevented does not compare with the value of human life, the moral demand is that a non-lethal means of prevention be found. Otherwise, individuals and/or society would be preventing a lesser evil by means of a greater one.

The crux of the problem remains the evaluation of the thief's life in relationship to property. The post-Tridentine moralists generally judged value on a monetary basis. They worked from a long-standing tradition that human life was not inviolable. Life can be taken in defense of life. They justified their position on property-defense by equating life and property of great value, however ambiguous the understanding of great value. It is this equation that is questioned on the basis of other considerations also present in the tradition. Specifically, the major oversight of the post-Tridentine moralists was the absence of a process whereby property would be divided according to the use it had, the needs it fulfilled. By this omission their teaching falls in line with the middle class use of Roman law theory on ownership. These moralists tend to make ownership absolute and inviolable. The inviolability of one's property on the basis of its monetary value or the comfort and convenience it provides is an erroneous position. Man has a "natural right" to life; he has a "natural right" to property. If the property at issue is not directly related to the preservation of life, in that its loss would be a definite threat to continued life, it is erroneous to give preference to the right to property over the right to life.

FOOTNOTES

FOOTNOTES

CHAPTER I

¹Alexander of Hales, Summa Theologia (Quaracchi: 1948), IV:3:2:3:2:1:2:5:1, p. 521. Thomas Aquinas, Summa Theologia, trans. Fathers of the English Dominican Province (New York: 1947), Vol. II, II-II:64:1. Bonaventure, Opera Omnia (Paris: 1863-1868), Vol. XII, Sermo VI, pp. 249-250. Alexander and Thomas both cite Augustine, De Civitate Dei, I:20. Cf. The City of God, trans. John Healy, ed. R. V. G. Tasker (London: 1945), Vol. I, I:19.
Although the Summa Fratris Alexandri will be cited as "Alexander, Summa" in this work, it should be noted that Part IV of the Summa is the work of William of Middleton, who died c. 1260. This fourth part was written 1257-1258, some thirty years after Alexander's death. The first three parts of the Summa were compiled between 1241-1245, by the disciples of Alexander. They were not always faithful to their master's opinions. Cf. Alexander, Summa, Liber Tertius Prolegomena (Quaracchi: 1930); Victorin Doucet, O.F.M., "A New Source of the Summa Fratris Alexandri," in Franciscan Studies, 6 (1946), pp. 403-417; Ignatius Brady, O.F.M., "General Introduction," in Philotheus Boehner, O.F.M., The History of the Franciscan School, Part I, Alexander of Hales (Detroit: 1947), pp. b-c.

²Friedrich Herr, The Intellectual History of Europe, trans. Jonathan Steinberg (London: 1966), p. 51; The Medieval World, trans. Janet Sondheimer (New York: 1962), p. 204.

³Bonaventure, Sermo VI, pp. 249-250.

⁴John Duns Scotus, Opera Omnia, ed. nova juxta editionem L. Waddingi (Paris: 1891-1895), Vol. XVIII, Oxon. IV:15:3, pp. 374-375.

⁵Cf. Ex. 22:2, 18-20, 22-24; Lev. 24:16-17, 21; Deut. 21:18-22; 22:20-26.

⁶Augustine, The City of God, I:20-21.

⁷Augustine, The Free Choice of the Will (De Libero Arbitrio), trans. Robert P. Russell, I:6-7, in The Fathers of the Church, ed. Roy J. Deferrari (Washington, D.C.: 1967), Vol. 59.

[8] Alexander, Summa, IV:3:2:3:2:1:2:5:3, p. 525; Thomas, Summa, II-II:64:2.

[9] Cf. infra, pp. 80-81.

[10] Alexander, Summa, IV:3:2:3:2:1:2:5:3, p. 525, Thomas, Summa, II-II:64:2.

[11] Gratian, Decretum, C.23, q.3 and c.36, C.23, q.4, in Corpus juris canonici, ed. E. Friedberg (Leipzig: 1879-1881).

[12] More than two centuries later Cajetan, citing this parable, will make the same point. Cf. Cajetan, Commentarium in summam theologicam S. Thomae Aquinatis, in St. Thomas Aquinas, Summa Theologica (Rome: 1773), Vol. V, II-II:64:2.

[13] Herr, Medieval World, p. 210.

[14] Alexander, Summa, IV:3:2:3:2:1:2:5:2:1, p. 528. Alexander refers to Augustine, "Letter 47:5" and "Letter 138:14," and to Gratian, c.8, C.23, q.5 and c.2, C.23, q.1, where Augustine is cited. Bonaventure, Sermo VI, pp. 249-250, and Vol. X, pp. 374-375.

[15] Cf. Augustine, "Letter 138," in The Fathers of the Church, Vol. 20, trans. Sister Wilfred Parsons, S.N.D., ed. Roy J. Deferrari (New York: 1953), p. 45.

[16] Herr, Medieval World, p. 62.

[17] Herr, Medieval World, p. 60; R. De Roover, "The Organization of Trade," in The Cambridge Economic History, Vol. III, Economic Organization and Policies in the Middle Ages, gen. eds. M. M. Postan and H. J. Habakkuk, eds. M. M. Postan, E. E. Rich, Edward Miller (Cambridge University Press: 1963), pp. 45-50; A. B. Hibbert, "The Economic Policies of Towns," in The Cambridge Economic History, Vol. III, pp. 185-187.

[18] C.23, q.3; c.36, C.23, q.4.

[19] Augustine, "Letter 133," in The Fathers of the Church, Vol. 20, pp. 6-8.

[20] Augustine, "Letter 139," in The Fathers of the Church, Vol. 20, pp. 53-57.

[21] c.3, C.23, q.5; cf. Augustine, "Letter 100," in The Fathers of the Church, Vol. 18, trans. Sister Wilfred

Parsons, S.N.D., ed. Roy J. Deferrari (New York: 1953), pp. 141-143.

[22]This particular phrase is omitted in c.3, C.23, q.5, but the parts of "Letter 100" actually quoted convey the same meaning.

[23]c.7, C.23, q.5.

[24]c.8, C.23, q.5, where Augustine, "Letter 47" is quoted. Cf. also c.33, C.23, q.8.

[25]c.29 and 31, C.23, q.5, for Jerome, Super Ezechielem, 4:22.

[26]Decretalium Collectiones, in Corpus juris canonici, ed. E. Friedberg (Leipzig: 1879-1881).

[27]Olim, X. 2.13.12; Significasti, X. 5.12.18.

[28]Huguccio died in 1210. His most famous work, Summa decreta, on the Decretum Gratiani, was written mainly in 1188-1190. An edition of this work is now in process. Cf. "Huguccio" in New Catholic Encyclopedia (New York: 1967), Vol. 7. (Hereafter: NCE.)

[29]D. 43.16.27, in Corpus juris civilis, ed. Joannes Ludovicus Guilielmus Beck (Leipzig: 1829). The same principle is found in c.7, D.I; X. 5.39.3, Si vero aliquis, De sententia excommunicationis. This decretal is taken from the writings of Pope Alexander III (1159-1181).

[30]E.g., c.7, C.23, q.5; Alexander, Summa, IV:3:2:3: 2:1:2:5:1 and 3 passim, pp. 521-528.

[31]Alexander, Summa, IV:3:2:3:2:1:2:5:2:2:1 and 2, pp. 531, 533; Bonaventure, Sermo VI, pp. 249-250; In III-IV Libros Sententiarum, Vol. V, p. 155b.

[32]Alexander, Summa, IV:3:2:3:2:1:2:5:3, p. 525.

[33]Alexander, Summa, IV:3:2:3:2:1:2:5:3, p. 526. Alexander gives a place to legitimate killing on the basis of Divine inspiration. Through inspiration God manifests his will and thus shares his authority over life. Certain occurrences in the Old Testament give rise to this teaching and to the distinction between the inspiration being consciously accepted or followed unknowingly. The Israelites in Canaan (cf. Book of Joshua) consciously acted under Divine inspiration; the Assyrians who punished the Israelites (Isaiah 10) acted as God's avengers unknowingly. Consequently, the Assyrians acted illicitly. The punitive

action was just; however, they themselves did evil because they did not act consciously as God's agents. (Obviously, only the Israelites were able to recognize the work of Yahweh in their punishment.) Thus to kill justly under Divine inspiration requires acknowledgment that the action performed is at the instigation of the Divine authority. And to be so conscious requires a recognition of God's law. Cf. Augustine, The City of God, I:20, c.49, C.23, q.5.

[34] Augustine, The City of God, I:20; The Free Choice of the Will, I:6-7. Cf. Scotus, Opera, XVIII, Oxon. IV:15:3, p. 374; Alexander, Summa, IV:3:2:3:2:1:2:5:3, p. 526.

[35] Augustine, "Letter 139"; Alexander, Summa, IV:3: 2:3:2:1:2:5:3, p. 525.

[36] Thomas, Summa, II-II:64:3. For Thomas' reasons why Mt. 5, etc. do not bind: II-II:40:1, and infra, pp. 67ff.

[37] Thomas, Summa, II-II:64:3.

[38] The benefit which may come from the punishment or lack of punishment can apply to not only the whole of society, but also to individuals within it. Thus public officials are invested with the responsibility and authority to defend not only the common good but also the individuals of the community. This defense can require the officials to act without any judicial process. Alexander (Summa, IV:3:2:3:2:1:2:5:2:2:2, p. 532), relying upon Augustine ("Letter 47") and Gratian (c.8, C.23, q.5), mentions as an exception to the rule of judicial process the case of a person being in immediate danger of death and an official having to kill to save him.
This recognition of public authority not always being able to follow the legal process of capture and conviction has already been mentioned in conjunction with the parable of the weeds and the wheat. The point is present when the evil person has a large following. (Cf. also c.31, C.23, q.4; c.9b, C.23, q.5.) Antoninus of Florence (d.1459) continues this teaching. Perhaps as a result of his experience with the warring city-states and resultant roaming bands of marauders, and the climate of vendetta and blood feuds on the part of powerful families (Cf. Lauro Martines [ed.], Violence and Civil Disorder in Italian Cities: 1200-1500 [Berkeley and Los Angeles: 1972], passim), Antoninus recognized that it was not always possible to capture and condemn by ordinary law someone very harmful to the community. This criminal could escape ordinary justice because of his power and following. As a consequence, Antoninus would tend to perpetuate the earlier teaching; when such a person is killed without formal conviction, it suffices that the death be merited and the ordinary means of punishment be impossible. Cf. Antoninus, Summa Theologica (Verona: 1740), 2:7:8:1:v. See also Hermann Busembaum,

Medulla Theologiae Moralis (Tournai: 1848), ed. Alphonsus Maria de Ligorio, I:3:4:1:2, where Ex. 22 and Rom. 13 are cited as Biblical foundation for bypassing the normal process. The exceptions which would give rise to such a need are mentioned in a footnote: if the crime is notorious, if there be danger of sedition, or if disgrace would come to the king if the judicial process would go on. (The "disgrace" envisioned here would seem to refer to information becoming known which would destroy the prestige of the king, either because of his own activity or that of someone connected with him. It appears to be the same idea as the "immunity" given to the advisors of United States' Presidents when, e.g., they are called to testify before a Congressional committee.) These exceptions are based upon the work of the Salamancans, *Cursus Theologiae Moralis* (Venice: 1728), VI:25:2:18. Busembaum lived 1600-1668; the Salamancans' work was done between 1665-1724. Thus it seems most likely that the footnote in Busembaum is the work of the editor, Alphonsus Ligouri. In his own work, Alphonsus uses both Ex. 22 and Rom. 13, and he gives the exceptions as they are in the Busembaum footnote. Cf. his *Theologia Moralis* (Rome: 1905), I:3:4:1:2, n. 376, 377. Thus the need to sometimes ignore the judicial process is both continued and broadened in the tradition through the eighteenth century.

[39] Raymund of Pennaforte, *Summa* (Verona: 1744), 2:1:1. His source is c.26, C.23, q.5, which is a quotation from Ambrose, *Commentaria ad c.9 Lucae*, Bk. 7. Cf. "Raymund of Pennafort," in *NCE*, Vol. 12.

[40] C.23, q.3.

[41] E.g., c.7, D.I; c.29, C.23, q.5; c.33, C.23, q.8.

[42] Alexander, *Summa*, IV:3:2:3:2:1:2:5:2:2:2, p. 531.

[43] Augustine, *The Free Choice of the Will*, I:5; D. 43.16.27.

[44] Augustine, "Letter 153"; cf. c.19, C.23, q.5.

[45] Hostiensis, *Commentaria super quinque libros decretalium* (Venice: 1581), on *Significasti*, *De homicidio*.

[46] Cf. *infra*, pp. 146-151.

[47] Bonaventure, *Sermo* VI.

[48] Raymund, *Summa*, 2:1:1.

[49] Thomas, *Summa*, II-II:64:7. Cf. *infra*, pp. 32-34.

⁵⁰Richard of Middleton, _Super quatuor libros sententiarum_ (Brescia: 1591), 3:37:3:2; _Commentum super quartum sententiarum_ (Venice: 1499), 25:5:3.

⁵¹Richard, _Super quatuor_, 3:37:3:2.

⁵²This is an example of the Scholastic effort to specify and compare various "goods." The precept of charity determines the value of the innocent person's bodily life as superior to the bodily life of the guilty person. But since the value of the soul's salvation is considered higher than that of bodily life, the salvation of another is to be preferred. This comparative process and the difficulty it raises for killing will receive continued examination by the authors in this inquiry.

⁵³Richard, _Super quatuor_, 3:37:3:2. He teaches the opposite in _Commentum_, 25:5:3. We will look at this discrepancy in the next chapter. Cf. _infra_, p. 54, nt. 42.

⁵⁴Cf., e.g., Bonaventure, _Sermo_ VI, p. 249; Richard, _Super quatuor_, 3:37:3:2.

⁵⁵Joannes Andreae, _Decretalium libros novellae commentaria_ (Venice: 1581), on _Significasti_, _De homicidio_, where he quotes C. 3.27, and its commentary by Baldus.

⁵⁶Joannes de Lignano, _Tractatus de bello_, LXXXIII, in _Tractatus Illustrium_ (Venice: 1584), Vol. XVI.

⁵⁷Jean Gerson, _Opera_ (Paris: 1606), II, _Regulae Morales_: _De praeceptis decalogi_; _Compendium theologiae_: _2 de decem praeceptis legis, expositio quinti praecepti_; _I, Errores circa praeceptum "non occides"_; Antoninus, _Summa_, 3:4:3:1; 2:7:8:1:v; Panormitanus, _Commentaria in libros decretalium_ (1522), on _Interfecisti_, _De homicidio_ and _Significasti_, _De homicidio_.

⁵⁸J. R. Hale, "Violence in the Late Middle Ages: A Background," in Martines, _Violence_, pp. 23-24, 34-35; John Larner, "Order and Disorder in Romagna: 1450-1500," in Martines, _Violence_, pp. 39-41, 48-50, 63-69; David Herlihy, "Some Psychological and Social Roots of Violence in the Tuscan Cities," in Martines, _Violence_, pp. 129-154; Gene A. Brucker, "The Florentine _Popolo Minuto_ and Its Political Role 1340-1450," in Martines, _Violence_, pp. 163-166; Cecilia Mary Ady, "Florence and North Italy, 1414-1492," in _The Cambridge Medieval History_, Vol. VIII, _The Close of the Middle Ages_, eds. C. W. Previté-Orton and Z. N. Brooke (Cambridge: 1936); C. G. Coulton, _Medieval Village, Manor and Monastery_ (New York: 1960).

⁵⁹Hale, "Violence," pp. 23-24.

⁶⁰Gerson, Regulae Morales; Antoninus, Summa, 3:4:3:1.

⁶¹Bernard Häring, The Law of Christ, Vol. I, trans. Edwin G. Kaiser (Westminster, Maryland: 1964), p. 16.

⁶²Panormitanus, Decretalium, on Significasti, De homicidio.

⁶³Antoninus, Summa, 2:7:8:2:4 and 5.

⁶⁴Sylvester Prieras, Summa (Venice: 1601), I, Bellum II, 1; Dominic Soto, De Justitia et Jure (Lyons: 1558), 5:1:8; Diego de Covarrubias y Leyva, Opera (Lyons: 1568), I, In Clementina, Si furiosus, De homicidio, pp. 782-783; Navarrus (Martin de Azpilcueta), Enchiridion sive Manuale Confessoriorum et Poenitentium (Venice: 1579), 15:3; Molina, De Justitia et Jure, in Opera Omnia (Geneva: 1733), III:4:3:11; Antoninus Diana, Coordinatus deu Omnes Resolutiones Morales (Lyons: 1680), 8:5:1; Busembaum, Medulla, I:3:4:1:3; Alphonsus, Moralis, I:3:4:1:3, n. 380.

⁶⁵Sylvester, Summa, Bellum II, 2. According to Haring, Law of Christ, Vol. I, p. 16, Sylvester's Summa ranks with the Summula of Cajetan as the best of the sixteenth century. Sylvester's extension of Panormitanus' teaching is based on the commentary of Bartolus on Item apud labeonem, ff., De injuria.

⁶⁶Covarrubias, In Clementina, p. 784. One who teaches this is Soto, De Justitia, 5:1:8; the illustrious person need not flee, while clerics and monks must.

⁶⁷Leonard Lessius, De Justitia et Jure (Lyons: 1653), 2:9:8, n. 44; Diana, Resolutiones, 8:5:1; Busembaum, Medulla, I:3:4:1:3.
Lessius (1554-1623) was a Jesuit moralist who taught at Louvain; his De Justitia et Jure is the most famous and original of his works, especially on issues of economics.

⁶⁸Lessius, De Justitia, 2:9:12.

⁶⁹Alphonsus, Moralis, I:3:4:1:3, n. 381-382.

⁷⁰Cf. infra, p. 130-131.

⁷¹Cajetan, Summa, II-II:64:7, repeats the teaching of Thomas that defensive killing is "consequent and per accidens." We will see further on that he applies this teaching to the defense of property. Thomas is also reaffirmed

by the Salamancans, <u>Cursus</u>, VI:25:1:4, n. 83, as he had been two centuries earlier by Antoninus, <u>Summa</u>, 2:7:8:1:v. Francisco de Vitoria (d.1546), <u>De Justitia</u> (Madrid: 1934), I, II-II:64:2, n. 10; II-II:64:7, n. 1, also agrees with Thomas; but he misunderstands him to be speaking of means, while Thomas is concerned with the end.

[72] Soto, <u>De Justitia</u>, 5:1:8; Navarrus, <u>Manuale</u>, 15; Molina, <u>Opera</u>, III:4:3:11; Diana, <u>Resolutiones</u>, 8:5:19; Lessius, <u>De Justitia</u>, 2:9:8, n. 53.

[73] Soto, <u>De Justitia</u>, 5:1:8, gives as authorizing his position, Aristotle, <u>Ethics</u>, Bk. 6. But this book is on virtue and the <u>mean</u>, the middle path, between extremes, it is not considering <u>means</u> to an <u>end</u>. Cf. Aristotle, <u>Ethics</u>, trans. J. A. K. Thomas (Baltimore: 1953).

[74] Thomas, <u>Summa</u>, I-II:8 and 11-16.

[75] In the seventeenth century Pascal answered these questions affirmatively and condemned the teaching. Cf. <u>The Provincial Letters</u>, trans. J. A. K. Thomson (New York: 1941).

[76] Cf. <u>supra</u>, pp. 20-21.

[77] Thomas, <u>Summa</u>, II-II:64-7.

[78] Cf. <u>supra</u>, pp. 27-32.

[79] Antoninus, <u>Summa</u>, 3:4:3:1. The earlier formulation of the due moderation principle by Joannes de Lignano is the equivalent of that of Antoninus: "the equivalent to that violence brought in quality of arms at the time." He states this definition to be "according to doctors commonly." Cf. Lignano, <u>Tractatus</u>,CXXI.

[80] Panormitanus, <u>Decretalium</u>, on <u>Significasti</u>, <u>De homicidio</u>.

[81] Cajetan, <u>Summa</u>, II-II:64:7, Sylvester, <u>Summa</u>, <u>Bellum</u> II, 1; Navarrus, <u>Manuale</u>, 15:3.

[82] Navarrus, <u>Manuale</u>, 15:3. In the next century Lessius gives the same explanation for due moderation. Cf. <u>De Justitia</u>, 2:9:8, n. 43.

[83] Diana, <u>Resolutiones</u>, 8:5:1. Diana is today considered a laxist, relying too heavily on external circumstances and too little upon moral principles. This case is a clear example of his emphasis.

FOOTNOTES

CHAPTER II

[1] c.5, C.33, q.2. Nicholas I was pope from 858-867.

[2] c.6, C.33, q.2.

[3] c.9, C.33, q.2, which quotes *De Adulterinis conjugiis*, 2:15. Cf. Augustine, *Adulterous Marriages*, in *The Fathers of the Church*, Vol. 27, trans. Charles T. Heugelmeyer, M. M. (New York: 1955), 2:15.

[4] Alexander, *Summa*, IV:3:2:4:1:6:2:3, p. 855.

[5] Thomas, *Summa*, Vol. III, *Supplement*, 60:1. The *Supplement* to the *Summa* of Thomas was an attempt to complete the unfinished work of Thomas by a compilation of material from his commentary on the fourth book of the *Sentences* of Peter Lombard. This commentary was completed by Thomas c. 1256, some ten years before the *Summa* was begun. 60:1 is from *IV Sentences*, 37.

[6] Thomas, *Supplement*, 60:1, where Thomas notes that according to civil law it was unlawful for a wife to kill her husband if she caught him in adultery. He concludes that since husband and wife are to be judged on a par (which, apparently, the civil law did not do), neither can a husband kill his wife. Cf. also c.33, C.32, q.5, which speaks of this parity.

[7] Bonaventure, *Opera*, Vol. VII, *IV Sent.*, 37:2:2.

[8] Cf. *supra*, pp. 3, 6-8, 20-1.

[9] Scotus, *Opera*, XVIII, *Oxon*. IV:15:3:8, p. 375. The commentary of Anthony Hickey, which appeared in 1637, mentions the possibility of public authority establishing the death penalty for adultery in cases where there is notable harm to society. This penalty would be licit because of the added evil (notable harm to society) to the original crime, not because of adultery taken simply in itself. Hickey arrives at this teaching on the basis of Scotus' position that a legislator may adopt the law of

some other legislator (e.g., Moses). Such a law, when established, has its authority not from the original legislator but from the one who established it. The difficulty with Hickey's teaching is that he ignores Scotus' statement that every human law must be compatible with Divine law. Since Scotus had declared killing for adultery contrary to Divine law, he would consider Hickey's application invalid; any human law which would impose death for adultery would be contrary to Divine law.

[10] The story of the adulterous woman in the Gospel of John (8:1-11) is today considered by Biblical scholars to be a later addition to the original Gospel text. The passage is said to have been introduced into the Gospel in the third century and to have gained liturgical acceptance by about the fifth century. The scholars agree in postulating as the reason for delayed acceptance the ease of forgiveness in the passage, which was difficult to reconcile with the stern penitential discipline of the early Church. The passage was accepted as authentic by the Western Church from the third century, but it was not incorporated into the standard Greek texts until about the tenth century. Jerome (d.419-420) had included the story in the Vulgate in the late fourth century. Cf. Raymond E. Brown, S.S., The Gospel According to John (I-XII), The Anchor Bible (Garden City, New York: 1966), pp. 335-338; Rudolf Schnackenburg, The Gospel According to St. John, Vol. I, trans. Kevin Smyth (New York: 1968), pp. 181-182; C. K. Barrett, The Gospel According to St. John (London: 1962), pp. 490-491; Rudolf Bultmann, The Gospel of John, gen. ed. G. R. Bensley-Murray, trans. R. W. N. Hoare and S. K. Riches (Philadelphia: 1971), p. 312.

The question which this passage raises for us, however, is why it was considered to be a _law_. Why would a particular event in the Gospel be accepted as law while other passages, such as the Sermon on the Mount, formulated in a more legalistic style (". . . but I say to you, do not . . .") not be taken as law? I would suggest that the reason was the context in which the passage entered the text of the Gospel. In the third century the rigorist movement called Montanism was widespread and, especially through Tertullian, attacking the Church for what it considered laxity in forgiving those guilty of sins of the flesh, specifically adultery. It appears likely that the Church would seek justification for its merciful approach to penitent adulterers. It would also be likely that such mercy would be understood as binding, as the "Gospel law," to reinforce the Church's rejection and condemnation of Montanist rigorism, specifically Tertullian's teaching that the Church had no power to forgive the sin of adultery. In his view, adultery was an irremissible sin, and, significantly, he does not mention the Johannine passage in his works cited below. Cf. Tertullian, On Penitence and on Purity, in Ancient Christian Writers, Vol. 28, trans. William P. Le Saint, S. J. (Westminster, Maryland: 1959); Bernard Poschmann, Penance and the Anointing of the Sick, trans. and rev. Francis Courtney, S.J. (New York: 1964), pp. 36-48; Paul F. Palmer, S.J., Sacraments and Forgiveness, in Sources of Christian Theology, Vol. II (Westminster, Maryland: 1959), p. 378.

[11] For a brief summary, Cf. Frederick Copleston, S.J., *A History of Philosophy*, Vol. 2, Part 2, *Albert the Great to Duns Scotus* (Garden City, New York: 1962), pp. 204ff; "Duns Scotus, John," in *NCE*, Vol. 4.

[12] *Supra*, p. 40; cf. c.9, C.33, q.2.

[13] Augustine, *Adulterous Marriages*, 2:6.

[14] Cajetan, *Summa*, II-II:64:2; cf. *infra*, pp. 46-47.

[15] Panormitanus, *Decretalium*, on *Interfecisti, De homicidio*; Antoninus, *Summa*, 2:7:8:8.

[16] *Authenticum, Ut nulli judicum*, Constitutio 128:10, *Corpus juris civilis*. The *Authenticum* is a collection of laws gathered after the publication of the revised Code of Justinian in 534 A.D. The last law incorporated dates from the year 556. The collection was given its name by medieval scholars. Cf. P. Vinogradoff, *Roman Law in Medieval Europe* (Oxford: 1929), p. 58; "Roman Law, History of," in *NCE*, Vol. 12, p. 594.

[17] Sylvester, *Summa, Homicidium* I, 5:5 and 6.

[18] Cajetan, *Summa*, II-II:64:2; Vitoria, *De Justitia*, II-II:64:2, n. 3, 4. 9.

[19] In Thomas' view of law, the Ten Commandments are the moral precepts governing Christian behavior; they are further specified for daily living by human reason. Cajetan and Vitoria follow him. Cf. *supra*, pp. 67-68.

[20] Vitoria, *De Justitia*, II-II:64:3, n. 3.

[21] Cf. *supra*, pp. 32-34, 35-36.

[22] Lessius, *De Justitia*, 2:9:5.

[23] Busembaum, *Medulla*, I:3:4:1:2, n. 1.

[24] Alphonsus, *Moralis*, I:3:4:1:2, n. 376.

[25] Henricus Denzinger and Adolfus Schönmetzer, S.J., *Enchiridion Symbolorum Definitionum et Declarationum De Rebus Fidei et Morum* (Barcelona: 1963), n. 2039. This proposition is one of a long list of laxist propositions condemned by Alexander VII (1665), nos. 2021-2065. For further examples of the attempt to remove laxism from moral teaching, see the propositions condemned by Innocent XI, nos. 2101-2166.

²⁶Because of the numerous references to the laws of the <u>Decretales</u>, these will not be explored until they are met in the various authors.

²⁷c.1-6, C.23, q.8. Cf. especially Pars I and c.6.

²⁸c.6, C.23, q.8.

²⁹Alexander, <u>Summa</u>, IV:2:3:2:1:2:5:2:2:2, pp. 532-533.

³⁰Alexander, <u>Summa</u>, IV:2:3:2:1:2:5:2:3, pp. 535-538.

³¹D.50, c.5.

³²D.50, c.36. Lérida (N. E. Spain) was the site of a Council in 546 A.D.

³³D.50, c.8.

³⁴Ex. 32:25-29.

³⁵I Mc. 2:23-26

³⁶Acts. 5:1-11.

³⁷c.12 and 13, C.15, q.1.

³⁸Alexander, <u>Summa</u>, IV:2:3:2:1:2:5:2:3, pp. 535-538; c.7-8, 18, C.23, q.8; <u>c.41</u>, C.23, q.5.

³⁹Hostiensis, <u>Decretalium</u>, on <u>Significasti</u>, <u>De homicidio</u>; Raymund, <u>Summa</u>, 2:1:8:5.

⁴⁰Hostiensis, <u>Decretalium</u>, on <u>Significasti</u>, <u>De homicidio</u>; Raymund, <u>Summa</u>, 2:1:1.

⁴¹<u>Significasti</u>, <u>De homicidio</u>, X. 5.12.18, does speak of the need for penance "just to be sure" (<u>ad cautelam</u>) in a case of licit killing by a priest.

⁴²Richard, <u>Commentum</u>, 25:5:3. In <u>Super Quatuor</u>, 3: 37:3:2, Richard says that a cleric cannot kill to defend himself because of "ecclesiastical regulation." His words are <u>nullatenus licet</u>" "it is never licit." Is this rule to be understood as making sinful self-defensive killing by a cleric? In the light of his remarks on <u>Interfecisti</u>, it would not seem so. <u>Interfecisti</u> says that penance is to be done "just in case"; penance is not required. Richard may be using <u>nullatenus licet</u> merely as an indication of the

presence of an ecclesiastical irregularity.

[43] D.50, c.5; Thomas, *Summa*, II-II:64:7.

[44] Thomas, *Summa*, II-II:64:4.

[45] Cf., e.g., II-II:64:5.

[46] Thomas, *Summa*, II-II:64:7.

[47] Thomas, *Summa*, II-II:64:3.

[48] Andreae, *Decretalium*, on *Significasti*, *De homicidio*.

[49] Lignano, *De Bello*, LXXXV.

[50] D.46, c.8.

[51] X. 5.12.10. This decretal will play an important role in the development of the teaching on killing in defense of property.

[52] X. 2.13.12.

[53] *In Clem.* 5.4.1.

[54] X. 5.39.3. This decretal repeats the principle of repelling force with force. There is no mention, however, of a cleric acting in self-defense. Consequently, the use of this law to support clerical self-defense is indirect: if a layman can kill to defend himself, a cleric can do the same. In conjunction with *Si furiosus* and the natural law principle, this conclusion might be drawn; but *Si vero aliquis* does not of itself refer to clerics.

[55] Herr, *Medieval World*, pp. 210-221.

[56] Lignano, *De Bello*, CXVII.

[57] Panormitanus, *Decretalium*.

[58] X. 5.12.6; 5.12.10; 5.12.18.

[59] The penalty is to be perpetually barred from the ministry of the altar, from reading liturgical lessons, and from chanting in the clerical choir. These clerics are to be banished to a monastery and are forbidden from entering a church for five or seven years.

⁶⁰Panormitanus remarks that to kill in self-defense carries no irregularity with it. The absence of irregularity is consistently rooted by others in Si furiosus, De homicidio (In Clem. 5.4.1); although Panormitanus does not refer to this decretal, it may be taken as the legal basis for his statement.

⁶¹Panormitanus does not expand this teaching beyond noting the lack of "inevitable necessity." When he comments on Significasti, De homicidio, he says that a cleric must flee when he can to avoid killing an aggressor. Thus it might be said that Panormitanus recognizes the possibility of flight as always present when property or someone else's life is at stake. Why there is no obligation to defend the endangered life of another is not explained.

⁶²It is in this context that Panormitanus' teaching on due moderation occurs: if one knows he cannot or is doubtful about his ability to observe moderation, he cannot repel with violence. Cf. supra, p. 35.

⁶³Antoninus, Summa, 3:4:3; cf. also 3:4:2:6, where Lignano is referred to as legitimating killing in self-defense by a cleric.

⁶⁴Antoninus, Summa, 3:4:2:6.

⁶⁵C.23, q.8, passim; X. 2.13.12.

⁶⁶A certain cynicism is a possible response to this teaching of Antoninus. But it also seems possible that what he was trying to avoid was clerical cooperation in ecclesiastically unauthorized warfare, i.e., either in a war against the pope or the Church, or in what would have been judged an unjust war. The teaching does not necessarily mean that clerics could only cooperate in wars fought by or for the pope.

⁶⁷Antoninus, Summa, 3:4:2:7. He refers to c.8, C.23, q.5; c.2, C.23, q.3; c.7, C.23, q.8. All of these are examples of Church prelates asking secular princes to fight in their behalf.

⁶⁸Cf. supra, pp. 55-56, Thomas, Summa, II-II:40.

⁶⁹Antoninus, Summa, 2:7:8:1.

⁷⁰Sylvester, Summa, Bellum II, 3; Homicidium I, 8; Cajetan, Summa, II-II:64:4 and 7; Vitoria, De Justitia, II-II:64:4, 1, 7, 9; Soto, De Justitia, 5:1:4 and 8; Covarrubias, In Clementina, p. 782; Molina, Opera, III:4:3:16 (where he incorrectly states that Covarrubias agrees with

him on the property-aspect of the question); Lessius, De Justitia, 2:9:11, n. 66-67, 72-73; Diana, Resolutiones, 8:5: 1 and 29; Busembaum, Medulla, I:3:3:1:3, n. 5; Alphonsus, Moralis, I:3:4:1:3, n. 380, 382.

[71] Soto, De Justitia, 5:1:4, also speaks of this restriction. His basis, however, is the Decretum, D.45, c.2 and 7; c.1, C.23, q.8, and not Thomas. For Soto the restriction is only an ecclesiastical one. Cf. Vitoria, De Justitia, II-II:64:4, n. 1.

[72] Diana, Resolutiones, 8:5:1; Alphonsus, Moralis, I:3:4:1:3, n. 380.

[73] X. 5.12.18.

[74] X. 2.13.12; 5.12.10; 5.12.2. This last decretal, Interfecisti, De homicidio, is most important in the development of the teaching on killing in defense of property. The full discussion of the various interpretations given to this law will be undertaken in the next chapter. Here there will be just an indication of its use in the question of clerics, which, as has been noted, was absorbed into the question of anyone killing to defend property.

[75] Sylvester, Summa, Bellum II, 1; Molina, Opera, III:4:3:16; Lessius, De Justitia, 2:9:11, n. 66; Diana, Resolutiones, 8:5:29.

[76] Cf. supra, p. 57.

[77] Cf. supra, pp. 57-58, 60-61.

[78] Covarrubias, In Clementina, p. 785; Molina, Opera, III:4:3:16.

[79] Cf. infra, pp. 119-120.

[80] Cf. supra, pp. 182-183, n. 42.

[81] Sylvester, Summa, Homicidium I, 8; Cajetan, Summa, II-II:64:7; Lessius, De Justitia, 2:9:11, n. 66.

[82] Cf. infra, pp. 115-119.

[83] Busembaum, Medulla, I:3:4:1:3, n. 5; Alphonsus, Moralis, I:3:4:1:3, n. 382.

[84] If the influence of Jn. 8:1-11 goes beyond the men mentioned, the ecclesiastical lawmakers and interpreters do not directly mention it.

[85] Thomas, _Summa_, I-II:90-114. For Questions 90-105, the edition used is Blackfriars, Vol. 28, ed. and trans. Thomas Gilby, O.P. (New York: 1966); Vol. 29, eds. and trans. Davis Bourke and Arthur Littledale (New York: 1969).
For a more lengthy yet concise summary of Thomas on the nature of law, cf. John T. Noonan Jr., _The Scholastic Analysis of Usury_ (Cambridge, Mass.: 1957), pp. 21-28.

[86] Thomas, _Summa_, I-II:91:1; 93:1.

[87] Thomas, _Summa_, I-II:94:2.

[88] Thomas, _Summa_, I-II:91:2.

[89] Thomas, _Summa_, I-II:91:3 and 4.

[90] Thomas, _Summa_, I-II:91:3; 97:1-4.

[91] Thomas, _Summa_, I-II:91:3.

[92] Thomas, _Summa_, I-II:91:4; 107:1 and 2.

[93] Thomas, _Summa_, I-II:106:1.

[94] Thomas, _Summa_, I-II:106:4; 108:2.

[95] Thomas, _Summa_, I-II:107:3; 100:1 and 2. According to Alexander, the moral precepts of the Gospel and the Old Law are generally **not** contained in the law of nature. The example he gives is the Gospel law of loving enemies in contrast to the love of friends demanded by the law of nature. He considers the natural law to be contained in the Law and the Gospel, but not that everything found in the Law and Gospel agrees with natural law. Cf. _Summa_, IV:3:2:4:1:4, pp. 843-844.

[96] Noonan, _Usury_, p.27, remarks: "Such an identification, it is clear, could work in one of two directions. On the one hand, any act prohibited by the Christian tradition could be treated as if it were evil by nature, not by positive law. On the other hand, any act not naturally demonstrable as evil could be considered as not prohibited by Christian teaching. The early scholastics—not without exceptions—incline to measure moral demands by what is demonstrably rational."

[97] The interdependence of the various types of law is expressed by Alexander as follows: natural moral law says what is to be done; human moral law tells the manner in which the "good" is to be done; Divine law gives the "final cause," the "because of which" the "good" is to be done. In the Old Law the final cause was reverence; in the New Law it

is love. Cf. *Summa*, IV:3:2:3:2:1:1:1, p. 415. Traces of the mutual dependence of types of law are also found in Bonaventure, Vol. V, *III Sent*. 37:1:3; Vol. VII, *Breviloquium*, V:9; Vol. VIII, *Compendium*, 5:59; Vol. IX, *Principium*, pp. 9b-10a; *Illuminationes*, *Sermo* XXI; Vol. VI, *IV Sent*. 37:2:2.

[98]Thomas, *Summa*, I-II:99.2.

[99]Thomas, *Summa*, I-II:91:5. Cf. also Alexander, *Summa*, IV:3:2:4:1:3, pp. 841-842; IV:3:2:4:1:5, pp. 845-846; IV:3:2:3:1:3:1, p. 398; Bonaventure, Vol. V, *III Sent*. 40: 1:1 and 3; Scotus, *Opera*, XV, *Oxon*. III:40, p. 1083.

[100]Thomas, *Summa*, I-II:99:2-4. Cf. also Alexander, *Summa*, IV:3:2:4:2, p. 880; Scotus, *Opera*, XV, *Oxon*. III: 40:1, p. 1084.

[101]Thomas, *Summa*, I-II:103:3.

[102]Thomas, *Summa*, I-II:108:2.

[103]Thomas, *Summa*, I-II:106:1.

[104]Thomas, *Summa*, I-II:107:1.

[105]Thomas, *Summa*, I-II:107:2; 92:1.

[106]Thomas, *Summa*, I-II:108:2. Cf. also Alexander, *Summa*, IV:3:2:4:1:8, p. 866.

[107]Thomas, *Summa*, I-II:108:1 and 2. He does say that some of the external acts which flow from the promptings of grace are necessarily connected with that grace. The example he gives is Mt. 10:32-33: "Whoever acknowledges me before men I will acknowledge before my Father in heaven. Whoever disowns me before men I will disown before my Father in heaven." This is considered by Thomas to be a binding precept. Scotus also understands the judicial precepts to be absent in the New Law. He says, however, that in the New Law the "law of gentleness and humanity is greater." Cf. *Opera*, XV, *Oxon*. III:40:1, p. 1084.

[108]Thomas, *Summa*, I-II:108:2, where Augustine, *De Sermo Domini in Monte*, 1:19, is cited. Cf. Augustine, *Commentary on the Sermon on the Mount*, *The Fathers of the Church*, Vol. 11, trans. Denis J. Kavanagh, O.S.A. (New York: 1951), p. 85.

[109]Thomas, *Summa*, I-II:108:4.

[110] Thomas, Summa, I-II:107:2.

[111] Thomas, Summa, I-II:108:3.

[112] It is interesting that Alexander, though teaching the same "internalness" for the Sermon on the Mount, remarks that the Old Law intended to order interior attitude by legislating exterior action. However, since the "ordering" of man proceeds from interior to exterior, the Gospel, as completing and fulfilling the Old Law, intends through interior disposition to order exterior acts. Cf. Summa, IV:3:2:4:1:3, p. 843. Despite this, Alexander, with Thomas, follows Augustine in teaching that "just vindication" is not sinful, though "it would be better" if none were taken. The "better" is in no way binding. Cf. Summa, IV:3:2:4:1:8, p. 866.

[113] Besides the need to deal with the teaching of the Sermon on the Mount witnessed by Thomas, Summa, I-II:106-108, and Alexander, Summa, IV:3:2:4:1:3-3:2:4:2:3:4:3, pp. 841-919, see for more contemporary approaches: Joachim Jeremias, The Sermon on the Mount, trans. Norman Perrin (London: 1961); K. Graystone, "Sermon on the Mount," in The Interpreter's Dictionary of the Bible, Vol. 4, ed. George Arthur Buttrick (New York: 1962), pp. 279-288; Archibald M. Hunter, A Pattern for Life: An Exposition of the Sermon on the Mount, rev. ed. (Philadelphia: 1965); Rudolf Schnackenburg, The Moral Teaching of the New Testament, trans. J. Holland-Smith and W. J. O'Hara (New York: 1971), pp. 59-88; John J. McKenzie, S.J., "Law in the New Testament," in The Jurist, 26 (1966), pp. 167-180; Günther Bornkamm, Jesus of Nazareth, trans. Irene and Fraser McLuskey with James M. Robinson (New York: 1960), pp. 221-225; Bernard Häring, "The Normative Value of the Sermon on the Mount," in The Catholic Biblical Quarterly, 29:3 (1967), pp. 69-79 (375-385); Charles E. Curran, "The Relevancy of the Ethical Teaching of Jesus," in his A New Look at Christian Morality (Notre Dame, Indiana: 1970), pp. 1-23. In these contemporary authors it is clear that the discussion is by no means over. It is also very clear that some definite relationship to behavior is recognized in the Sermon on the Mount.

[114] Jeremias, Sermon, pp. 32-33; Graystone, "Sermon," p. 288b; Bornkamm, Jesus, pp. 224-225; Hunter, Pattern, pp. 114-118.

[115] Jeremias, Sermon, pp. 20-24, 30-31; Hunter, Pattern, pp. 114-118; Schnackenburg, Moral Teaching, pp. 87-88; McKenzie, "Law," pp. 171, 176; Häring, "Normative Value," pp. 70-72.

[116] Schnackenburg, Moral Teaching, pp. 83-84; Hunter, Pattern, pp. 95-96; McKenzie, "Law," p. 176.

[117] Jeremias, *Sermon*, pp. 27-29; Graystone, "Sermon," p. 287b; Schnackenburg, *Moral Teaching*, pp. 77-78, 80-82.

[118] Jeremias, *Sermon*, pp. 27-28, who understands this command to refer specifically to refraining from making a complaint under civil law in a matter concerning profession of faith; Graystone, "Sermon," p. 287b, which grasps the teaching to be "do not seek damages for injury"; Hunter, *Pattern*, p. 57, where he speaks of non-retaliation in cases of being personally wronged; Häring, "Normative Value," p. 77, who views the statement to be the fundamental directive on non-violence "in the sense of the ultimately all-conquering power of intense and selfless love."

[119] Häring, "Normative Value," pp. 74-76. His term is <u>goal commandments</u>, which are norms for an organized action toward clearly defined goals; these norms are contrasted with the limitative, <u>fulfillment commandments</u> of the Decalogue, which are minimal standards.

[120] The obligatory character of the statements of Jesus in the Sermon on the Mount—that they obligate behavior and not simply attitude—is also present in the medieval Scholastics, but it is there in the "objections," which are then refuted or "distinguished" into merely internal disposition—and thus into practical oblivion.

[121] Hunter, *Pattern*, p. 49; Schnackenburg, *Moral Teaching*, p. 88.

[122] Alexander, *Summa*, IV:3:2:4:2, p. 880, says that the Sermon on the Mount contains moral precepts binding on all. But he continues to the common position of making "binding" equal "counsel," with the "perfect-imperfect" dichotomy.

[123] Cf. also Bonaventure, Vol. VIII, *Compendium*, LXX; Alexander, *Summa*, IV:3:2:4:1:8, p. 866; IV:3:2:4:2:3: 2:1, pp. 899-902.

[124] Curran, "Relevancy," p. 14; cf. also Raymund of Pennaforte's position, <u>supra</u>, pp. 21-22.

[125] There is current among theologians and ethicists a debate over the relationship between Christian morality and a guide for behavior based on a valid natural morality. What is it that distinguishes Christian morality? The trend in this discussion is toward viewing the Gospel as giving man a vision of his total vocation, in which what is authentically human becomes more explicit and more discoverable. From this vision and discovery follow attitudes and intentions on which can be built a manner of accomplishing moral tasks which the Christian has in common with others. In stating that the Sermon on the Mount constitutes the

Christian people, I mean to say that these passages of the Gospel are expressive of attitudes and intentions that must lead to a concrete manner of living. The Cross remains the essentially Christian model for living a moral life; it speaks of the "authentically human" in most explicit terms: self-giving. The type of self-giving which the Sermon on the Mount demands is not contrary to what natural law demands, but, in the Christian vision, it brings natural law to its fulfillment by making what is truly human more explicit. Cf. Charles E. Curran, "Is There A Distinctively Christian Social Ethic?" in *Metropolis: Christian Presence and Responsibility*, ed. Philip D. Morris (Notre Dame, Indiana: 1970). The same article may be found in *Chicago Studies* 9 (1970), pp. 59-80; Richard A. McCormick, S.J., "Notes on Moral Theology," in *Theological Studies*, 32:1 (1971), pp. 71-78; John Macquarrie, *Three Issues in Ethics* (New York: 1970); and the bibliographies in McCormick and Macquarrie.

[126] Thomas, *Summa*, I-II:91:4; 100:2.

[127] Thomas, *Summa*, I-II:95:1.

[128] Thomas, *Summa*, I-II:96:2.

[129] Thomas, *Summa*, I-II:96:2.

[130] Despite the abrogation of the Old Law's judicial precepts, we will find in the next chapter a continuous use of one of these precepts (Ex. 22:1-2) as the basis for killing in defense of property.

[131] Thomas, *Summa*, I-II:108:1. Thomas gives an example of "precepts necessary for an operative faith," Mt. 10:32-33 (cf. *supra*, nt. 107). Any further specification of actions necessarily flowing from the profession is not undertaken. Other "acts" are considered "not necessarily opposed to, or in keeping with faith that works through love."

[132] Cf. *supra*, p. 7.

[133] Cajetan, *Summa*, II-II:64:2.

FOOTNOTES

CHAPTER III

[1] Raymund, *Summa*, 2:5:1, 2:6:1; Hostiensis, *Summa Aurea*, *Quid fit furtum*, *De furtis*, and *Quis fit raptor*, *De raptoribus rerum*; Joannes Andreae, *Decretalium*, on *Fures*, *De furtis*; Panormitanus, *Decretalium*, on *Fures*, *De furtis*.

[2] Alexander, *Summa*, IV:2:3:2:1:2:7:1, p. 559, and IV: 2:2:2:2:1:3:4:1:5:2, pp. 699-700; Bonaventure, *Opera*, Vol. V. *IV Sent.*, 3:37:7; Vol. VII, *Centiloquium*, 1:31; Thomas, *Summa*, II-II:66:3 and 4; Scotus, *Opera*, XVIII, *Oxon.* 4:15: 3:8, p. 375.

[3] Panormitanus, *Decretalium*, on *Fures*, *De furtis*; Scotus, *Opera*, XVIII, *Oxon.* 4:15:3:8, p. 375; Thomas, *Summa*, II-II:66:3 and 4.

[4] In this study it will always be clear if the notion of force is present, whether or not the term "robbery" is used. Most often I use "thief" or "theft," as these are the most frequent terms used by the tradition.

[5] Cf. *supra*, pp. 9-36.

[6] If greater good comes to the innocent by not harming the evil, one is to refrain from harming them. Cf. *supra*, pp. 5-6.

[7] Thomas, *Summa*, II-II:64:2; Antoninus, *Summa*, 2:7: 8:1:v.

[8] Aristotle, *Politics*, I:2; *Ethics*, VII:6, in *The Basic Works of Aristotle*, ed. Richard McKeon (New York: 1941).

[9] Thomas, *Summa*, II-II:64:3.

[10] Thomas, *Summa*, II-II:66.

[11] Thomas, *Summa*, II-II:66; X. 5.12.2, *Interfecisti*,

De homicidio; 5.17.1, De illis autem, De raptoribus; Raymund, Summa, 2:1:1; Joannes Andreae, Decretalium, on Interfecisti, De homicidio; Panormitanus, Decretalium, on Interfecisti, De homicidio. The same teaching can be found in the late seventeenth century: Salamancans, Cursus, VI:25:1:4, n. 81.

[12] Cf. e.g., Thomas, Summa, I-II:100:8. We might note that the thief killed in the act of theft was not to be prayed for. Cf. c.31, C.13, q.2; Hostiensis, Decretalium, Fures, De furtis. The policy is a blanket one, with no reference to gravity of fault. Obviously, the sin was considered grave.

[13] Thomas, Summa, II-II:66:4.

[14] This translation is from The New American Bible, trans. Members of the Catholic Biblical Association of America (New York: 1970). The note on 22:1ff. says: "This seems to be a fragment of what was once a longer law on housebreaking, which has been inserted here into the middle of a law on stealing animals."
The Jerusalem Bible, gen. ed. Alexander Jones (Garden City, New York: 1966), emphasizes the notion of "blood vengeance," which will be pursued below: "If a thief is caught breaking in and is struck a mortal blow, there is to be no blood-vengeance for him, but there shall be blood-vengeance for him if it was after dawn." The translation of The New English Bible (Oxford and Cambridge: 1970) stresses the idea of legitimacy: "If a burglar is caught in the act and is fatally injured, it is not murder; but if he breaks in after sunrise and is fatally injured, then it is murder."
Bernard S. Jackson, Theft in Early Jewish Law (Oxford: 1972), pp. 203-204, gives the context of this law to be a situation in which the thief is caught on the premises; the law's purpose is to govern the owner's right to defend on his own.
The concept of "bloodguilt" is interpreted by Jackson as "has no blood" and "has blood," the subject being the thief. The sense is: "The killer conquers the blood of the slain opponent. Thus here when the thief is killed at night, the owner may acquire his blood. But when he is killed during the day, such a conquest of blood is illegitimate. The kin of the slain thief may carry out the blood feud, thus delivering the blood of the owner to the thief, who thus again 'has blood.'"

[15] Babylonian Talmud, gen. ed. Rabbi Dr. I. Epstein (London: 1935-1960). It may be noted that according to Baba Kama, 79b (trans. E. W. Kirzner, pp. 451-452), the distinction between the thief and the robber is based on the stealth of the thief and the public nature of the robber's crime. There is no mention of the presence or absence of weapons.

¹⁶Jackson, Theft, pp. 208-209, holds the most important question left open by Ex. 22:1-2 to be the significance of the day-night distinction. The Tannaim (Rabbis of c. 50 B.C. to 200 A.D., whose dicta are to be found in Mishnah, Tosephta, and Baraitha; the Babylonian Talmud is a commentary on the Mishnah and a collection of Baraitha) held that the purpose of the law was to allow the owner to take action to protect his life and the lives of his household, not to protect his property. The very presence of an intruder was a threat to life, for it was impossible to know if he had come to steal or to kill. Even though the provision originally referred not to a house but to intrusion into a sheepfold, the threat to the shepherd's life remains the point.

¹⁷The New American Bible translation is somewhat different. The second part, "in the night he is as a thief," is contained in v. 15b. The whole is: "When there is no light the murderer rises, to kill the poor and needy [v.14]. . . . In the night the thief roams about, and he puts a mask over his face [v.15b]; in the dark he breaks into houses [16a]."

¹⁸Pesahim 2b (trans. Rabbi Dr. H. Freedman, p. 3). The bracketed words are the work of the translator.

¹⁹Yoma 85a (trans. Rabbi Dr. Leo Jung, p. 420).

²⁰Trans. Rabbi Dr. H. Freedman, II, pp. 491-492.

²¹Jackson, Theft, pp. 209-210, judges the opinion which forbids killing when there is doubt to be a minority dissent which was rejected by the majority of teachers. The trend in rabbinic interpretation was to extend the rights of the owner. The effect of allowing killing when doubtful would be minimal in nighttime cases, as it would be easy to claim doubt regarding intention. The effect on daytime situations would be greater. A literal reading of the Biblical text held the defender always liable; the interpretation according to intention would have created a whole category of cases in which the defender would not be liable for daylight killing.

²²Sanhedrin, 72a (II, p. 489), teaches that the thief is to be assumed to have considered opposition by the victim and to have decided to kill if opposed.

²³The issue which arises from the text is whether the distinction between day and night was to make conclusive presumptions as to the intruder's intent, so as to allow the ignoring of other factors, or were the presumptions rebuttable, as the Tannaim understood. Cf. Jackson, Theft, pp. 209-210.

[24] Mekhilta, ad Ex. 22:2. Cited by Jackson, Theft, p. 209.

[25] Mekhilta, ad Ex. 21:13. Cited by Jackson, Theft, p. 209.

[26] Mekhilta, ad Ex. 22:2. Cited by Jackson, Theft, p. 212.

[27] D. 28.8.9. The Lex Cornelia dates from 67 B.C.

[28] D. 48.8.9, nt. Y, in Digestum Novum seu Pandectarum Juris Civilis (Venice: n.d.). Accursius was one of the outstanding glossators in the first half of the thirteenth century (d.1263). His work of selecting from and resolving conflicts in earlier glosses received wide acceptance. His glosses are known as the Glossa ordinaria, or simply the Glossa. These were added to all the stereotype Bolognese manuscripts of the Corpus Juris Civilis, and were reprinted in many editions of the Corpus Juris Civilis up to 1627. Cf. "Roman Law, History of" in NCE, Vol. 12, p. 604.

[29] D. 47.2.56.

[30] The Twelve Tables was the earliest Roman legislation, traditionally dated 450-449 B.C. It was not a comprehensive code, but a statement of more important legal provisions. Cf. "Roman Law, History of" in NCE, Vol. 12, p. 586.

[31] D. 47.2.56, nt. T, in Digestum Novum.

[32] D. 9.2.4. The Lex Aquilia dates from 286 B.C.

[33] C. 8.4.1.

[34] C. 3.27.1.

[35] X. 5.12.3.

[36] Innocent IV, In quinque libros decretalium (Venice: 1570), on Si perfodiens, De homicidio; Hostiensis, Decretalium, on Si perfodiens, De homicidio; Raymund, Summa, 2:6:2.

[37] Alexander, Summa, IV:3:2:3:2:1:2:5:2:2:2, p. 531.

[38] Alexander, Summa, IV:3:2:3:2:1:2:5:2:2:2, p. 532.

³⁹Alexander, *Summa*, IV:3:2:4:1:5—3:2:4:1:6:1, pp. 845-848. Cf. Thomas, *Summa*, I-II:108:2; and *supra*, pp. 68-69.

⁴⁰Alexander, *Summa*, IV:2:3:2:2:1:3:4:3, p. 695.

⁴¹Alexander, *Summa*, IV:2:3:2:2:1:3:4:3, p. 695. "Robber" is here understood to employ the use of force and weapons, and so to create a threat to life.

⁴²Thomas, *Summa*, II-II:64:7.

⁴³E.g., Cajetan, *Summa*, II-II:64:7; Vitoria, *De Justitia*, II-II:64:2 and 7; Salamancans, *Cursus*, VI:25:1:4, n. 83; Alphonsus, *Moralis*, I:3:4:1:3, n. 380. Covarrubias, *In Clementina*, p. 785, understands Thomas to legitimate killing for property only when there is a threat to life present.

⁴⁴Aristotle, *Ethics*, I:8-10; IV:1, in which wealth provides the means to the virtue of generosity. Cf. Hans Baron, "Franciscan Poverty and Civic Wealth as Factors in the Rise of Humanistic Thought," *Speculum* 13 (1938), p. 3.

⁴⁵Thomas, *Summa*, I-II:59:3, II-II:125:4. In both places Thomas makes frequent reference to Aristotle's *Ethics*; such reference is absent in II-II:64:7. Cf. Herr, *Intellectual History*, pp. 146-153. Herr also refers to Thomas, *Quodlibetalis*, VI:10:14, and *Summa Contra Gentiles*, III:123-126, 136, for attacks on the condemnation of wealth and the glorification of poverty.

⁴⁶John F. McGovern, "The Rise of New Economic Attitudes—Economic Humanism, Economic Nationalism—During the Later Middle Ages and the Renaissance, A.D. 1200-1550," *Traditio* 26 (1970), pp. 224-225; Baron, "Franciscan Poverty," pp. 3-4; P. Boissonnade, *Life and Work in Medieval Europe*, trans. Eileen Power (New York: 1964), pp. 162-194.

⁴⁷Thomas, *Summa*, II-II:108:1-3.

⁴⁸"Revenge" is the word used by the Dominican edition of the *Summa* for the Latin Vulgate quoted by Thomas, II-II:108:1. The Vulgate has: *Deus non faciet vindictam electorum suorum*. . . .

⁴⁹Thomas, *Summa*, II-II:108:1.

⁵⁰Thomas, *Summa*, II-II:108:2.

⁵¹Thomas, *Summa*, II-II:108:2.

[52] Thomas, *Summa*, II-II:108:3.

[53] Thomas, *Summa*, II-II:108:3.

[54] Cf. Larner, "Order and Disorder," in Martines, *Violence*, pp. 65-67.

[55] Richard, *Super Quatuor*, III:37:3:2.

[56] Cf. *supra*, p. 23; and "Richard of Middleton," in *NCE*, Vol. 12.

[57] Scotus, *Opera*, XVIII, *Oxon.* 4:15:3:8, p. 375.

[58] Scotus, *Opera*, XVIII, *Oxon*, 4:15:3:8, p. 375. Scotus adds what may have been a precautionary note for his position. He says that even if it were true that Mosaic law had allowed killing for theft alone, this law would have been revoked by the mercy of the Gospel. This mercy was clearly at work in the case of adultery (cf. *supra*, pp. 42-44), and even in the Old Testament adultery had been viewed as a more serious crime than theft (Proverbs 6). According to Scotus, since the rigor of the law was lessened in the more serious case, the less serious offense would also be the recipient of Gospel mercy.

[59] Andreae, *Decretalium*, on *Si perfodiens*, *De homicidio*.

[60] D. 9.2.4, *Itaque*, *Ad Legem Aquiliam*; 47.2.56, *Si pignore*, *De furtis*.

[61] "Bartolo de Sassoferrato," in *NCE*, Vol. 2.

[62] Bartolus a Sassoferrato, *Omnium Juris Interpretum Antesignani, Commentaria* (Venice: 1615).

[63] Bartolus, *Commentaria*, Vol. VI, D. 48.8.9.

[64] The same teaching is found in Bartolus' comments on *Unde vi*, C. 8.4.1, *Commentaria*, Vol. VIII: "A person can kill for goods if they cannot otherwise be saved."

[65] McGovern, "New Economic Attitudes," pp. 224-225; Alfred von Martin, *Sociology of the Renaissance,* trans. W. L. Luethens (London: 1944), p. 30.

[66] McGovern, "New Economic Attitudes," pp. 225, 230.

[67] Paolo de Messer Pace da Certaldo, *Il Libro di bouoni costumi* (Florence: 1921). Cf. Christian Bec, *Les Marchands Escrivains a Florence, 1375-1434* (Paris: 1967), pp. 95-111. Bec dates Certaldo's work c. 1360.

[68] Certaldo, *Il Libro,* par. 89, 352, 356, 251.

[69] Certaldo, *Il Libro*, par. 381, 105.

[70] Certaldo, *Il Libro*, par. 276.

[71] Certaldo, *Il Libro*, par. 331, 334, 119.

[72] Bec, *Les Marchands*, pp. 110-111.

[73] von Martin, *Sociology*, pp. 1-8.

[74] von Martin, *Sociology*, pp. 31-40.

[75] Bec, *Les Marchands*, p. 439. Two centuries after the merchant-writers, Covarrubias, *In Clementina*, p. 783, cites Cicero as approving only self-defensive killing. In the next century, three hundred years after the merchant-writers, the Salamancans, *Cursus*, VI:25:1:4, n. 81, refer to Cicero as approving killing to defend property.

[76] Cicero, *De Officiis*, II:21:22, in Richard Schlatter, *Private Property: The History of an Idea* (New Brunswick, New Jersey: 1951), p. 25.

[77] Cicero, *De Officiis*, I:7:16, in Schlatter, *Private Property*, p. 25. Schlatter understands this ambiguity in Cicero to be the consequence of his sympathy with the Stoic theory that equality was the rule in the "golden age of nature."

[78] Schlatter, *Private Property*, p. 26, attributes this idea more directly to Seneca, "Letter 90."

[79] "Things become the private property of individuals in many ways; for the titles by which we acquire ownership in them are some of them titles of natural law, which as we said, is called the law of nations, while some of them are titles of civil law." Justinian, *Institutes*, II:1, quoted by Schlatter, *Private Property*, p. 21.

[80] Schlatter, *Private Property*, p. 32 and ch. 4. For the early Christian period, cf. ch. 3 of Schlatter.

[81] Cf. e.g., Alexander, *Summa*, IV:2:2:3:2, pp. 347-348; Thomas, *Summa*, I-II:57:3, 94:5, 105:2; Schlatter, *Private Property*, pp. 44-45.

[82] Aristotle, *Politics*, II; cf. also Schlatter, *Private Property*, p. 47.

[83] Thomas, *Summa*, I-II:57:3, 94:5, 105:2.

[84] While private ownership might be natural and the more perfect form of ownership for Thomas, he considers common ownership or none at all the most perfect, the most natural form. Sin (and the Fall) makes this most perfect form accessible to only a few, viz., religious. Cf. *Summa Contra Gentiles*, III:2:131-135, and Schlatter, *Private Property*, pp. 54-55.

[85] Giles of Rome wrote his *De Ecclesiastica Potestate* in 1301, to defend and extend Church and papal rights over property in opposition to the claims of temporal rulers. Cf. Giles of Rome, *De Ecclesiastica Potestate* (Scientia Aalen: 1961), esp. II:4.

[86] Cf. John Moorman, *A History of the Franciscan Order From Its Origins to the Year 1517* (Oxford: 1968), esp. Part II, chs. 12-17; Part III, chs. 25-30; Schlatter, *Private Property*, pp. 58-62; Herr, *Intellectual History*, p. 136, mentions Roger Bacon as already expressing in the mid-thirteenth century a typical criticism of the Spiritual Franciscans against the Curia in Rome: "the Curia in Rome has been perverted by the laws of Roman emperors and by secular Roman law."

[87] William of Ockham, *Opus nonaginta dierum*, in *Opera Politica*, ed. J. G. Sikes (Manchester: 1940-1963), Vol. I and II. The *Opus* was probably written in 1333, according to Moorman, *A History*, pp. 323-324; Copelston, *A History*, Vol. 3, Part 1, p. 123, gives that date as probably 1332.

[88] Ockham, *Opus*, ch. 14, in *Opera*, Vol. II. Ockham is said by Herr to be the forerunner of Locke in as much as he is the prophet of the two essential natural rights of humanity: property and freedom. Cf. *Intellectual History*, p. 169.

[89] Copelston, *A History*, Vol. 3, Part 1, p. 125.

[90] Herr, *Intellectual History*, p. 170, mentions the Universities of Paris, Wittenberg, and Erfurt.

[91] Lignano, *De Bello*, CXIIII, CXVII, CXVIII, CXXII.

[92] C. 8.4.1; D. 9.2.45.

[93] Lignano, *De Bello*, CXIIII.

[94] Lignano, *De Bello*, CXIIII. A century later Sir John Fortescue wrote in England: "In the sweat of thy brow thou shalt eat bread; in which words was granted to man a property in the things he should acquire by his labour. . . . For since the bread which a man gained by labour was his own, and no man could eat bread without the sweat of his own brow, every man who toiled not was prohibited from eating the bread which by his own sweat another man had acquired; wherefore property in the bread so gained accrued only to the man who toiled for it . . . and in this way property capable of descent first took rise. . . . Property takes the place of the man's bodily integrity . . . and so thenceforth accompanies his blood." Quoted by Schlatter, *Private Property*, p. 73, from *De Natura Legis Naturae*, in Fortescue's *Works*, II, 32. According to Schlatter, Fortescue provided the combination of medieval theories which would serve the purposes of bourgeois apologists for the next 300-400 years. Cf. *Private Property*, p. 72.

[95] Lignano, *De Bello*, CXVII.

[96] Thomas, *Summa*, I-II:57:3, 94:5, 105:2; cf. Schlatter, *Private Property*, pp. 49-50.

[97] Lignano, *De Bello*, CXXII. The Roman law is found in D. 48.8.9. In making his own case for killing in defense of property at this point, Lignano cites Jacobus de Aretio as one who teaches the same: as long as due moderation is observed, killing is licit for property when there is no other means to recover the impending loss. Despite much searching, I have not been able to identify Jacobus de Aretio. There are references to him in Antoninus, *Summa*, III:4:3:1, and in Sylvester, *Summa*, *Bellum* II, 1, where he is used as Lignano uses him. Cf. also *infra*, nt. 160, p. 203 for a possible reference by Joannes Andreae.

[98] A further limitation is the demand that the person actually possess the goods in question and not just be hoping to possess them sometime in the future; Lignano, *De Bello*, CXVIII. Joined to this demand is the requirement that the person be capable of valid ownership; servants, monks, et al. are excluded from licit killing in defense of property because they cannot own property; *De Bello*, CXVII.

[99] On pp. 57-59, we saw Lignano's teaching on clerics being able to kill in self-defense or for property. There his basis was Church law; here it is Roman law. There he established legitimate self-defense by rejecting New Testament texts; here there is no mention of the New Testament, just a linking of property and self. The initial

rejection remains applicable because of the linkage of self and property: defense of the latter is defense of the former. The absence of the New Testament here may be another indication of the "counsel-character" of the New Testament: it is taken into consideration when clerics, the "more perfect," are the subjects.

[100] Gerson, Opera, I, Errores circa praeceptum "non occides."

[101] Panormitanus, Decretalium, on Si perfodiens, De homicidio.

[102] Panormitanus, Decretalium, on Interfecisti, De homicidio.

[103] D. 9.2.4.

[104] Further weight to the conclusion I have drawn is found in the consistent acceptance of Panormitanus as an opponent of killing for property alone. Cf. Sylvester, Summa, Excommunicatio VI:6:9; Navarrus, Manuale, 15:3; Molina, Opera, III:4:3:16; Diana, Resolutiones, VIII:5:29. Panormitanus' case is opposite that of Thomas (cf. supra, pp. 90-95. If we accept the later understanding of Thomas, he then appears contradictory. With Panormitanus, if we reject the later acceptance of his teaching he is self-contradictory.

[105] Antoninus, Summa, II:7:8:1, p. 864.

[106] The entire passage is: "Fur nocturnus, si discerni, non poterat, quod ad furandum, et non ad occidendum venisset, nec alias poterat deprehendi; potuit occidi. . . ." Antoninus, Summa, II:7:8:1, p. 864.

[107] X. 5.18.2.

[108] Antoninus, Summa, III:4:3:1, p. 225.

[109] Cf. Navarrus, Manuale, 15:3; Lessius, De Justitia, 2:9:11, n. 66. Further grounds for this conclusion can be drawn from Antoninus' position regarding clerics and property. He holds that clerics can kill to defend property. If they can, it seems logical that the laity could. Cf. supra, p. 61. By way of contrast, Panormitanus forbade clerics to kill in this case. Cf. supra, pp. 60-61.

[110] Supra, pp. 29-34, 62.

[111] Cf. Noonan, Usury, pp. 126-128.

[112] Cf. supra, nt. 61, p. 177.

[113] In 1477. Cf. "St. Antoninus," in *NCE*, Vol. 1.

[114] Herr, *Intellectual History*, p. 206.

[115] Lauro Martines, *The Social World of the Florentine Humanists: 1390-1460* (Princeton, New Jersey: 1963), pp. 18-25.

[116] Martines, *Social World*, pp. 283-284. Bruni published a new Latin translation of the *Ethics* in 1417.

[117] von Martin, *Sociology*, pp. 48-51, 77.

[118] Noonan, *Usury*, p. 71.

[119] Noonan, *Usury*, p. 6.

[120] Noonan, *Usury*, pp. 199ff.

[121] M. J. Tooley, "Political Thought and the Theory and Practice of Toleration," in *The New Cambridge Modern History*, Vol. III, *The Counter-Reformation and the Price Revolution, 1559-1610*, ed. R. B. Wernham (Cambridge: 1968), pp. 481, 505-506.

[122] Noonan, *Usury*, pp. 199ff.

[123] H. R. Trevor-Roper, "Religon, the Reformation and Social Change," in his *Religion, the Reformation and Social Change* (London: 1967), esp. pp. 24ff.

[124] Hale, "Violence in the Late Middle Ages," in Martines, *Violence*, pp. 23-35.

[125] F. C. Spooner, "The Economy of Europe 1559-1609," in *The New Cambridge Modern History*, Vol. III, pp. 14-39; Hale, "Violence in the Late Middle Ages," in Martines, *Violence*, p. 23; Larner, "Order and Disorder," in Martines, *Violence*, pp. 39-41.

[126] Hale, "Violence in the Late Middle Ages," in Martines, *Violence*, p. 23.

[127] Sylvester, *Summa*, *Homicidium* I:5:5 and 6, I:8; *Bellum* I:3, II:1, 2 and 8; Cajetan, *Summa*, II-II:64:2 and 7; Navarrus, *Manuale*, 15:3; Molina, *Opera*, III:4:3:11 and 16.

[128] Covarrubias, In Clementina, p. 785.

[129] Sylvester, Summa, Homicidium I:5:5 and 6.

[130] Sylvester, Summa, Bellum I:3, II:1, 3, 8.

[131] Cajetan, Summa, II-II:64:7.

[132] Cf. infra, pp. 121-125.

[133] Navarrus, Manuale, 15:3.

[134] Navarrus, Manuale, 15:5.

[135] Molina, Opera, III:4:3:16.

[136] Molina, Opera, III:4:3:16.

[137] D. 9.2.4.

[138] D. 48.8.9.

[139] Molina, Opera, III:4:3:16, gives as his basis Sed etsi, Ad Legem Aquiliam.

[140] Covarrubias, In Clementina, pp. 785-787.

[141] Covarrubias, In Clementina, p. 786.

[142] D. 47.2.56; 9.2.4; 48.8.9.

[143] Schlatter, Private Property, p. 124. For a discussion of the perfection of the theory of individual rights to property, cf. Private Property, pp. 124-238.

[144] Lessius, De Justitia, 2:9:11, n. 65-67. In n. 66, Lessius teaches that a person who kills a daytime thief who is not defending himself with a sword will be held accountable in the external forum, but he will be excused in the forum of conscience if there was no probable hope of recovery. We have come full circle from Alexander of Hales, cf. supra, p. 89. Diana, Resolutiones, VIII:5:29; Salamancans, Cursus, VI:25:1:4, n. 77-78, 81; Busembaum, Medulla, I:3:4:1:3:4; Alphonsus, Moralis, I:3:4:1:3, n. 380, 382-383.

[145] Lessius, De Justitia, 2:9:11, n. 66; Salamancans, Cursus, VI:25:1:4, n. 81; Busembaum, Medulla, I:3:4:1:3:4; Alphonsus, Moralis, I:3:4:1:3, n. 380, 383.

[146] Lessius, *De Justitia*, 2:9:11, n. 66, Busembaum, *Medulla*, I:3:4:1:3:4; Alphonsus, *Moralis*, I:3:4:1:3, n. 383.

[147] *In VI°*, 5.11.6. The *Liber Sextus* was promulgated by Pope Boniface VIII in 1298.

[148] Lessius, *De Justitia*, 2:9:11, n. 66; Salamancans, *Cursus*, VI:25:1:4, n. 81; Alphonsus, *Moralis*, I:3:4:1:3, n. 383. This decretal is referred to by earlier authors in different contexts. Hostiensis, *Decretalium*, on *Suscepimus*, *De homicidio*, and Andreae, *Decretalium*, on *Suscepimus*, *De homicidio*, use the decretal as justification for clerics calling upon the secular arm of government to defend property. Covarrubias, *In Clementina*, p. 783, regards it as justifying self-defensive killing.

[149] Cf. *supra*, p. 88.

[150] X. 5.12.2.

[151] Hostiensis, *Decretalium*, on *Interfecisti*, *De homicidio*.

[152] Hostiensis, *Decretalium*, on *Suscepimus*, *De homicidio*.

[153] *In VI°*, 5.11.6.

[154] Hostiensis, *Decretalium*, on *Significasti*, *De homicidio*.

[155] Cf. *supra*, pp. 60-61.

[156] C. 8.4.1; D. 9.2.45.

[157] X. 5.12.3. Cf. *supra*, pp. 88-89.

[158] Raymund, *Summa*, 2:1:1; Richard, *Commentum*, 25:5:3; Andreae, *Decretalium*, on *Interfecisti*, *De homicidio*; Panormitanus, *Decretalium*, on *Interfecisti*, *De homicidio*.

[159] *Interfecisti*, *De homicidio*, is, of course, dealt with in the *Decretalium* of Innocent IV; but his comments have no bearing upon the *te tuaque* phrase.

[160] In his statements on this decretal, Andreae rejects the opinion of one whom he terms "Jo." This may be a reference to Joannes de Lignano, who justified killing in defense of property alone. Andreae also refutes a like position of "Ja," who could be Jacobus de Aretio.

[161] _Supra_, pp. 109-113.

[162] Sylvester, _Summa_, _Homicidium_ I:8; Cajetan, _Summa_, II-II:64:7; Molina, _Opera_, III:4:3:16.

[163] Covarrubias, _In Clementina_, pp. 785-786. He mentions Cajetan as teaching the opposite and rejects his opinion.

[164] Lessius, _De Justitia_, 2:9:11, n. 66; Diana, _Resolutiones_, VIII:5:30; Salamancans, _Cursus_, VI:25:1:4, n. 80.

[165] X. 5.12.10.

[166] Hostiensis, _Decretalium_, on _Suscepimus_, _De homicidio_; Andreae, _Decretalium_, on _Suscepimus_, _De homicidio_; Panormitanus, _Decretalium_, on _Suscepimus_, _De homicidio_.

[167] Covarrubias, _In Clementina_, p. 785; Sylvester, _Summa_, _Homicidium_ I:8; _Excommunicatio_ IX:6:9; Molina, _Opera_, III:4:3:16.

[168] Salamancans, _Cursus_, VI:25:1:4, n. 80; Alphonsus, _Moralis_, I:3:4:1:3, n. 383; Diana, _Resolutiones_, VIII:5:29, who refers to _Suscepimus_, _De homicidio_, only in the context of Panormitanus' forbidding clerics to kill in defense of property. Diana rejects this position on the basis of _Olim_, _De restitutione spoliatorum_, X. 2.13.12.

[169] _Supra_, pp. 4-6,14ff., _passim_. The source of this hierarchy is Augustine, _Free Choice_, I:5.

[170] Sylvester, _Summa_, _Excommunicatio_ VI:6:9.

[171] Cajetan, _Summa_, II-II:64:7; Vitoria, _De Justitia_ I, II-II:64:7, n. 6; Navarrus, _Manuale_, 15:3; Molina, _Opera_, III:4:3:16; Lessius, _De Justitia_, 2:9:8, n. 51; Salamancans, _Cursus_, VI:25:1:4, n. 80, 81-84; Alphonsus, _Moralis_, I:3:4:1:3, n. 382-383. The argument on preferring life to goods is also mentioned by Diana, _Resolutiones_, VIII:5:29, but he does not directly answer it. His position is that goods are a means of sustaining life; so one can kill to protect them.

[172] Covarrubias, _In Clementina_, pp. 785-786.

[173] Thomas, _Summa_, II-II:32:5.

[174] Thomas, _Summa_, II-II:32:5. Italics are mine.

[175] Cf. e.g., Vitoria, *De Justitia*, I, II-II:64:7, n. 6. This position would have been reinforced by the seventeenth century condemnation by Innocent XI of the proposition which said that one could steal not only in extreme necessity but also in "grave need." Denzinger-Schönmetzer, *Enchiridion*, n. 2136. Lessius, *De Justitia*, 2:12:12 and Diana, *Resolutiones*, V:8:23, held this condemned opinion.

[176] Cajetan, *Summa*, II-II:64:7. He terms the obligations "common" (own property) and "special" (other's life).

[177] Molina, *Opera*, III:4:3:16; Diana, *Resolutiones*, VIII:5:30; Salamancans, *Cursus*, VI:25:1:4, n. 82; Alphonsus, *Moralis*, I:3:4:1:3, n. 382. It is curious that in I:2:3:2:2, n. 28, Alphonsus understands charity to oblige a person to act in cases of urgency. The examples he gives include the "hope of an enemy's salvation" and "spiritual necessity." His position in n. 382 can only be understood to eliminate "urgency" when the person puts himself in danger. The obligation would thus be removed, and n. 28 would not bind.

[178] Alphonsus, *Moralis*, I:3:4:1:3, n. 383.

[179] There are two other interesting elements in this principle as it is stated and interpreted by Alphonsus. These will be mentioned briefly because of Ligouri's importance for the moral tradition which followed him.

In speaking of the obligation to prefer life over goods only when there is extreme need, Alphonsus says that the obligation is rooted in the "precept of charity." Charity obliges the preference be given to a higher good in the case of extreme need. If the need were extreme, would it not be justice that would oblige? In extreme need a person has a right to what he needs. We are in the area of a right to life; and this cannot be dealt with except by way of comparing rights, viz., the right to life and the right to property. It is the area of comparative values, which will be examined in the next chapter.

Alphonsus also remarks that if it were not licit to kill for property, it would not be licit to kill an aggressor seeking to take a person's life. This statement does not appear quite evident. The right to defend life by taking an aggressor's life is a question of comparing equal values: life with life. When the comparison is life and a material thing, the values are unequal. We will follow in the next chapter the effort to equate the values, an effort we have already seen begun by Lignano's teaching that a person and his goods are joined together. The task will involve the determination of when a lower value is to be preferred to a higher value, i.e., when a lower value becomes in a particular situation the higher value.

[180] Of course, the requirement of due moderation remains, as does the need for the property protected to be "of great value." How great value is determined will be pursued in the next chapter.

[181] Sylvester, Summa, Excommunicatio VI:6:8; Molina, Opera, III:4:3:16; Salamancans, Cursus, VI:25:1:4, n. 82; Alphonsus, Moralis, I:3:4:1:3, n. 382.

[182] Scotus, Opera, XVIII, Oxon, IV:15:3, p. 366.

[183] Molina, Opera, III:4:3:16; Lessius, De Justitia, 2:9:11, n. 67; Salamancans, Cursus, VI:25:1:4, n. 82. There was mention of this idea by Alexander of Hales, who quoted Jerome. Cf. supra, p. 8.

[184] Noonan, Usury, pp. 222-225; for a full treatment of the Triple Contract, pp. 202ff.

[185] The fifteenth century appears to be the time in which the shift to killing in defense of property was still a matter of conjecture. In the sixteenth century the major authorities are almost unanimous in legitimating the killing. An example of the practical, concrete living situation in the fifteenth century is given by Larner, "Order and Disorder," in Martines, Violence, pp. 50-69. He discusses the area of Romagna, which was subjected to Florentine expansion in the fifteenth century. It was very difficult to obtain justice in this area, as there was neither a constant standard of justice nor an efficient police force. Consequently, the effort to control the lower classes was minimal; the powerful were not controlled at all. Blood feuds and vengeance (the latter being legitimated by the Statutes of the city of Faenza in 1410) continued Romagna's long history of treacherous violence. Larner remarks that the predominance of individual morality was not a rebirth of the Roman bourgeois man, but rather a breaking free of barbarism from law. The Church was powerless to change this trend. One wonders if the criteria established for defense of both self and property were not perhaps efforts to tighten up actual practice.

[186] In his article "Crime and Punishment in Ferrara, 1440-1500," in Martines, Violence, pp. 108-122, Werner L. Gundersheimer remarks that theft was the most prevalent crime of this period. It was not related to scarcity or famine, but was a fairly constant feature of the urban scene. Theft and robbery were not crimes of the higher social classes, and these lower class criminals were dealt with harshly by regimes supported by men of property.

Theft was a capital crime, and Gundersheimer incorporates some statistics on executions from the period 1441-1557. During this time, one hundred eighteen were executed for theft alone, twenty-one for theft-homicide, and seventy for homicide alone. Between 1441-1460, forty-three were executed for theft alone. After this date, these executions decreased: thirty-nine between 1461-1480, thirty-six between 1481-1500. The highest single year was 1454, when eight persons died for the crime of theft.

In Florence, the thief was sometimes hanged if he were an habitual criminal (cf. Brucker, "The Florentine Popolo Minuto," in Martines, Violence, p. 165), while somewhat earlier statistics from Venice show the sentence of death for theft to appear to depend on the kind of theft and the value of the goods. Of seventeen hanged for theft between 1350-1370, ten were habitual thieves, one had robbed a church, four were slaves who had taken from their masters, and two had stolen large sums of money. Thieves were also maimed: loss of hands, eyes, nose, lips; they were also branded, as Alexander of Hales mentioned (cf. supra, p. 90). Cf. Stanley Chojnacki, "Crime, Punishment and the Trecento Venetian State," in Martines, Violence, pp. 225-226.

These statistics speak only to official sentences of death. Yet the death penalty for a crime says something of the gravity of that crime in the eyes of a society. In the fourteenth-fifteenth century areas mentioned here, the "eyes" of society were the ruling property class, seeking to protect that which they valued so highly.

FOOTNOTES

CHAPTER IV

[1] Accursius in the thirteenth century and Bartolus in the fourteenth so taught. Cf. supra, pp. 85, 96-97.

[2] Lignano and Antoninus. Cf. supra, pp. 101-102, 105-108.

[3] Lignano, De Bello, CXIIII; cf. supra, pp. 101-102.

[4] Alexander, Summa, IV:3:2:3:2:1:2:5:1, p. 521; Thomas, Summa, II-II:64:1.

[5] Sylvester, Summa, Homicidium I, 5: Bellum II, 1; Excommunicatio VI, 6, 9; Cajetan, Summa, II-II:64:7; Navarrus, Manuale, 15:3. Cajetan does say that property is necessary for life, but he does not make the decisive move which creates the later issue: which property is so necessary?

[6] Vitoria, De Justitia, I, II-II:64:7, 6, where he says this may be done when the goods are not necessary for the life of the person stealing (cf. also supra, pp. 121-124); Soto, De Justitia, 5:1:8; Molina, Opera, III:4:3:16.

[7] From the use of authors cited in this study I understand a "ducat" to be equivalent to a "gold piece."

[8] The amounts for Soto and Molina are arrived at by taking their statements that a particular amount is not sufficient value to kill for and using the next unit of value as the permissible sum. E.g., Soto says that two or three ducats are not enough; thus four ducats would create "great value." The Salamancans, Cursus, VI:25:1:4, n. 86, do this with Soto. They cite him as holding three, four, or five ducats to be great value. We have seen Soto to actually say that two or three ducats are not great value. In any case, the process is clear.

[9] Cf. e.g., Cajetan, Summa, II-II:64:7, and what was said about the necessity of preferring another's life to

one's own goods, supra, pp. 121-124.

[10] Denzinger-Schönmetzer, Enchiridion, n. 2131, which is proposition 31 of Sanctissimus Dominus Noster, March 2, 1679.

[11] Busembaum, Medulla, I:3:4:1:3:4; Salamancans, Cursus, VI:25:1:4, n. 85; Benjamin Elbel, Theologia Moralis, ed. Irenaeus Bierbaum (Paderborn: 1891), II:4, n. 64, who adds it would be against charity and sane reason; Alphonsus, Moralis, I:3:4:1:3, n. 383, who remarks that three, four, or five ducats are not sufficient for great value. He attributed this opinion to the Salamancans, among others. However, the Salamancans actually held that it was a probable opinion that three, four or five ducats do constitute great value.

Benjamin Elbel (d.1756), whom we meet for the first time, was a Franciscan moral theologian. He followed the system of probabilism, and in an age of severe moral disputes was noted for the lack of controversy associated with his name. Cf. "Elbel, Benjamin," in NCE, Vol. 5.

[12] Busembaum, Medulla, I:3:4:1:3:4; Salamancans, Cursus, VI:25:1:4, n. 87. A "probable opinion" is one which leads a person to assent to it on the basis of the weight of its arguments. If the arguments offered are well-founded, the opinion is probable, even though other arguments might be "more probable." Cf. Häring, Law of Christ, Vol. I, pp. 169-189.

[13] Salamancans, Cursus, VI:25:1:4, n. 85.

[14] Elbel, Moralis, II:4, n. 64-65. He says that Cardenas is the source of the absolute-relative distinction. Juan de Cardenas was a Jesuit moral theologian (d.1684) who was important in the "probability" controversies of his age. He defended a moderate probabilism in opposition to both laxism and rigorism. Cf. "Cardenas, Juan de," in NCE, Vol. 3.

[15] Lessius, De Justitia, 2:9:11, n. 67.

[16] While Lessius gives canonical (Interfecisti, De homicidio, Olim, De restitutione spoliatorum, Dilecto, De sententia excommunicationis), Scriptural (Ex. 22:1-2) and civil (Furem nocturum, Ad Legem Corneliam de sicariis, Itaque, Ad Legem Aquiliam) law sources for the basic legitimacy of killing for property, he gives no sources for the further specification of that legitimacy to be applicable only when the property is necessary for a decent life. Cf. De Justitia, 2:9:11, n. 67, and supra, pp. 113-119.

[17] The work contains Lessius' lectures from 1593 and 1595; it was published in 1605. Cf. Ch. van Sull, S.J., *Leonard Lessius* (Louvain: 1930), p. 185.

[18] van Sull, *Lessius*, p. 188.

[19] J. P. Cooper, "General Introduction," to *The New Cambridge Modern History*, Vol. IV, *The Decline of Spain and the 30 Years' War*, ed. J. P. Cooper (Cambridge: 1970), pp. 11-14; Spooner, "The Economy of Europe," pp. 67-71.

[20] For the role played by Lessius in the revision of the understanding of usury, cf. Noonan, *Usury*, *passim*.

[21] Noonan, *Usury*, p. 88; for a full discussion of the concept of just price, pp. 82-99.

[22] Thomas, *Summa*, II-II:77:3.

[23] Lessius, *De Justitia*, 2:21:1-4; cf. also van Sull, *Lessius*, p. 189; Cecil H. Chamberlain, S.J., "Leonard Lessius," in Gerard Smith, S.J., ed. *Jesuit Thinkers of the Renaissance* (Milwaukee: 1939), pp. 143-144.

[24] Chamberlain, "Lessius," p. 140.

[25] Thomas, *Summa*, II-II:32:6. The context of the statement is almsgiving; cf. *supra*, pp. 122-123.

[26] Thomas, *Summa*, II-II:32:6.

[27] Sylvester, *Summa*, *Excommunicatio* VI, 6, 9; Soto, *De Justitia*, 5:1:8.

[28] Cajetan, *Summa*, II-II:118:1. Cf. *infra*, p. 162.

[29] Chamberlain, "Lessius," pp. 133ff.; van Sull, *Lessius*, pp. 30-79; H. Koenigsberger, "The Empire of Charles V in Europe," in *The New Cambridge Modern History*, Vol. II, *The Reformation*, 1520-1559, ed. G. R. Elton (Cambridge: 1965), pp. 301-333.

[30] It is interesting that Anthony Hickey, the commentator on Scotus, who wrote only fourteen years (1637) after the death of Lessius, should be of such a different opinion. He teaches that no thief is to be killed for a theft which inflicts no other harm besides that suffered by the one who endures the loss. He attempts to show that such authors as Cajetan misunderstand Scotus, attributing to him the opinion that no thief is to be killed. Hickey

responds by saying that if the thief is also an attacker of a person or his theft is gravely harmful to the common good, Scotus would allow him to be killed. It is the simple thief who cannot be killed. But Hickey also says that Cajetan and others too often presume grave harm to the common good to be present in all theft, an opinion which Hickey himself rejects. Cf. Scotus, Opera, XVIII, Oxon. VI:15:3, pp. 380-382.

[31] Diana, Resolutiones, VIII:5:32. Diana rejects certain attempts to specify great value at, e.g., one, two, or four gold pieces.

[32] Salamancans, Cursus, VI:25:1:4, n. 77, 87.

[33] Elbel, Moralis, II:4, n. 64-65.

[34] The absolute-relative distinction of Elbel was not used by Alphonsus, although he does cite him frequently on other points. However, the distinction was carried on into the nineteenth and twentieth centuries. Cf. Henry Davis, S.J., Moral and Pastoral Theology, Vol. II, Commandments of God, Precepts of the Church, seventh edition, ed. L. W. Geddes, S.J. (London: 1958), p. 154; Marcellino Zalba, S.J., Theologia Moralis Specialis: Tractatus de Mandatis Dei et Ecclesiae, Vol. II of E. F. Regatillo and M. Zalba, S.J., Theologiae Moralis Summa (Madrid: 1953), p. 277; Patrick Sporer, O.F.M., De Justitia de Contractibus, Vol. II of his Theologia Moralis, second edition, ed. Irenaeus Bierbaum, O.F.M. (Paderborn: 1903), p. 295; Anthony Ballerini, S.J., De Justitia et Jure, Vol. III of his Opus Theologicum Morale, third edition, ed. Dominic Palmieri (Prati: 1899), pp. 276-277; Thomas Iorio, S.J., De praeceptis Decalogi et Ecclesiae, Vol. II of his Theologia Moralis, fourth edition (Naples: 1954), p. 116.

[35] Elbel, Moralis, II:4, n. 65.

[36] Cooper, "Introduction," pp. 8-9, 36-49, 56-59; D. C. Coleman, "Economic Problems and Policies," in The New Cambridge Modern History, Vol. V, The Ascendency of France: 1648-88, ed. F. L. Carsten (Cambridge: 1961), pp. 21-22, 41-42; Stephen Skalweit, "Political Thought," in The New Cambridge Modern History, Vol. V, pp. 118-120; R. Mousnier, "The Exponents and Critics of Absolutism," in The New Cambridge Modern History, Vol. V, pp. 120-126, where he speaks of the limit on the king's absolutism by the demand that the natural right of property, an absolute and inviolable right, be respected; Spooner, "The Economy of Europe," p. 75.

[37] Coleman, "Economic Problems," p. 42; Juan Reglá, "Spain and Her Empire," in The New Cambridge Modern History, Vol. V, p. 370.

[38] Mousnier, "Exponents," pp. 124-126; Schlatter, *Private Property*, pp. 124-238.

[39] For a discussion of the various systems, cf. Häring, *Law of Christ*, Vol. I, pp. 169-189; *NCE*: "Moral Theology, History of" and "Morality, Systems of," in Vol. 9; "Laxism," in Vol. 8; "Probabilism" and "Probabiliorism," in Vol. 11; "Rigorism," in Vol. 12; and the appropriate titles in John Macquarrie, ed., *Dictionary of Christian Ethics* (Philadelphia: 1967).

[40] *Supra*, p. 181, nt. 25, and this chapter, p. 210, nt. 10.

[41] Denzinger-Schönmetzer, *Enchiridion*, n. 2363. The condemnation was by Alexander VIII in 1690. Cf. Pascal, *Provincial Letters*, esp. Letters 5, 7, 13, where he opposes probable opinions as too lax.

[42] Alphonsus, *Moralis*, I:3:4:1:3, n. 383. He refers this teaching to Roncaglia, an early eighteenth-century moralist (d.1737). Cf. Constantinus Roncaglia, *Universa Moralis Theologia* (Venice: 1736), I:11:3:5:1.

[43] Alphonsus understands Molina and the Salamancans to have taught that up to five ducats is *not* great value. We have seen that what was taught by Molina was that in a case of another person's property one could kill for this amount. The Salamancans acknowledged the "probable" status of the opinion which permitted killing for five ducats, though they themselves preferred the relative process of evaluation. Cf. Alphonsus, *Moralis*, I:3:4:1:3, n. 383, and *supra*, pp. 129-131.

[44] Alphonsus, *Moralis*, I:3:4:1:3, n. 383. He attributes this position to Domenico Viva, a Jesuit who died in 1726, and Alexander Natalis. Natalis (d.1724) was a Dominican theologian and polemecist, who was involved in the controversies over Gallicanism, probabilism-laxism, and Jansenism. After having some of his writing condemned and being suspected of Jansenism, he died within the ranks of the Church. Cf. "Natalis, Alexander," in *NCE*, Vol. 10; "Viva, Domenico," in *NCE*, Vol. 14.
The understanding which Alphonsus has of the teaching of Elbel does not agree with my reading of Elbel's position. As I understand it, Elbel uses "sustenance" only as an example of relatively grave harm, not as an exclusive criterion.

[45] Alphonsus, *Moralis*, I:3:4:1:3, n. 383. He cites Lugo for this opinion, and, curiously, does not mention the Salamancans. Juan de Lugo (d.1660) was a Jesuit cardinal and theologian, mainly esteemed as a moralist of profound theoretical and social insight. Cf. "Lugo, Juan de,"

in *NCE*, Vol. 8.

Alphonsus understands Lugo's position differently than do the Salamancans, *Cursus*, VI:25:1:4, n. 85, who consider him to have sanctioned killing for a value less than one gold piece. They include him among those condemned in proposition thirty-one of Innocent IV.

[46] The Salamancans, for example, use "notable harm" without any indication that this harm is to be equated or related to sustenance. Cf. *Cursus*, VI:25:1:4, n. 77, 87.

[47] Alphonsus, *Moralis*, I:3:4:1:3, n. 383.

[48] Cf. *supra*, pp. 34-36.

[49] Cf. *supra*, pp. 109-115.

[50] Cf. *supra*, p. 128.

[51] Soto, *De Justitia*, 5:1:8.

[52] Lessius, *De Justitia*, 2:9:11, n. 66.

[53] Busembaum, *Medulla*, I:3:4:1:3:4; Alphonsus, *Moralis*, I:3:4:1:3, n. 382.

[54] Diana, *Resolutiones*, VIII:5:29.

[55] Salamancans, *Cursus*, VI:25:1:4, n. 78.

[56] Cf. *supra*, pp. 121-124.

[57] Thomas, *Summa*, II-II:32:6.

[58] Hostiensis, *Decretalium*, on *Significasti*, *De homicidio*; Lignano, *De Bello*, CXIII; Antoninus, *Summa*, III:4:3:1:2, p. 225.

[59] Sylvester, *Summa*, *Bellum* II, 1 and 7; *Excommunicatio* VI, 6, 9.

[60] Soto, *De Justitia*, 5:1:8.

[61] Covarrubias, *In Clementina*, p. 787. He also forbids the killing of a fleeing attacker of a person; there is no longer need for defense, cf. p. 783.

[62] Molina, *Opera*, III:4:3:16. It has been noted that in the case of a fleeing thief, when the property belongs

to another, up to five ducats is not considered great value by Molina. A person can kill for less value when it is his own property or a person's direct responsibility. Molina also quotes a Spanish civil law, A Sabiendas, from the Nova Collectio, 8:23:4, which confirms his position. The law is seemingly not quoted from the beginning; it is to be understood as legitimating what it "excepts." "Except if he kill a thief whom he meets at night in his house, stealing or breaking in; or if he meets him fleeing with what he has stolen and if he does not want to go to prison, or if he finds him stealing his property and he does not want to leave it."

[63] Lessius, De Justitia, 2:9:11, n. 73; Diana, Resolutiones, VIII:5:29 and 30, who rejects Covarrubias' opinion explicitly; Busembaum, Medulla, I:3:4:1:3:7.

[64] Lessius, De Justitia, 2:9:11, n. 69.

[65] Thomas, Summa, II-II:25:8 and 9. Cf. supra, pp. 5-8, 69-71.

[66] Cf. supra, pp. 121-124.

[67] Lessius, De Justitia, 2:9:11, n. 73; Diana, Resolutiones, VIII:5:29.

[68] Salamancans, Cursus, VI:25:1:4, n. 88, 89, 93; Alphonsus, Moralis, I:3:4:1:3, n. 382.

[69] Alphonsus, Moralis, I:3:4:1:3, n. 383. The Salamancans, Cursus, VI:25:1:4, n. 88, require that the thief be forewarned and there be no other hope of recovery. In n. 89, they say that one may kill if he forewarns or there is no hope of recovery. The use of "or" would seem to separate the requirements of warning and recovery possibilities. Yet it does not appear that the Salamancans would justify killing simply on the basis of the thief's refusal to halt. They demand at least doubt of recovery to legitimate killing.

[70] Elbel, Moralis, II:4, n. 54.

[71] Hostiensis, Decretalium, on Significasti, De homicidio; Lignano, De Bello, CXIII; Sylvester, Summa, Homicidium I; Bellum II, 7; Soto, De Justitia, 5:1:8; Molina, Opera, III:4:3:16; Lessius, De Justitia, 2:9:11, n. 74; Diana, Resolutiones, VIII:5:29, 30, 31; Busembaum, Medulla, I:3:4:1:3:7; Salamancans, Cursus, VI:25:1:4, n. 91, 92; Alphonsus, Moralis, I:3:4:1:3, n. 382.

[72] Lignano, *De Bello*, CXIII; Sylvester, *Summa*, *Bellum* II, 7.

[73] Cf. *supra*, pp. 132-133, 134-139.

[74] Lessius, *De Justitia*, 2:9:11, n. 74.

[75] Diana, *Resolutiones*, VIII:5:30; Busembaum, *Medulla*, I:3:4:1:3:7; Alphonsus, *Moralis*, I:3:4:1:3, n. 382. Diana teaches that Lessius permits killing if the thief resists; cf. VIII:5:31. Lessius' position is not that simply stated. Diana does not acknowledge the "disorder" fear that Lessius has, nor does he consider Lessius' statement that one cannot use the thief's resistance as an excuse to kill.

[76] Salamancans, *Cursus*, VI:25:1:4, n. 92.

[77] Salamancans, *Cursus*, VI:25:1:4, n. 91.

[78] Salamancans, *Cursus*, VI:25:1:4, n. 92; Thomas, II-II:66:3; 66:5.

[79] Cf. *supra*, p. 145.

[80] Cf. *supra*, pp. 5-6, 29-30.

[81] Alexander, *Summa*, IV:2:3:2:1:2:5:1, p. 521; Raymund, *Summa*, 2:6:1; Hostiensis, *Summa Aurea*, *Quis fit raptor*, *De raptoribus rerum*; *Quid fit furtum*, *De furtis*.

[82] E.g., Lessius, *De Justitia*, 2:9:11, n. 66; Salamancans, *Cursus*, VI:25:1:4, n. 81; Alphonsus, *Moralis*, I:3:4:1:3, n. 383.

[83] Cf. *supra*, pp. 98-100.

[84] Schlatter, *Private Property*, pp. 56-69.

[85] Cf. *supra*, pp. 97-100.

[86] Schlatter, *Private Property*, pp. 63-75, and chapter two.

[87] Schlatter, *Private Property*, pp. 77-238.

[88] Schlatter, *Private Property*, pp. 85-87, where Thomas More in England and Luther in Germany are shown to give evidence of this recognition.

[89] Schlatter, *Private Property*, pp. 47ff. It is in the same fourteenth century that killing in defense of property began to be legitimated on the basis of Roman law glosses and the linking of person and property. Given the unanimous recognition of stealing to be against the natural law (a violation of the Decalogue), would not the judging of the possession of private property to be a natural right have increased the evil perceived in stealing?

[90] For example, the concern of the merchants and bankers with whom Lessius worked was productive wealth. The same focus is evident in the reevaluation of usury theory between the fifteenth and eighteenth centuries. Cf. Noonan, *Usury*, pp. 199-364.

[91] The position of Molina, ultimately condemned as overly lax, would be an exception to this general trend.

[92] Cf. *supra*, pp. 129-143.

[93] Cf. *supra*, pp. 34-36.

[94] Cf. *supra*, p. 125.

[95] Cf. *supra*, pp. 29-30.

[96] Clement of Alexandria, "Who is the Rich Man that Shall be Saved?" in *The Ante-Nicene Fathers*, Vol. II, eds. the Rev. Alexander Roberts, D.D., and James Donaldson, LL.D. (New York: 1925), pp. 591ff.; John Chrysostom, "Homily 66 on Matt. 20:29-30," in *Library of the Fathers, The Homilies of S. John Chrysostom on the Gospel of St. Matthew*, Part III, trans. Members of the English Church (Oxford: 1851), pp. 889-900; Augustine, "Exposition on Psalm 147," in *Library of the Fathers, Expositions on the Book of Psalms*, Vol. VI, trans. Members of the English Church (London: 1857), p. 393; "Letter 153" and "Letter 155," in *The Fathers of the Church*, Vol. 20, *Letters*, Vol. III, gen. ed. Roy J. Deferrari, trans. Sister Wilfred Parsons, S.N.D. (New York: 1953), esp. p. 302.

[97] Augustine, "Psalm 147," "Letter 153," "Letter 155," Thomas, *Summa*, II-II:66:2; 118:1.

[98] Thomas, *Summa*, II-II:118:1.

[99] Cajetan, *Summa*, II-II:118:1.

[100] Cajetan published his commentary on Thomas' Secunda Secundae in 1517. Lessius' De Justitia was printed in 1605. Lessius uses "decent life" and Cajetan speaks of "opportune conveniences" in conjunction with a definition of what meaning is to be applied to "life" in terms of preserving life. The concepts appear related, though Lessius acknowledges no dependence on Cajetan.

[101] Thomas, Summa, II-II:118:1; 117:3; I-II:2:1. Yet Thomas also says in 118:1 that all external goods can be valued in terms of money.

[102] Cf. supra, pp. 129-143.

[103] Cf. supra, pp. 133-134.

BIBLIOGRAPHY

BIBLIOGRAPHY

Ady, Cecilia Mary. "Florence and North Italy, 1414-1492." In *The Cambridge Medieval History*. Vol. VIII, *The Close of the Middle Ages*. Edited by C. W. Previte-Orton and Z. N. Brooks. Cambridge: University Press, 1936.

Alexander of Hales. *Summa Theologica*. Quaracchi, 1924-1948.

Alphonsus de Ligouri, St. *Theologia Moralis*. Rome, 1905.

Andreae, Joannes. *Decretalium libros novella commentaria*. Venice, 1581.

Antoninus of Florence, St. *Summa Theologica*. Verona, 1740.

Aristotle. *The Basic Works*. Edited by Richard McKeon. New York, 1941.

_____. *Ethica Nicomachea*. Translated by W. D. Ross, *Ed. cit.*

_____. *Politica*. Translated by Benjamin Jowett, *Ed. cit.*

Augustine, St. *Adulterous Marriage* (*De incompetentibus nuptiis*). In *The Fathers of the Church*, Vol. 27. Translated by Charles T. Huegelmeyer, M.M. Edited by Roy J. Deferrari. New York: Fathers of the Church, Inc., 1955.

_____. *City of God* (*De civitate Dei*). Translated by John Healey. Edited by R. V. G. Tasker. 2 vols. New York, 1947.

_____. *The Free Choice of the Will* (*De libero arbitrio*). In *The Fathers of the Church*, Vol. 59. Translated by Robert P. Russell, O.S.A. Edited by Roy J. Deferrari. Washington, D.C.: The Catholic University of America Press, 1967.

_____. *Letters*, Vol. I (1-82). In *The Fathers of the Church*, Vol. 12. Translated by Sister Wilfred Parsons, S.N.D. Edited by Roy J. Deferrari. New York: Fathers of the Church, Inc., 1951.

Augustine, St. Letters, Vol. II (83-130). In The Fathers of the Church, Vol. 18. Translated by Sister Wilfred Parsons, S.N.D. Edited by Roy J. Deferrari. New York: Fathers of the Church, Inc., 1953.

_____. Letters, Vol. III (131-164). In The Fathers of the Church, Vol. 20. Translated by Sister Wilfred Parsons, S.N.D. Edited by Roy J. Deferrari. New York: Fathers of the Church, Inc., 1953.

_____. Expositions on the Book of Psalms. Vol. VI (126-150). In Library of the Fathers. Translated by Members of the English Church. Oxford: John Henry Parker, 1857.

_____. Commentary On the Lord's Sermon On the Mount. In The Fathers of the Church, Vol. 11. Translated by Denis J. Kavanagh, O.S.A. Edited by Roy J. Deferrari. New York: Fathers of the Church, Inc., 1951.

Babylonian Talmud. Edited by Dr. I. Epstein. London: The Soncino Press, 1935-1960.

Ballerini, Antonius, S.J. Opus Theologicum Morale. 7 vols. Third edition. Edited by Dominic Palmieri. Prato: Giachetti, 1898-1899.

_____. De Justitia et Jure. Vol. III, ed. cit.

Baron, Hans. "Franciscan Poverty and Civic Wealth as Factors in the Rise of Humanistic Thought." Speculum 13 (1938), pp. 1-37.

Barrett, C. K. The Gospel According to St. John. Fifth edition. London: S.P.C.K., 1962.

Bartolus a Sasoferrato. Omnium Juris Interpretum Antesignani, Commentaria. Venice, 1615.

_____. Digestum Novum. Vols. I and VI, ed. cit.

_____. Codex. Vol. VIII, ed. cit.

Bec, Christian. Les Marchands Ecrivains a Florence, 1375-1434. Paris: La Haye, 1967.

Beck, Hans-Georg, et al. From the High Middle Ages to the Eve of the Reformation. Vol. IV of Handbook of Church History. Translated by Anselm Biggs. Edited by Hubert Jedin and John Dolan. New York: Herder and Herder, 1970.

Becker, Marvin B. "The Florentine Territorial State and Civic Humanism in the Early Renaissance." In Florentine Studies, Politics and Society in Renaissance Florence. Edited by Nicolai Rubinstein. Evanston: Northwestern University Press, 1968.

Bindoff, S. T. "The Greatness of Antwerp." In _The New Cambridge Modern History_. Vol. II, _The Reformation, 1520-1559_. Edited by G. R. Elton. Cambridge: University Press, 1965.

Boehner, Philotheus, O.F.M. _The History of the Franciscan School_. Part I, _Alexander of Hales_. Detroit: Duns Scotus College, 1947. Mimeo.

Boissonnade, P. _Life and Work in Medieval Europe_. Translated by Eileen Power. Preface to the Torchbook edition by Lynn White, Jr. New York: Harper and Row, 1964. First published in English translation by Kegan Paul. London: Trench, Trubner and Co., 1927.

Bonaventure, St. _Opera Omnia_. Paris: Ludovicus Vives, 1864-1871.

_____. _Breviloquium_. Vol. VII, _ed._ _cit_.

_____. _Centiloquium_. Vol. VII, _ed._ _cit_.

_____. _Compendium Theologicae Veritatis_. Vol. XIV, _ed._ _cit_.

_____. _De Paupertate Christi Contra Magistrum Guilelmum_. Vol. XIV, _ed._ _cit_.

_____. _De Septem Itineribus Aeternitatis_. Vol. VIII, _ed._ _cit_.

_____. _Expositio in Caput Sextum Evangelii S. Matthaei_. Vol. X, _ed._ _cit_.

_____. _Expositio in Evangelium S. Lucae_. Vol. X, _ed._ _cit_.

_____. _Illuminationes Ecclesiae in Hexaemeron_. Vol. IX, _ed._ _cit_.

_____. _In II Librum Sententiarum_. Vol. III, _ed._ _cit_.

_____. _In IV Librum Sententiarum_. Vol. VI, _ed._ _cit_.

_____. _In III-IV Libros Sententiarum_. Vol. V, _ed._ _cit_.

_____. _Principium Sacrae Scripturae_. Vol. IX, _ed._ _cit_.

_____. _Sermones De Decem Praeceptis_. Vol. XII, _ed._ _cit_.

Bornkamm, Günther. _Jesus of Nazareth_. Translated by Irene and Fraser McLuskey with James M. Robinson. New York: Harper and Row, 1960.

Bowsky, William M. "The Anatomy of Rebellion in Fourteenth-Century Siena: From Commune to Signory?" In *Violence and Civil Disorder in Italian Cities: 1200-1500.* Edited by Lauro Martines. Berkeley and Los Angeles: University of California Press, 1972.

Brentano, Robert. "Violence, Disorder, and Order in Thirteenth-Century Rome." In *Violence and Civil Disorder in Italian Cities: 1200-1500.* Edited by Lauro Martines. Berkeley and Los Angeles: University of California Press, 1972.

Brodrick, J., S.J. *The Economic Morals of the Jesuits.* London: Oxford University Press, 1934.

Brown, Raymond E., S.S. *The Gospel According to John (I-XII). The Anchor Bible.* Garden City, New York: Doubleday and Company, Inc., 1966.

Brucker, Gene A. "The Florentine *Popolo Minuto* and Its Political Role 1340-1450." In *Violence and Civil Disorder in Italian Cities: 1200-1500.* Edited by Lauro Martines. Berkeley and Los Angeles: University of California Press, 1972.

Bultmann, Rudolf. *The Gospel of John: A Commentary.* Translated by R. W. N. Hoare and S. K. Riches. Edited by G. R. Beasley-Murray. Philadelphia: The Westminster Press, 1971.

Busembaum, Hermann. *Medulla Theologiae Moralis.* 2 vols. Edited by S. Alphonso Maria de Ligorio. Tournai, 1848.

Cajetan. *Commentarium in summam theologicam S. Thomae Aquinatis.* In St. Thomas Aquinas, *Summa Theologica.* Rome, 1773.

Chamberlain, Cecil H., S.J. "Leonard Lessius." In *Jesuit Thinkers of the Renaissance.* Edited by Gerard Smith, S.J. Milwaukee: Marquette University Press, 1939.

Chojnacki, Stanley. "Crime, Punishment, and the Trecento Venetian State." In *Violence and Civil Disorder in Italian Cities: 1200-1500.* Edited by Lauro Martines. Berkeley and Los Angeles: University of California Press, 1972.

Chrysostom, John, St. "Homily 66 on Matt. 20:29-30." In *Library of the Fathers. The Homilies of St. John Chrysostom on the Gospel of St. Matthew,* Part III. Translated by Members of the English Church. Oxford: John Henry Parker, 1851.

Clement of Alexandria, St. "Who is the Rich Man that Shall
Be Saved?" In The Ante-Nicene Fathers. Vol. II.
Edited by the Rev. Alexander Roberts, D.D. and
James Donaldson, LL.D. New York: Charles Scribner's
Sons, 1925.

Coleman, D. C. "Economic Problems and Policies." In The
New Cambridge Modern History. Vol. V, The Ascendency of France: 1648-88. Edited by F. L. Carsten.
Cambridge: University Press, 1961.

Cooper, J. P. "General Introduction." In The New Cambridge Modern History. Vol. IV, The Decline of
Spain and the 30 Years War. Edited by J. P. Cooper.
Cambridge: University Press, 1970.

Copleston, Frederick, S.J. A History of Philosophy.
Image Books. Garden City, New York: Doubleday and
Company, Inc., 1962.

⎯⎯⎯⎯⎯. Albert the Great to Duns Scotus. Vol. 2, Part 2,
ed. cit.

⎯⎯⎯⎯⎯. Ockham to the Speculative Mystics. Vol. 3,
Part 1, ed. cit.

Corpus juris canonici. Edited by Aemilius Friedberg.
Leipzig, 1922.

Corpus juris civilis. Edited by Joannes Ludovicus Guilielmus
Beck. Leipzig, 1829.

Coulton, G. G. Medieval Village, Manor, and Monastery.
Harper Torchbooks. New York: Harper and Row, 1960.
First published as The Medieval Village. Cambridge:
University Press, 1925.

Covarrubias y Leyva, Diego de. Opera. Lyon, 1568.

⎯⎯⎯⎯⎯. In Clementina. Vol. I, ed. cit.

Curran, Charles E. "Is There A Distinctively Christian
Social Ethic?" In Metropolis: Christian Presence
and Responsibility. Edited by Philip D. Morris.
Notre Dame: Fides Publishers, Inc., 1970. Also
found in Chicago Studies 9 (1970), pp. 59-80.

⎯⎯⎯⎯⎯. "The Relevancy of the Ethical Teaching of Jesus."
In his A New Look at Christian Morality. Notre
Dame: Fides Publishers, Inc., 1970.

da Certaldo, Paolo de Messer Pace. Il Libro di bouoni
costumi. Florence: Le Monnier, 1921.

Davis, Henry, S.J. Moral and Pastoral Theology. 4 vols.
Seventh edition. Edited by L. W. Geddes, S.J.
London: Sheed and Ward, 1958.

Davis, Henry, S.J. Commandments of God, Precepts of the
    Church. Vol. II, ed. cit.

Denzinger, Henricus and Schönmetzer, Adolfus, S.J.
    Enchiridion Symbolorum Definitionum et Declarationum
    De Rebus Fidei et Morum. Thirty-second edition.
    Barcelona: Herder and Herder, 1963.

de Roover, Raymond. "Labour Conditions in Florence Around
    1400: Theory, Policy and Reality." In Florentine
    Studies, Politics, and Society in Renaissance
    Florence. Edited by Nicolai Rubinstein. Evanston:
    Northwestern University Press, 1968.

_____. "The Organization of Trade." In The Cambridge
    Economic History. Vol. III, Economic Organization
    and Policies in the Middle Ages. General editors,
    M. M. Postan and H. J. Habakkuk. Edited by M. M.
    Postan, E. E. Rich, Edward Miller. Cambridge:
    University Press, 1963.

Derrett, J. D. M. "Law in the New Testament: The Story
    of the Woman Taken in Adultery." New Testament
    Studies (Cambridge) 10 (1963-1964), pp. 1-26.

Diana, Antoninus. Coordinatus seu Omnes Resolutiones
    Morales. 12 vols. Lyon, 1680.

Digestum Novum seu Pandectarum Juris Civilis. Venice, n.d.

Doucet, Victorin, O.F.M. "A New Source of the Summa
    Fratris Alexandri." Franciscan Studies 6 (1946),
    pp. 403-417.

Duns Scotus, John. Opera Omnia. Editio nova juxta
    editionem L. Waddingi.

_____. In Librum Tertium Sententiarum. Vol. XV, ed.
    cit.

_____. In Librum Quartum Sententiarum. Vol. XVIII,
    ed. cit.

Elbel, Benjamin, O.F.M. Theologia Moralis. 3 vols.
    Edited by Irenaeus Bierbaum, O.F.M. Paderborn,
    1891.

Elton, G. R. "Introduction: The Age of the Reformation."
    In The New Cambridge Modern History. Vol. II, The
    Reformation, 1520-1559. Edited by G. R. Elton.
    Cambridge: University Press, 1965.

Gerson, Jean. Opera. Paris, 1606.

_____. Alius sermo contra assertionem magistri Joannis
    Parvi, circa praeceptum 'non occides.' Vol. I,
    ed. cit.

Gerson, Jean. *Compendium theologiae: tractatus 2 de decem praeceptis legis*. Vol. II, ed. cit.

_____. *Errores circa praeceptum 'non occides.'* Vol. I, ed. cit.

_____. *Opusculum Tripertitum eiusdem, de praeceptis decalogi, de confessione et de arte moriendi.* Vol. II, ed. cit.

_____. *Regulae Moralis: De praeceptis decalogi*. Vol. II, ed. cit.

Giles of Rome. *De Ecclesiastica Potestate*. Scientia Aalen, 1961.

Grabmann, Dr. Martin. *Thomas Aquinas*. Translated by Virgil Michel, O.S.B. New York: Russell and Russell, Inc., 1963.

Graystone, K. "Sermon on the Mount." In *The Interpreter's Dictionary of the Bible*. Vol. 4. Edited by George Arthur Buttrick. New York: Abingdon Press, 1962.

Gundersheimer, Werner L. "Crime and Punishment in Ferrara, 1440-1500." In *Violence and Civil Disorder in Italian Cities: 1200-1500*. Edited by Lauro Martines. Berkeley and Los Angeles: University of California Press, 1972.

Hale, J. R. "Armies, Navies and the Art of War." In *The New Cambridge Modern History*. Vol. III, *The Counter-Reformation and Price Revolution, 1559-1610*. Edited by R. B. Wernham. Cambridge: University Press, 1968.

_____. "Violence in the Late Middle Ages: A Background." In *Violence and Civil Disorder in Italian Cities: 1200-1500*. Edited by Lauro Martines. Berkeley and Los Angeles: University of California Press, 1972.

Häring, Bernard, C.SS.R. *The Law of Christ*. 3 vols. Translated by Edwin C. Kaiser, C.PP.S. Westminster, Maryland: The Newman Press, 1961-1966.

_____. "The Normative Value of the Sermon on the Mount." *The Catholic Biblical Quarterly* 29:3 (1967), pp. 69-79 (375-385).

Herlihy, David. "Some Psychological and Social Roots of Violence in the Tuscan Cities." In *Violence and Civil Disorder in Italian Cities: 1200-1500*. Edited by Lauro Martines. Berkeley and Los Angeles: University of California Press, 1972.

Herr, Friedrich. *The Intellectual History of Europe*. Translated by Jonathan Steinberg. London: Weidenfeld and Nicolson, 1966.

Herr, Friedrich. *The Medieval World: Europe 1100-1350*. Translated by Janet Sondheimer. New York: The New American Library, Inc. Reprint of edition published by The World Publishing Company, 1962.

Hibbert, A. B. "The Economic Policies of Towns." In *The Cambridge Economic History*. Vol. III, *Economic Organization and Policies in the Middle Ages*. General editors, M. M. Postan and H. J. Habakkuk. Edited by M. M. Postan, E. E. Rich, Edward Miller. Cambridge: University Press, 1963.

Hostiensis (Henry Bartholomew of Susa). *Commentaria super quinque libros decretalium*. Venice, 1581.

_____. *Summa Aurea*. Turin: Bottega D'Erasmo, 1963.

Hunter, Archibald M. *A Pattern for Life: An Exposition of the Sermon on the Mount*. Revised edition. Philadelphia: The Westminster Press, 1965.

Hurstfield, J. "Social Structure, Office-Holding and Politics, Chiefly in Western Europe." In *The New Cambridge Modern History*. Vol. III, *The Counter-Reformation and Price Revolution, 1559-1610*. Edited by R. B. Wernham. Cambridge: University Press, 1968.

Hyde, J. K. "Contemporary Views on Faction and Civil Strife in Thirteenth and Fourteenth-Century Italy." In *Violence and Civil Disorder in Italian Cities: 1200-1500*. Edited by Lauro Martines. Berkeley and Los Angeles: University of California Press, 1972.

Ilardi, Vincent. "The Assassination of Galeazzo Maria Sforza and the Reaction of Italian Diplomacy." In *Violence and Civil Disorder in Italian Cities: 1200-1500*. Edited by Lauro Martines. Berkeley and Los Angeles: University of California Press, 1972.

Innocent IV. *In quinque libros decretalium*. Venice, 1570.

Iorio, Thomas, S. J. *Theologia Moralis*. 3 vols. Fourth edition. Naples: M. D'auria, 1954.

_____. *De praeceptis Decalogi et Ecclesiae*. Vol. II, The Clarendon Press, 1972.

Jackson, Bernard S. *Theft in Early Jewish Law*. Oxford: The Clarendon Press, 1972.

_____. "Evolution and Foreign Influence in Ancient Law." *The American Journal of Comparative Law* 16:3 (1968), pp. 372-390.

Jarrett, Bede, O.P. *Social Theories of the Middle Ages: 1200-1500*. Westminster, Maryland: The Newman Press, 1942. First printing 1926.

Jeremias, Joachim. *The Sermon on the Mount*. Translated by Norman Perrin. University of London: The Athlone Press, 1961.

Koenigsberger, H. G. "The Empire of Charles V in Europe." In *The New Cambridge Modern History*. Vol. II, *The Reformation, 1520-1559*. Edited by G. R. Elton. Cambridge: University Press, 1965.

──────. "Western Europe and the Power of Spain." In *The New Cambridge Modern History*. Vol. III, *The Counter-Reformation and Price Revolution, 1559-1610*. Edited by R. B. Wernham. Cambridge: University Press, 1968.

Kossmann, E. H. "The Low Countries." In *The New Cambridge Modern History*. Vol. IV, *The Decline of Spain and the 30 Years War*. Edited by J. P. Cooper. Cambridge: University Press, 1970.

Larner, John. "Order and Disorder in Romagna: 1450-1500." In *Violence and Civil Disorder in Italian Cities: 1200-1500*. Edited by Lauro Martines. Berkeley and Los Angeles: University of California Press, 1972.

Laski, Harold J. "Political Theory in the Later Middle Ages." In *The Cambridge Medieval History*. Vol. VIII, *The Close of the Middle Ages*. Edited by C. W. Previté-Orton and Z. N. Brooks. Cambridge: University Press, 1936.

Latourette, Kenneth Scott. *The Thousand Years of Uncertainty, AD 500-AD 1500*. Vol. 2 of *A History of the Expansion of Christianity*. Grand Rapids, Michigan: Zondervan Publishing House, 1970. First published in 1938.

Le Bras, Gabriel. "Conceptions of Economy and Society." In *The Cambridge Economic History*. Vol. III, *Economic Organization and Policies in the Middle Ages*. General editors, M. M. Postan and H. J. Habakkuk. Edited by M. M. Postan, E. E. Rich, Edward Miller. Cambridge: University Press, 1963.

Lessius, Leonard. *De justitia et jure ceterisque virtutibus cardinalibus libri quatuor ad 2.2. D. Thomae a questione 47 usque ad questionem 171*. Lyon, 1653.

Lignano, Joannes de. *Tractatus de bello*. In *Tractatus Illustrium*. Vol. XVI. Venice, 1584.

McCall, John. "The Writings of John of Leganno with a List of Manuscripts." *Traditio* 23 (1967), pp. 415-437.

McCormick, Richard A., S.J. "Notes on Moral Theology." *Theological Studies* 32:1 (1971), pp. 71-78.

McGovern, John F. "The Rise of New Economic Attitudes— Economic Humanism, Economic Nationalism—During the Later Middle Ages and the Renaissance, AD 1200- 1550." *Traditio* 26 (1970), pp. 217-253.

McKenzie, John L., S.J. "Law in the New Testament." *The Jurist* 26 (1966), pp. 167-180.

McNally, R. E. *The Bible in the Middle Ages*. Westminster: The Newman Press, 1959.

Macquarrie, John. *Three Issues in Ethics*. New York: Harper and Row, 1970.

_____ (ed.). *Dictionary of Christian Ethics*. Philadelphia: The Westminster Press, 1967.

Martines, Lauro. "Introduction: The Historical Approach to Violence." In *Violence and Civil Disorder in Italian Cities: 1200-1500*. Edited by Lauro Martines. Berkeley and Los Angeles: University of California Press, 1972.

_____. *Lawyers and Statecraft in Renaissance Florence*. Princeton: Princeton University Press, 1968.

_____. "Political Violence in the Thirteenth Century." In *Violence and Civil Disorder in Italian Cities: 1200-1500*. Edited by Lauro Martines. Berkeley and Los Angeles: University of California Press, 1972.

_____. *The Social World of the Florentine Humanists: 1390-1460*. Princeton: Princeton University Press, 1963.

_____ (ed). *Violence and Civil Disorder in Italian Cities: 1200-1500*. Berkeley and Los Angeles: University of California Press, 1972.

Miller, Edward. "Introduction" to "The Economic Policies of Governments." In *The Cambridge Economic History*. Vol. III, *Economic Organization and Policies in the Middle Ages*. General editors, M. M. Postan and H. J. Habakkuk. Edited by M. M. Postan, E. E. Rich, Edward Miller. Cambridge: University Press, 1963.

Molina, Louis. *Opera Omnia*. Geneva, 1733.

_____. *De justitia et jure*. Vol. III, *ed. cit.*

Moorman, John. *A History of the Franciscan Order From Its Origins to the Year 1517*. Oxford: The Clarendon Press, 1968.

Mousneir, R. "The Exponents and Critics of Absolutism." In
    The New Cambridge Modern History. Vol. IV, The
    Decline of Spain and the 30 Years War. Edited by
    J. P. Cooper. Cambridge: University Press, 1970.

Navarrus (Martin de Azpilcueta). Enchiridion sive Manuale
    Confessoriorum et Poenitentium. Venice, 1579.

New Catholic Encyclopedia. New York: McGraw-Hill Book
    Company, 1971.

Nineham, D. E. (ed.). The Church's Use of the Bible Past
    and Present. London: S.P.C.K., 1963.

Noldin, H. and Schmitt, A., S.J. Summa Theologiae Moralis.
    3 vols. Thirty-fourth edition. Prepared by G.
    Heinzel, S.J. Innsbruck: Felicianus Rauch, 1963.

_____. De Praeceptis. Vol. II, ed. cit.

Noonan, John T., Jr. The Scholastic Analysis of Usury.
    Cambridge: Harvard University Press, 1957.

Ockham, William. Opera Politica. 3 vols. Edited by J.
    G. Sikes. Manchester: University Press, 1940-
    1963.

_____. Opus nonaginta dierum. Vols. I and II, ed. cit.

Palmer, Paul F., S.J. (ed. with a commentary). Sacraments
    and Forgiveness. Sources of Christian Theology.
    Vol. II. Westminster: The Newman Press, 1959.

Panormitanus (Nicolaus de Tudeschis). Commentaria in
    libros decretalium. 1522.

Pascal, Blaise. Pensees—The Provincial Letters. Trans-
    lated by Thomas M'Crie. New York: The Modern
    Library, 1941.

Pearce, G. J. M. "Augustine's Theory of Property."
    Studia Patristica 6 (1962), pp. 496-500.

Pirenne, Henri. "The Low Countries." In The Cambridge
    Medieval History. Vol. VIII, The Close of the
    Middle Ages. Edited by C. W. Previté-Orton and
    Z. N. Brooks. Cambridge: University Press, 1936.

Poschmann, Bernhard. Penance and the Anointing of the
    Sick. Translated and revised by Francis Courtney,
    S.J. New York: Herder and Herder, 1964.

Previté-Orton, C. W. "Epilogue." In The Cambridge Medi-
    eval History. Vol. VIII, The Close of the Middle
    Ages. Edited by C. W. Previté-Orton and Z. N.
    Brooks. Cambridge: University Press, 1936.

Raymund of Pennaforte, St. *Summa*. Verona, 1744.

Reglá, Juan. "Spain and Her Empire." In *The New Cambridge Modern History*. Vol. V, *The Ascendency of France: 1648-88*. Edited by F. L. Carsten. Cambridge: University Press, 1961.

Richard of Middleton. *Commentum super quartum sententiarum*. Venice, 1499.

_____. *Super quatuor libros sententiarum*. Brescia, 1591.

Roly, H. J. "Roman Law." In *The Cambridge Medieval History*. Vol. II, *The Rise of the Saracens and the Foundation of the Western Empire*. Edited by H. M. Gwatkin and J. P. Whitney. Cambridge: University Press, 1936.

Roncaglia, Constantinus. *Universa Moralis Theologia*. Venice, 1736.

Sabetti, Aloysius, S.J. *Compendium Theologiae Moralis*. Twenty-eighth edition. Edited by Timothy Barrett, S.J. New York: Frederick Pustet Co., Inc., 1919.

Salamancans. *Cursus Theologiae Moralis*. 6 vols. Venice, 1728.

Schlatter, Richard. *Private Property: The History of an Idea*. New Brunswick, New Jersey: Rutgers University Press, 1951.

Schnackenburg, Rudolf. *The Gospel According to St. John*. Vol. I. Translated by Kevin Smyth. New York: Herder and Herder, 1968.

_____. *The Moral Teaching of the New Testament*. Translated by J. Holland-Smith and W. J. O'Hara. New York: Herder and Herder, 1971.

Skalweit, Stephan. "Political Thought." In *The New Cambridge Modern History*. Vol. V, *The Ascendency of France: 1648-88*. Edited by F. L. Carsten. Cambridge: University Press, 1961.

Smalley, Beryl. "The Bible in the Medieval Schools." In *The Cambridge History of the Bible*. Vol. II. Edited by G. W. H. Lampe. Cambridge: University Press, 1969.

_____. *The Study of the Bible in the Middle Ages*. New York: The Philosophical Library, 1952.

Soto, Anthony, O.F.M. "The Structure of Society According to Duns Scotus." *Franciscan Studies* 11 (1951), pp. 194-212; 12 (1952), pp. 71-90.

Soto, Dominic. *De justitia et jure*. Lyon, 1558.

Spooner, F. C. "The Economy of Europe 1559-1609." In The New Cambridge Modern History. Vol. III, The Counter-Reformation and Price Revolution, 1559-1610. Edited by R. B. Wernham. Cambridge: University Press, 1968.

_____. "The European Economy 1609-1659." In The New Cambridge Modern History. Vol. IV, The Decline of Spain and the 30 Years War. Edited by J. P. Cooper. Cambridge: University Press, 1970.

Sporer, Patrick, O.F.M. Theologia Moralis. 3 vols. Second edition. Edited by Irenaeus Bierbaum, O.F.M. Paderborn: Bonifaciana, 1903.

_____. De Justitia et Contractibus. Vol. II, ed. cit.

Sylvester Prieras. Summa summarum quae Sylvestrinae merito nuncupatur. Pars Prima. Venice, 1601.

Tertullian. On Penitence (De Paenitentia) and On Purity (De Pudicitia). Ancient Christian Writers. Vol. 28. Translated and annotated by William P. Le Saint, S.J. Edited by Johannes Quasten and Walter Burghardt, S.J. Westminster: The Newman Press, 1959.

Thomas Aquinas, St. Catena Aurea. Oxford: John Henry Parker, 1841.

_____. Summa Theologica. 5 vols. Edited by Cardinal Joseph Pecci. Paris, n.d.

_____. Summa Theologica. 60 vols. Blackfriars. New York: McGraw-Hill Book Company, 1964—

_____. Summa Theologica. 3 vols. Translated by Fathers of the English Dominican Province. New York: Benziger Brothers, Inc., 1947-1948.

Thrupp, Sylvia L. "The Gilds." In The Cambridge Economic History. Vol. III, Economic Organization and Policies in the Middle Ages. General editors, M. M. Postan and H. J. Habakkuk. Edited by M. M. Postan, E. E. Rich, Edward Miller. Cambridge: University Press, 1963.

Tilley, Arthur A. "The Renaissance in Europe." In The Cambridge Medieval History. Vol. VIII, The Close of the Middle Ages. Edited by C. W. Previté-Orton and Z. N. Brooks. Cambridge: University Press, 1936.

Tooley, M. J. "Political Thought and the Theory and Practice of Toleration." In The New Cambridge Modern History. Vol. III, The Counter-Reformation and Price Revolution, 1559-1610. Edited by R. B. Wernham. Cambridge: University Press, 1968.

Trevor-Roper, H. R. "Religion, the Reformation and Social Change." In his <u>Religion, the Reformation and Social Change</u>. London: Macmillan, 1967. First printed in <u>Historical Studies IV</u>. Papers read before the 5th Irish Conference of Historians. Edited by G. A. Hayes-McCoy.

_____. <u>The Rise of Christian Europe</u>. London: Thames and Hudson, 1965.

Turrecremata, Johannes A. <u>Gratiani Decretorum</u>. Rome, 1726.

van Sull, Ch., S.J. <u>Léonard Lessius</u>. Louvain, 1930.

van Werveke, H. "The Rise of the Towns." In <u>The Cambridge Economic History</u>. Vol. III, <u>Economic Organization and Policies in the Middle Ages</u>. General editors, M. M. Postan and H. J. Habakkuk. Edited by M. M. Postan, E. E. Rich, Edward Miller. Cambridge: University Press, 1963.

Vinogradoff, Paul. <u>Roman Law in Medieval Europe</u>. Third edition. Oxford: University Press, 1929.

Vitoria, Francis de. <u>De Justitia</u>. 3 vols. Edited by Vicente Beltran de Heredia, O.P. Madrid, 1934.

von Martin, Alfred. <u>Sociology of the Renaissance</u>. O-P Book. University Microfilms, Inc., Ann Arbor, Michigan, 1960. Translated by W. L. Luethens. London: Kegan Paul, Trench, Trubner and Co., Ltd., 1944.

Wilks, M. J. "The Problem of Private Ownership in Patristic Thought and an Augustinian Solution of the Fourteenth Century." <u>Studia Patristica</u> 6 (1962), pp. 533-542.

Zalba, Marcellino, S.J. <u>Theologia Moralis Specialis: Tractatus de Mandatis Dei et Ecclesiae</u>. Vol. II of E. F. Regatillo and M. Zalba, S.J. <u>Theologiae Moralis Summa</u>. 3 vols. Madrid: Biblioteca De Autores Cristianos, 1953.

AMERICAN ACADEMY OF RELIGION
DISSERTATION SERIES

Series Price: $4.50

($3.00 to Members of Sponsoring Societies)

Payment must accompany order: orders from individuals cannot be invoiced. Please send orders, with check made out to SCHOLARS PRESS.

The Theological Development of Edwards Amaska Park: Last of the "Consistent Calvinists"
Anthony C. Cecil, Jr.

Authority in the Church: A Study in Changing Paradigms
T. Howland Sanks

Moment of Truth for Protestant America: Interchurch Campaigns Following World War One
Eldon Ernst

A Complex Inheritance: Henry James and Henry James, Sr.
James G. Moseley, Jr.

Moral Action, God and History in The Thought of Immanuel Kant
Carl A. Raschke

The Sociality of Christ and Humanity
Clifford Green

Freud as Student of Religion
Reuben M. Rainey

The Religious Language of Nicholas of Cusa
James E. Biechler

Passion, "Knowing How," and Understanding
Andrew J. Burgess

Three Uses of Christian Discourse in John Henry Newman
Jouett L. Powell

The Hermeneutic of Dogma
Thomas B. Ommen

Theory and Religious Understanding
Charles M. Wood

The Responsible God: A Study of the Christian Philosophy of H. Richard Niebuhr
Donald E. Fadner

Nazism and the Pastors
James A. Zabel

Killing in Defense of Private Property
Shaun J. Sullivan

Man in the World: The Theology of Johannes Baptist Metz
Roger Dick Johns

Domesticating the Clergy: The Inception of the Reformation in Strasbourg, 1522-1524
William S. Stafford

SCHOLARS PRESS
UNIVERSITY OF MONTANA
MISSOULA, MONTANA 59801